MEETING THE ENEMY

ARTHUR RATHBURN

brite publishing

4308 Blueberry Road
Fredonia, Wisconsin 53217

This novel is based on the life experiences of real people as related to the author. However, even though every attempt was made to adhere to these experiences it was necessary, as in all material based on memories, for the author to speculate and guess, even invent in order to give the story coherence and shape. Many of the names were changed to protect the privacy of others. The author cannot guarantee historical accuracy.

Copyright © 2003 Arthur Rathburn

ALL RIGHTS RESERVED
Brite Publishing
4308 Blueberry Road
Fredonia, Wisconsin 53217
Published in the United States of America

Cataloging in publication
Rathburn, Arthur
    Meeting the Enemy

    ISBN: 1-891400-70-3

    1. Fiction

Library of Congress Control Number: 2002115980

MEET YOUR ENEMY AS A FRIEND
AND YOU WILL HAVE NO ENEMY.

ACKNOWLEDGMENT

To start a novel, to say nothing of finishing it, takes a strong friend and supporter to encourage you along the way. I am fortunate to have such a person in my loving wife, Ursula. I also am lucky enough to have two supportive daughters, Christine and Heidi, and good friends such as Manfred, Juergen, Rick Jerry, and Horst that read and commented on my rough drafts. I especially want to thank my big brother Carl who has always been my biggest critic (good and bad) as well as a role model for me.

Lastly I would be remiss to not pay tribute to some fine teachers along the way that did not give up on this less than stellar student. People such as Jack Bibb from my ancient Portola High School days, the late Dr. Joe Brewer of California State University Stanislaus whose encouragement made me actually believe that some day I could write in this strange language called English, and the late Dr. Granville Jensen of Oregon State University, the rock I clung to in the rapids called grade school.

CONTENTS

FOREWORD. 6

SECTION I	AFRIKA KORPS 9
Chapter One	On the Offense 10
Chapter Two	On the Defense 19
Chapter Three	Escalation of Hate 23
Chapter Four	Taking Command 35
Chapter Five	Meeting Americans 40
Chapter Six	Airborne Assault 47
Chapter Seven	My War Ends 55

SECTION II	TRANSPORTED TO THE LAND OF THE ENEMY 73
Chapter One	The Cruise 74
Chapter Two	Working With the Enemy 83
Chapter Three	The Storm 93
Chapter Four	Otto's Fate 97
Chapter Five	Last Days Aboard Ship 103

SECTION III	PRISONER OF WAR 109
Chapter One	Welcome to America .110
Chapter Two	Journey to the Wild West. 127
Chapter Three	On the Great American Frontier 135
Chapter Four	Prisoner or Tourist? 162
Chapter Five	Among the Mormons .175
Chapter Six	The Magic Valley. 196

SECTION IV	ENGLAND 233
Chapter One	Return to England 234
Chapter Two	An Old Friend 236
Chapter Three	Settling into Prisoner Life in England 240
Chapter Four	Vera's Story 245
Chapter Five	A New Way of Thinking 258
Chapter Six	Last Days in England .265

SECTION V	DER VATERLAND 269
Chapter One	On German Soil 270
Chapter Two	A Prisoner in One's Own land 274
Chapter Three	The Long Walk Home 287
Chapter Four	The Circle is Closed 312

EPILOGUE 317

FOOTNOTES. 319

FOREWORD

I met Erich at a wine festival along the Rhine River in the fall of 1964. I was in the army and was stationed in a small Kaserne near Mainz. Erich was an English instructor in a middle school, but he also taught night classes to adults, at a Volkshochschule in a small town in the area. We instantly struck up a friendship that led me to become his unpaid assistant at the night classes. It was a wonderful way for me to meet local people other than the drunks and whores that hung around the Gasthauser where many American soldiers congregated when off duty.

My friendship with Erich also led me to a far greater understanding of the strange phenomenon known as war. Erich had risen to the rank of Hauptmann (captain) in the German military during World War II. He was a paratrooper, and thus had been in the Luftwaffe (air force), rather than in the Wehrmacht (army). In the African Campaign he had served in a heavy infantry unit, a unit he eventually commanded. Not long after we came to know each other he began to tell me his story. He told it to me over a period of about a year, as we would meet together on weekends or after classes. I encouraged him at that time to write it for posterity, because of its unusual nature. He promised to do so, but never did.

The impact his story had on me was profound, partly because I was a soldier and war was of obvious interest to me. However, more than that, his conversations with me were my first glimpse of World War II from the view of a soldier from the "other" side. I had grown up during the time of patriotic movies where the Americans were always victorious and the Germans were mean, vicious, killers who waved Nazi swastika banners. The heroes of my childhood were patriotic soldiers who fought for love of freedom and home, not out of hate. This was my first time to meet the enemy, and lo and behold he was telling me about his experiences as he met the enemy. I had never even considered that my countrymen could actually be "the enemy." This is the story of Erich meeting his enemy on the battlefield as well as on the home ground and sanctuaries of the enemy, far from the conflict. This look through the eyes of a German at our World War II allies, and at America with our diverse culture, was an eye opener for me, as I hope it is for any of the people who choose to read this book.

This is not a biography. I took no notes during my meetings with Erich, and he never made any attempt to tell his experiences in a chronological order. After Erich's early death I promised myself that someday I would try to write a novel loosely based on his life. The story that follows is my recollection of his conversations with me along with bits and pieces of stories by other German veterans. I have tried not to overembellish the actual events that took place. I have had to do my best to relate actual conversations and feelings that took place during those events and experiences.

As you read, please just imagine yourself as a young American soldier in a foreign land, sitting in a Gasthaus listening to this story.

Section I
AFRIKA KORPS

CHAPTER ONE

ON THE OFFENSE

The **Volkshochschule** class had been released early and Erich had taken me to the local **Weinkeller** for a glass of Riesling. He was in a very serious mood. I could tell something was on his mind. Erich had appeared to me to be a man who avoided the serious side of life. In fact he used to kid me when I would become serious, by saying, "Art, you must try to look at the wonder of life, not the difficulties. If I were to have dwelled on the difficulties in my life I would not have survived to be such a handsome, charming fellow." Indeed a handsome, charming fellow he was with his full, immaculately combed dark hair with distinguishing streaks of gray. That night though, he let the laugh lines be dominated by a firm set jaw, and slight wrinkles in his forehead. After we made our first **Prost** and went through the local ritual of sampling the wine, with me faking it as if I knew a good one from a bad one, he lit a cigarette (he was a chain smoker), sat a moment in silence, then suddenly began to tell me his story.

Art, being that you are a soldier, I want to tell you about my time in the war. You, of course, realize that your parents and I were once enemies. I don't mean on a personal basis, but from the standpoint of our nationalities. I want to tell you this story because you of all the Americans I have met seemed to want to know about the true German. Please do not think I am trying to justify Germany's, or for that matter my, role in the war. Frankly I had joined the military with a strong feeling of nationalism and the belief that Adolf Hitler's dream for a Gross Deutschland was a moving and wonderful goal. It was not until Africa that I learned what war was, and the price I and the German people had to pay to strive for this dream.

It may be difficult for me to tell you about Africa. Africa is mostly a haze of dust and heat waves in my mind. That is what the African campaign was. My time in Africa was dominated by long boring night moves through endless miles of dust. During the day we tended to sleep or sit gazing out on to a world nearly void of the color green and never in focus. Though one could see for many kilometers, the shimmering heat waves gave everything a surreal look as if the camera lens was always out of focus just a bit, and the operator had a shaky hand.

We were not the only ones trying to survive the unforgiving elements and endless maneuvering against a relentless enemy. The English were on the same chessboard. That's what the struggle for Northern Africa was—a giant chess game between Rommel and Montgomery. It was a constant game of move, counter move, faint, and bluff. In the game the small, heavy infantry units like mine were the knights. Feldmarschall Rommel would use us to move deep into enemy territory, strike a quick blow, and move out. We also would be used to create a temporary block on a key access point. The regular infantry units were the pawns used to probe for weak points or as decoys to draw the enemy into a vulnerable position so that the bishops (the Luftwaffe), and the queen (the panzer units) could make swift and deadly strikes. The artillery was the rook that could strike out at great distance or remain in solid protection of the king. One problem with this analogy is that I am not really sure I, or any of the other common German soldiers, knew who or where the king was on that African game board. We were not conscious of trying to protect anything or anyone. My immediate cohorts and I were just fighting an enemy. Victory was ours to win and lose on each given day. There was no grand prize in mind other than survival. This, I suppose, means that death was defeat. Strange! I have never really thought of it as that until now.

Most of my time in Africa is lost in that dust haze. When I think of Africa or try to tell someone like you about it. It seems like the time was incredibly short, because all I can remember or tell about is a series of events that in total encompass only a few days. It is not that these were the only days of action. There are many days where conflict took place that just seem to flow together. That is because of the sameness of these skirmishes. In the desert one avoids battle during the middle of the day because of the heat—its destructive force upon men and equipment can be as deadly as any enemy weapon—and the threat of air strikes. Due to lack of cover, and because of the telltale evidence given by dust plumes, movement during the day is deadly. Night battle is nearly impossible. Units can be moved in convoy at night, but swift cross-country movement, so necessary in battle, is nearly impossible. Therefore nearly all combat took place at dawn or dusk. During the night we, and the English, would be on the move. During the midday we both would hunker down and sleep.

Rather than go about describing the many battles, let me tell you of a couple in a general sort of way. Actually, I am not sure if I can describe many specific firefights. They all seem to just flow together in my mind. As an example of a typical offensive action perhaps I can remember a bit of a scrape. Ah, yes! There was that time right before I took over the company.

We moved out on patrol soon after dark. I was to take my platoon cross-country to a large wadi where it was thought that a fuel depot was located. We took two small Schwimmwagen (the equivalent to your jeep) and a lorrie. The first few hours went swiftly because we followed a track well known to us. We left the track right before reaching a line of high hills. The pass over the hills was held by our troops, but since it was a familiar track we knew the Englander would be well entrenched on the other side. Therefore it was my plan to skirt around through an area that seemed on the maps to be passable, but due to its lack of cover should be void of dug-in English troops. The reality of war hits you not when the first shot is fired, but when you first go into the unknown. In this case it was just as we reached the crest of the hills that, at that time, could probably have been properly described as the line between the opposing forces. That moment of exposure as one tops a rise is an eternity. Due to noise I could not suddenly increase speed and rush across the top in an all-out dash for the relative safety of the down slope, but had to slowly creep across, even stopping occasionally and turning off the engines to listen for danger. Nor did I dare send a scout to walk over first. If the enemy is watching the crest he can see people as well as vehicles and will then be alerted and have the artillery primed and ready. So I just took my entire convoy in one unit slowly across the crest. At least if there was resistance I could charge forward as a group or retreat in force according to the size of the threat. If it is possible to hold one's breath for about ten minutes, I have done so many times on each of these forays. What always made me mad at myself was that when we stopped to listen it seemed like minutes went by before I could hear anything but my heart beating furiously in my chest. I was always afraid my men would hear it and know what a coward they had for an officer.

On this night, as in all but two of my forays into enemy territory, we met no resistance. One would think a wave of relief would have come over me as we descended down the slope, but such was not the case. When the hair-raising fear of the crossing subsides, a sense of regret and dread sets in. If we would have met resistance we could have scurried back to safer ground and gone home, mission complete. Now we were committed. Each moment from that time on carried us further into the grasp of the enemy. No longer could we scurry back. No matter what, we would have to sneak back or find a hiding place in an area that I had chosen to cross because of its lack of hiding places. Slowly we descended. I did not stop until we reached the bottom of the hill. There I got out, listened, and let the troops relieve themselves one last time. We crossed over what I hoped was relatively smooth ground toward the broken-up area where I expected to find the fuel dump.

We crossed the flat fairly quickly, stopping only once to listen for any tiny sound that would alert us to awaiting death. As we reached the rough ground I immediately began to look for a place to cache the vehicles. The trick was to find a deep wadi not too far from the flat so a quick exit would be possible. I soon came across one. This was, as always, by sheer luck since in the dark, with less than accurate maps, predetermining small points of geography is not possible. I sent men out in both directions, left and right, to place small flags. These, though obviously visible to the enemy, were necessary for us to find our vehicles again in this featureless landscape. I proceeded immediately with my entire group to go forward on foot. There was no necessity in leaving a guard or two since any enemy patrol that would venture out into this jumble of rock and gullies would be large enough to easily overpower a couple of guards. We moved rather quickly. It is actually

13

faster to cover such ground on foot at night than it is to drive it, even in daylight. We would stop and listen occasionally. The English were never good at noise discipline.

Soon we were rewarded with the sound of a petrol can being banged into another. We slowly crawled forward until we found a good place to get down out of sight and settle in for the last few hours of darkness. It is odd how the body can focus on one task and shut out all other sensations. Often a day or two after one of these patrols one would find bruises and punctures inflicted upon the hands, elbows, and knees during these nighttime crawls. At first one would wonder how the hell such punishment could have taken place, until the night exercise is recalled.

The waiting is the hard part. I can still remember the urge to have a cigarette that would come over me every time I would get in such a situation. I bet there were as many soldiers killed because they lit up a cigarette than any other cause. I had to keep constant vigil on my men to keep some idiot from trying to sneak a smoke. I don't seem to remember on that particular night having any smokers violate our security, but I did have my usual problem with Oberfeldwebel (platoon sergeant) Schmidt. Schmidt had been at war since Poland in '39 and had sort of adjusted to it. He never seemed to get nervous. In fact he would sit those tense moments out by falling asleep. The only problem was that he snored loud enough to simulate a panzer. On that night he started up like a whole convoy. It seemed like minutes before several of us descended on him to wake him. I knew that the enemy had to have heard us. It was only then that I realized that his snores came right as an English convoy approached the fuel dump. For some reason the enemy outposts must have not recognized Schmidt's loud snorts as snoring.

The approach of the convoy created a whole new problem. These fuel dumps were not big areas full of petrol tanks, but rather small caches of petrol cans. They were normally guarded by a small contingent. They were there just to give a patrol or convoy enough fuel to extend their range a few more kilometers than we Germans would be expecting. The arrival of the convoy, despite the fact that it seemed to be only a few lorries and one armored vehicle of some type, meant additional weaponry to oppose us. I had to decide rather to carry on or pull out before first light. I believe you Amis say "put up or shut up." I was about to pull out when one of my men said, "Sir, it sounds like they are unloading more cans." So that was it. It was a resupply convoy. That meant that they were building up the dump for a bigger convoy to come through. The need to disrupt that activity was now more vital. Besides, if the lorries were carrying petrol it was an indication that they were not full of troops. Perhaps, I deduced, they would not have an overabundance of fire power. I decided to proceed with my attack.

My plan had been to rush the dump in a small tight group to gain maximum penetration, thus hoping to get in close enough, fast enough, to blow up most of, or at least enough of, the petrol to make the dump of little use to anything but a very small patrol. However, the presence of the armored vehicle would mean such a bold move would be suicide. Therefore, I decided on the oldest trick in the books. I spread out my men with the idea that the enemy would think we were a much bigger unit than we were. Hopefully, they would decide that their best bet was to get the hell out of there. At the least, they would know that we knew the location of this dump and that might cause them to alter any plans of a large movement in this direction.

There were some very anxious moments as my men spread out. Any movement that close to dawn was very dangerous. As I told you earlier, most action occurred at dawn or dusk when one can see close objects, but when one looks toward the distance the whole world looks gray and yellow brown. Therefore any guards or outposts are normally at their utmost vigilance at that time. Luck was with us, probably because of the noise being made by the men unloading petrol cans. I just had to wait those last agonizing minutes. The sweat rolled constantly down into my eyes, and the urge to urinate grew. I must have looked at my watch every ten seconds. At last my designated time suddenly appeared on my watch. It is funny how one can wait so impatiently for the action to begin, and then when it is actually there one is surprised at how fast it arrived.

I signaled the Panzerfaust team and they let a round go into the middle of the wadi. At the same time nearly all of my men fired rifle grenades. I didn't expect anyone to hit anything; in fact, I knew the grenades would probably fall well short of doing any damage, but the idea was to create a sudden gut-wrenching noise. Rifle fire takes one a moment to recognize; thus it loses its shock value. But, if one suddenly thinks that a full-blown assault is under way, I guarantee that even the bravest soul will dive for cover and crap his pants. I remember cussing myself for not packing in a large Granatwerfer (what I believe you call a mortar), but that regret passed on our hasty return to the vehicles. The weight of a Granatwerfer would have seriously slowed us down. On quick strikes I had learned that heavy weapons could be a detriment. Our bold move paid off. The English at first just froze and then many started to panic. There was much shouting, but little return fire. Unfortunately the commander of the armored vehicle was evidently an old veteran because it was not long before we were receiving some nasty return machine-gun fire. I could soon hear the "pop pop pop" of their slower firing machine gun. They had located the area my Panzerfaust team was in. It took them little time to silence my team. Due to the fact that my men were so spread out we were able to pour some rifle fire into the wadi, hopefully injuring or killing some of the enemy and puncturing some petrol cans. There was not an instant fireball like one sees in the movies, but points of flame sprang up indicating some success. From the screams of pain, I also knew that we hit several soldiers. When the English panzer began to maneuver to find a way out of the wadi to get around us, I called for the quick withdrawal I had preplanned with my men. This is a particularly vulnerable time. If the enemy had any artillery or mortar support we would always get blasted on the way out. My men, as directed, stayed spread out on the move back. (Strange, we never did use the word Rueckzug, retreat.) One didn't use such terms in Rommel's Afrika Korps.

It was on the run back out of a firefight that the weight of command hits you. On the way in I was busy planning the assault in my mind. I was just doing my job. On the way out the realization hits you that you may have lost some of your men. As we ran, with the angry whine of bullets flying about us, I began to imagine that I was alone except for the few men I could see jumping, running, and dodging. We didn't make one of the wonderful organized withdrawals one practices while in training. No by-the-fire team movements. No brave one-man stands. In fact, we didn't return any fire. The idea was to get the hell out of there as fast as possible. We knew the English would not follow immediately. They were not dumb. One does not leave a fortified position to chase armed soldiers into an unknown area.

As we gathered at the vehicles there was an ever tightening knot in my gut as I waited and counted my men. It was difficult to do because the men instantly spread out and took firing positions in the odd chance that the English would follow us. Usually the last in was Schmidt, not because of his bravery, or his fatherly feeling toward the men; he was just the slowest man in the unit. Two of the men managed to get back despite being wounded. They were quickly being attended to by the medic, actually a priest.[1] Two men, those of the Panzerfaust team, did not arrive. We waited a few minutes to see that we were not going to be set upon just as we loaded into the vehicles, and in hopes the last two were not killed or captured and would make it back. At the last minute Jaeger Oster came staggering in carrying his buddy, Jaeger Schweikard. Schweikard was in very bad condition. I ordered the men to quickly board the lorrie. We headed out. I knew that it was too late in the day to cross the flat leading up to the pass, so I turned just on the edge of the flat. There we could travel faster, but could duck into the broken ground if necessary. Surprisingly, no artillery came thundering down around us. I only went a short distance before leading the other vehicles back into the broken area to find a place to hide out through the daylight hours. We were not long in place when a pair of spitfires were to be seen flying low in hopes of catching us crossing the hills. They never spotted us.

That day was a long one. We sat quietly and kept a lookout for enemy patrols. Schweikard's condition was deteriorating and I was sure that he would not make it back to camp alive. The other two were in great pain, but not in immediate danger of dying. I sent out a couple of men to sneak back toward the ammo dump. Their mission was to see if a convoy arrived and determine how big it was. They came back much later and informed me that the area was deserted. Our discovery of the dump must have upset the British plan and the men at the dump must have reloaded the petrol and moved out in the early light, just as we had. I could report back a successful mission even though we could not confirm that we had destroyed the objective.

That was a fairly typical way things worked in that vast struggle.

Hours of sitting and waiting and short minutes of intense fear, exhilaration, and furious action. One has to really concentrate to remember the boring aspect of war.

There is something I should tell you about my experience in the war. I think of it here because I remember thinking about it as I sat out in that godforsaken piece of African landscape watching one of my men die. Several of the soldiers, especially Oster, as could be expected, were very vocal about their hate for the Englanders. They did not seem to take into consideration the fact that they had tried to kill us because we had attacked and tried to kill them. I had spent many months studying in England before the war. I had learned to appreciate the English, despite their rather haughty ways, and their general superior attitude toward Germans. In war they had become enemies and I did not try to defend them as good people to my men, but I, to that point, can say I really didn't hate them. In my mind I was meeting the enemy in battle, not Englishmen. I hope you can understand the difference. Probably not. Perhaps you have to have been in battle to know that difference.

As the last light faded and the desert landscape went back into its nondescript yellow-brown condition before it totally disappeared into the black of an African night, we moved out toward our company encampment. The trip back, as far as I can remember, was uneventful. Schweikard never made it.

CHAPTER TWO

ON THE DEFENSE

As the weeks went by we found ourselves more and more on the defense. Manning a defensive position in war is an entirely different feeling as is experienced when on the offense. The concept is the same except one important element is missing: the exhilaration. The boring hours are there. In fact they are doubled. The fear is still there, and so are the short bursts of action. In truth the control of a battle is in the hands of the commander of the defense. It is his battlefield. In order for the offense to win they must find a way to wrest the control away from the defensive force. However, even when knowing this and having this driven home to me during officer training, I always felt a bit helpless as we had to sit and wait for the enemy to make his move. On the other hand when I was on an offensive patrol or a strike I felt more in control. I decided when to hit and where to hit. In truth the enemy most often determined this by his action or nonaction. Whereas there was that feeling of excitement as one descended on the enemy, the feeling of sitting and defending against an attack only brought fear. Yes, there was some satisfaction when the attack was repelled, but the overall feeling at the end of the battle was one of relief. You knew they would be back. The Englander always came back. What persistent bastards they were.

Once our position was located by the enemy they came around, dawn after dawn, and dusk after dusk. The worst time was dawn. An attack at dusk was normally a harassment tactic that would end with darkness. The dawn attacks were most often of a more furious nature. The enemy had only an hour or so to overrun us, or force us out of our position. If they didn't do this they had to pull back in daylight, a dangerous maneuver, or dig temporary positions, making themselves vulnerable to counterattack.

Being a small, relatively lightly armed unit we were normally assigned to set up a block or delay point on minor transportation routes. Rommel was a panzer commander, and seemed never to really be sure what to do with a small heavy infantry unit such as we had become since getting to Africa. The entire African campaign had very flexible, if not totally nebulous front lines, and our capability as paratroopers was nearly totally

19

lost. Unfortunately for us, we were often used as a decoy. We were strong enough to defend ourselves against even fortified company-sized strikes, but had little chance against an armored unit. Therefore, we would be put out in a position that invited armored attack so that Rommel could make his famous blitz-pincher movement. English armor was more maneuverable but if forced, or led, into a restricted area it was no match for the heavier German panzer.

I remember one situation that we were placed in that was particularly dangerous. The setting was a long narrow valley, bordered on one side by small but rugged hills, and on the other by a large area of very broken rocky terrain. We were ordered to block the head end of this valley. Luckily the enemy either did not discover us or were concentrating on more accessible routes for some time. This allowed us to dig in and camouflage quite well. After one is dug in and holds a position for a short time in the desert, the wind and dust do their job and coat everything, and everyone, with a masking layer that renders all nearly invisible. Soon though, our rest was interrupted by the normal angry wasp attacks of Englander patrols and probing strikes. Day after day we endured the morning routine of awaking a couple hours before dawn, repelling an attack, leisurely eating our morning bread, taking a nice long nap in the shade of our camouflage, and getting set for an evening of snipers and small probes. As the attacks persisted and yet never seemed to increase in size, it became clear the enemy was just keeping us occupied until a large scale offensive against us, or some other point in this particular range of mountains, was organized. This tactic was an English tradition in World War I, and the Englander, in their tradition-bound way, carried it into the early part of this war. Rommel and his staff seemed to thrive on this habit of the Englander.

As the intensity of the attacks slackened off I was ordered by my company commander, Hauptmann Werner, to take my platoon and a squad from the heavy weapons platoon down to a small gap in the hills that bordered the one side of the valley. As we got there we were joined by a rather large unit of friendly armor that dug in and camouflaged behind our position. The trap was lain. For the next two days no patrols or any attacks came. This was my first experience before a big battle and I was feeling rather let down. I was almost anxiously awaiting what I had expected war to be—

a massive clash of forces with the glory of seeing the enemy whither before the might of the Vaterland's superior army. Instead there was the same boredom.

On the third day the boredom was interrupted with the drone of overhead aircraft in the very first hint of a dawn sky. I knew how fast planes flew, having had quite some experience with them as a Fallschirmspringer,[2] but it seemed in war that they creep across the sky, laughing at the inability of the antlike earthbound victims to disrupt the flow of death they expel from their bellies. Before the drone of the planes was drowned out by the terrifying rumble of their exploding eggs, a more piercing whine of engines and clanking of dust-worn wheels and tracks came charging up the valley. Just as the head end of the valley erupted into blinding flashes, smoke, and dust created by the bombers, we could make out many tanks and men moving across our front. We remained quiet and out of sight as ordered. It takes strong discipline to see the enemy so vulnerable in your sights without firing. I was sure that at any moment one of my men would crack and start shooting prematurely.

As my superiors had predicted, the second rank of enemy vehicles made a sudden turn toward us. Knowing that they were hidden from our main emplacement at the head end of the valley by all of the dust from the bombardment, and the fire from the proceeding rank of tanks, they headed for the notch in the hills we were hiding in, in order to try to outflank our forces at the head end of the valley. The enemy was using the first rank as a ploy to cover their planned flanking strike. As they came into range the tanks to our rear broke camouflage and charged through my position. The lighter English tanks, being caught in an untenable position, quickly reversed fields and headed back toward where they had come from, losing several of their numbers as burning hulks on the battlefield. The German tanks formed a block in the valley which I rushed my men into in support. We awaited the outcome of the battle being pitched between us and our main force. As stragglers of the first enemy force realized that they were in a trap they headed into the badlands where they could eventually find their way slowly, and at great cost in time and equipment, back to their own lines. Though not many enemies died on that day, the victory was a big one because of the expenditure of fuel on the enemy side. This was one of the main strategic goals of

Rommel. The weakness of this philosophy was that the enemy had too many supplies. This was double so with the coming of the Americans.

We did not stay in our temporary fighting position in the middle of the valley for long. To do so was to invite air attack. As we were moving out we spotted the English medical vehicles moving up to search for dead and wounded. We ignored them and proceeded to scoot out of the valley. This was normal early in the defense of Africa. After a battle both sides would send in their medical corps to retrieve the wounded. Often they would pass each other on the same track. It was not unheard of for one side to signal the other the location of one of the opposition's wounded. This was not just a matter of gallantry, but also one of practicality. In the desert, wounded were a burden. It was enough of a problem to have to try to care for, and eventually evacuate, one's own wounded. To take on the responsibility for the enemy wounded was foolish if you could get their own medical corps to haul them back to tie up and utilize their own valuable resources. This was, of course, not the case as the struggle wore on.

Don't get the idea that all of our defensive actions were as successful as this one. More than once we found ourselves falling back as fast as our vehicles would take us. Being without armored vehicles my outfit was quite prepared to let the English have a piece of real estate if they were seen to be coming toward us with tanks. Our job was done when they chose to burn up their valuable petrol to chase us around.

Resources: petrol, ammunition, food, and especially water, were the keys to victory. On the smaller scale it became a reason to fight. Simply put, if one killed an enemy one could take his vehicle, petrol, and water. We never did put much of a value on the English rations. If as a people they could not even set a decent table, by German standards, in their homes, how could they be expected to do so in the field of battle? One exception for me was tea. I, having spent so much time in England, had developed a taste for tea. My men would drink it, but only if coffee was not available.

Oh yes! There was one more valued booty of war—cigarettes. Cigarettes were not only valued for their worth as occupiers of time, soothers of nerves, and necessities of habit. They were a major item of currency. A pack of cigarettes would get one most anything he needed from other soldiers or, when on leave, from women.

CHAPTER THREE

ESCALATION OF HATE

When I actually make the effort to calculate the time I spent in Africa, I realize that it was not very long. But as I remember it, it was a very long time. It was an eternity, a lifetime all rolled into slightly more than a year. It was a time when I transformed from a boy to a hardened warrior who probably deserved the title a commander has among his men: "the Old Man". Partly this was due to the strain of command with its isolation from the rest of the troop. But it was also due to a transformation within myself. As I stated earlier, I started the war viewing the enemy not with hate, but as opposing soldiers. I viewed the fact that they were English with regret. The English were not the enemy; the enemy forces just happened to be English. I tried to hide this from my comrades because not to hate the English would have been viewed as heresy. It was bad enough that I had, upon first arriving in the unit, spoken of my time as a student in England before the war. For some time I was labeled the "English lover" behind my back. It took me some time to gain the confidence of my troops.

However, as the first year wore on this mental separation of past feelings and present duty changed. I don't know exactly when it happened, but I realize now that slowly the English did become the enemy. I replaced my hate of a faceless enemy with a hate for the English. Part of it was their persistence. It got so that all one looked forward to was some respite from the constant jab and parry of their patrols. Why wouldn't they soon realize that the German war machine was superior and just give up?

Since I spoke fluent English, I was often called upon to interrogate prisoners. It became increasingly difficult to interview a prisoner in a civil manner when one had just written to parents about the death of their son, or had just viewed the broken body of a soldier under your command. It did not help that so many of the prisoners, especially the young ones, were so damn cocky. They tended not to view me as an officer in an opposing army, but as some evil bloodthirsty monster who was a personal representative of Adolf Hitler, a person they seemed to equate with the devil himself. I still at that time looked at Adolf Hitler as der Fuehrer; the esteemed leader of a country that was just trying to take its rightful place in the world. There are a few events that stick out as focal points in my changing view of the English. One of these was the bombing of the hospital.

During a break in what had seemed unending action since we landed in Africa (as I said one forgets the hours of boredom), our unit was moved back to a relatively quiet zone for some rest and resupply. I took the time to request a chance to visit some of our wounded. Hauptmann Werner let me, along with Oberfeldwebel Schmidt, go back to a small hospital near Tripoli to do this. It also let me get some long overdue rest. I was diligently engaged in that endeavor when my world shattered and I no longer had any doubt that the English were a race of cowardly bastards, as most of my men already considered them to be.

I was lying up on the roof of a small hut near the hospital catching what little bit of afternoon breeze there was. Someone had constructed a tattered canvas awning so that I was somewhat protected from the blazing rays of the desert sun. I was not even feeling guilty that I had ordered Schmidt to remain with the Schwimmwagen. One could not trust it to be left alone. We may have been in a German Kaserne, but in war any unoccupied piece of equipment is fair game for booty rights. The fact that Schmidt had to be the one who sat out the day in the dust under our vehicle while I enjoyed the breeze atop the hut was not a question. I was the officer. In the German army it was not the privilege of the officers to enjoy a better life, it was the unquestionable right. It was a very quiet afternoon as it usually was in Africa. In the villages, afternoon is also the quiet time. It seems that even the goats and chickens take an afternoon nap. The Kaserne where the hospital was located was rather small. There was no fortification, and the only other military presence was a small prisoner of war compound. Sequestered in it were only a few dozen bedraggled English prisoners. The area was supported by a large cistern. Around the cistern was also perhaps ten huts full of locals. There was also one large hut or, if one stretched the term, house. This served as a house of prostitution when girls were available. This was a common occurrence around a hospital area. The German command saw to it that all important rear area functions were taken care of.

I remember lying there on my pad and listening to a large blowfly circling under the awning. I was thinking that I could write to my mother about how loud the African flies are. As I tried to figure out how to write the sound that big creature was making so that my mother could fully appreciate its sleep disturbing nature, I noticed that the sound suddenly grew in intensity. Before my brain could connect reality to my half dream world, the buzzing of the fly erupted into the roar of a spitfire flashing low right over my head. Before I could even jump up I was flung upward by the earth-shattering jolt of an explosion under me in the hut. I managed to crawl to the edge of the roof and look over the ledge. I saw two more flashes of silver coming directly at me. For some reason I did not duck but watched in horror as the two spitfires dove seemingly directly at me. At the last minute I could tell that I was not their target. I watched as from each plane an object detached itself and tumbled in a gentle arc right toward the hospital. The hospital, as was the custom, was whitewashed with a large red cross painted on its side that nearly covered the entire two stories. One bomb hit the dirt in front of the building and skipped into it, exploding just as the other bomb disappeared into the side of the structure. The entire wall seemed to shatter as the roof lifted upward and then crashed down with such force that the building collapsed. It all seemed to happen in slow motion.

I screamed, "Nein Frank ist da drin." Unteroffizier (Corporal) Frank was a young soldier who, because he was from the Potsdam area near my home in Germany, was one of the men I allowed myself to get a little closer to—a dangerous trait in war. He was in the hospital only to be treated for heat exhaustion. Without thinking I jumped over the ledge around the roof and hit the ground rolling in the airborne manner. Just as I did, the roof took the full force of a strafing run by an enemy aircraft, presumably the first spitfire that had set off the rude alarm clock under me, as it had circled back for the usual strafing run. I laid there a moment in shock and then sprang up and ran toward the hospital. As I watched the dust cloud rise over the remains of the hospital I heard Schmidt screaming, "Herr Leutnant, runter, runter, Flugzeug." I dove for a pile of rocks. As I hit the dirt the angry wish-snap of large bullets whizzed by me. I watched in terror as several men running in front of me collapsed like rag dolls. The majority of the rounds slammed into the now smoldering pile of rubble that had been the hospital.

I jumped back up on to my feet and ran on to the hospital. When I reached it I began to grab chunks of the mud bricks it had been made of, throwing them aside. I saw a hand among the rubble and grabbed it. As I pulled, it, and the part of the arm it was attached to, came loose and I just stood there in shock and looked at it. A man near me took the body part from me gently and said, "Dig sir, you can't help this man." I realized later that the reason I could not see what I was doing is that I was crying. We came across many shattered bodies, one being that of Frank. Schmidt and I carried his remains back to an area where the dead were being laid out. As I did I looked up to see the English prisoners lined up at the barbed wire watching us.

I began to scream and ran toward them. As I reached the fence I grabbed the wire and shook it not aware of the barbs ripping my flesh. They stumbled backward with fearful looks on their faces. I began to scream. "You dirty murdering swine. Do you see what you bastard English have done? Could you not see the red cross?" Just as a guard ran to me and tried to get between me and the fence, I heard an old Englishman say to me in German: "Schwein." I am not sure if the guard said anything to me or not. I am not sure if I even saw him. What I did see was his rifle. I grabbed it and tried to wrestle it away from him. I wanted to shoot the pig that had spoken to me from the compound. I was beyond reasoning and hated him with all of the anger that should have been directed at the pilots, not that poor wretch. Just as I got the rifle free of the stunned young guard Schmidt slammed into me knocking me to the ground. He wrenched the rifle back away from me and threw it to the guard. He jumped back on me and kept talking to me in a calm voice until I just laid there gasping for breath. When he at last let go I stood up, dusted myself off, and walked calmly back to my hut, not even glancing back at the prisoners.

As I reached the hut I ducked around the corner out of sight and threw up. After I regained control I staggered into the hut heading for my bunk. As I started to fall into it in the half light of the dust-filled interior, I froze. It was then that I became conscious that the room was a mess; part of the wall was missing and there sticking into the wall centimeters above the remains of the bunk was a piece of shrapnel about 15 cm long. The oppressive heat had saved me. Had I not escaped up to the roof to get some breeze, that piece of shrapnel would be sticking in (or would have passed through) my body.

I don't know if I passed out or just staggered out of the hut in a trance. The next thing I remember was sitting in the Schwimmwagen and being handed a bottle of cognac by Schmidt. He then spoke the only words to me that I was to hear about my behavior. He said in a very fatherly tone: "It also took me awhile to hate the assholes."

We left the hospital area and proceeded on into Tripoli as was our plan. That evening we found a canteen and for the first time in my military career I got drunk with a subordinate. This was very frowned on in the German forces. However, the deep understanding that had been created between us by Schmidt's nonreaction to my weakness at the site of the bombing was strong enough to erase the natural barrier between us. Schmidt was from a town not far north of Potsdam. He had been a baker before the war and had joined earlier than I, having seen action in Poland and Czechoslovakia. He had distinguished himself there and been one of the few soldiers allowed to transfer from the Wehrmacht to the Luftwaffe. He wanted to go fallschirmspringer school. He had joined my platoon when we were still in France. I had never really gotten to know him. He was a quiet man, and was just one of those noncommissioned officers who are there when you need them. With a drink or two in him he was not so quiet. I had always thought of him as one who enjoyed war, since he was often volunteering for extra duty. He always seemed to be in the thick of a firefight. However, I was a bit shocked to learn how much he hated war and the people responsible for it. I was happy that we had picked an out-of-the-way bistro in which to drink (we had done so because of the difference in our rank). Had we been with other Germans we probably would have been arrested for his not-so-kind words for Adolf Hitler, and more so propaganda specialist Goebels.

The next morning we were sitting at a sidewalk cafe drinking the sweet mud that the locals sold as coffee when a young attractive girl came by selling flowers. As I was flirting with her in my poor schoolboy French the waiter brought the plate of rolls we had ordered. I saw the look of hunger

27

and envy on the face of the girl as she stared at the plate. I invited her to sit with us. She hesitated, then came around and started to sit. She looked about, caught the scowl on the faces of the local men who were sitting at other tables, turned red, and fled down the street. I could not enjoy the rolls as the memory of her face kept appearing in my mind.

Upon leaving the cafe we began to walk toward the canteen where we had overindulged the night before. I suddenly stopped at a stand and purchased a baguette. Schmidt laughed and said, "Herr Leutnant, do you think we should have a snack already?" I just grinned and proceeded on with the long crusty bread under my arm. Soon I spied a nice salami which I also purchased. By this time Schmidt had caught the spirit and declared that he would get the wine. In fact, he bought two bottles (one for each us) so, as he put it, "the officer and gentleman would not have to drink from the same bottle as a mere Oberfeldwebel." This jibe at our different stations would have never been made under normal circumstances.

Soon afterward I spotted who I then realized I had been unconsciously looking for: the flower girl. She started to hurry away but I stopped her with my yelled request for flowers. She shyly came up and offered me a bouquet. I meticulously looked over her small bunch of blooms and inquired loud enough for all of the merchants in the street to hear, "Have you more? I need a large bouquet."

She at first said in a small voice, "I am sorry monsieur, but this is all I have." Then with a bit more bravado she said, "But, I know where more are to be had."

I winked at Schmidt and said, "Well lead on Miss Flower Girl."

She motioned to us and we began to follow her. As we passed out of earshot of the curious merchants I whispered to her, "Please do not be afraid, but we will buy all of your flowers if you will take us somewhere private where we can all have some of this bread and meat."

She stopped and turned toward me. With a very frightened look on her face she quietly but firmly said, "I am only a flower girl."

"I want only to buy your flowers," I assured her. "But we have been fighting in the sun too long and only want a shady, quiet place to eat and perhaps talk with someone besides a soldier."

Her eyes strayed to the baguette. "Then you shall eat," she declared.

She then turned and walked away. We followed her at a respectful distance. She suddenly ducked into a small pathway between buildings. We followed. Soon we found ourselves in a small glen of olive trees overgrown with weeds.

"My sisters and I come here when we want to be alone," she said as she gestured for us to sit. "Now buy my flowers and I will leave you to eat in peace," she said as she held the flowers out to me.

"Please, I will buy your flowers but first you must join us for bread," I offered.

She at first looked as if she would run, then squared her shoulders, and said, "Very well, I have not had my midday meal anyway. I will have a little."

After we all settled ourselves into the soft tall grass, I started to cut the bread. I suddenly realized that we had no way to pull the corks out of the wine bottles. As I bemoaned this oversight, Schmidt just laughed and produced from one of his many pockets a corkscrew. This brought a giggle from the girl. I handed her a generous slice of bread, turned to Schmidt and gave him one. As I looked back I realized that her piece was gone. I cut myself a small piece and then her another large one; she devoured it without even looking up. I glanced at Schmidt and he just nodded. We continued to enjoy our quiet picnic in near silence. The girl ate most of the salami and bread and Schimdt drank most of the wine. I was kept busy cutting the portions for the girl.

As the last of the bread and meat disappeared the girl smiled and said, "Perhaps I was a bit more hungry than I thought." She then laid gently on to her back in the sun and stretched. As she did I became even more aware of her fine figure and long brown legs. Her dress had pulled up showing a generous potion of firm thigh. She caught me gazing at her and sat up quickly.

"You must give me my money for the flowers so I can go," she abruptly said.

"But can't you stay just awhile?" I asked.

"No I am sorry, but I have to sell more flowers to help feed my mother and sisters," she declared as she lithely sprang to her feet.

As I handed her a bill much too large for her price I said, "Have you a friend or sister as beautiful as you?"

Before she realized the implication of what I had said, her eyes still being on the generous money, she said, "Yes, my older sister is home watching our small sister as Mama tends the garden."

I then boldly said to her, "Please understand Flower Girl, we are starved for the companionship of people who are not soldiers and will buy every flower in your garden if you and your sister will come out to dinner with us."

She seemed almost to cry and exclaimed, "I am only a flower girl."

I saw the uncertainty in her eyes and said, "I don't mean to insult you. You talk it over with your sister and come to the Red Camel canteen tonight at dusk if you want." With that we parted.

Dusk comes late and slow in Tripoli. It is a time of great activity and enjoyment. The shops open and the inhabitants who have been hiding from the daytime heat emerge to shop and stroll the streets. The loafers, such as we were, swarm to the sidewalk cafes to have a casual before-dinner drink and watch the crowds, especially the girls, go by. As the last light began to fade Schmidt sipped his cognac and shook his head.

"That is why I like you despite your rank my dear Herr Leutnant," he declared. "You are the optimist in this tragic theater. Did you really think the pretty young thing would come?"

I tried to look unaffected by my minor defeat and pass it off with humor. I used my most haughty tone as I remarked, "I should have realized that if I am going to hang out with an old uncouth bum like you, I must lower my standards. Do we eat first or do you go down to the whorehouse at the docks first?" This only solicited a hearty laugh.

As I looked around to motion the waiter for the bill, I saw them. Much to my delight, and Schmidt's surprise, out of the shadows came my flower girl and a plain but attractive older girl.

"We have come to sell our flowers," the younger girl said in a very businesslike tone. She then added, "And I have brought my sister to assist me as you asked."

The sister then surprised us with a fair German greeting of "Guten Abend Herr Leutnant, Herr Oberfeldwebel."

Schmidt's smile lighted up the whole alley as he replied: "Guten Abend Fraenlein Schwester, Du sprichst sehr gut Deutsch."

She continued in fair German, "I have had some dealings with soldiers of your army, thank you."

After a few more formalities we invited the girls to sit. The older sister, in a voice loud enough for the curious neighboring tables to hear, answered, "Well perhaps we can join you for one glass of wine, since you are such good buyers of our flowers."

Several glasses later, older sister said very loud, more to the rest of the canteen than to us, "Well we have many more flowers to sell. Please come with us to pick up your order so we can see our many other customers."

During this entire time my little flower girl (already I thought of her as "mine") said very little but kept her eyes on the floor, glancing up only occasionally to give me an appraising look. If she saw me catch her glance she would blush and look back down.

As we left the canteen I asked her, "Aren't you going to join us for dinner?"

She answered rather hesitatingly, "My mother said that since you are buying all of our flowers at a good price…You are, aren't you?" she quickly added. I nodded. "Then you should join us for dinner."

The girls led us on a long walk through the narrow street and alleys, obviously to confuse us. We began to linger in the shadows getting the idea that we were not to be seen. At last we ducked into a doorway that led us down a very dark passageway. I tapped Schmidt and he whispered, "Yes I know this is not smart. Be on your toes for trouble." At last we went through another doorway and entered a dimly lit room. There we were met by an older lady who bowed to us and gestured for us to sit on the spread carpets around a low table. She backed out of the room.

Older sister said very charmingly, "Please sit and do excuse our humble belongings. Mother will now serve us." For some reason I suddenly felt that too much planning had gone into this for it to be a casual spur-of-the-moment courtesy. I could tell by Schmidt's warning look to me that he felt the same way. I asked Little Flower Girl (no names had been given, nor seemed appropriate), "Do you often sell your, ah, wares like this?"

"No!" she declared quickly. "I only sell flowers on the street."

"Then why are we so fortunate to be invited here?" I inquired.

She looked down and said quietly: "You must believe me. I came home and told my sister and mother how nice you were today to give me bread and meat, and how generous you were with your payment for my flowers. Mother then decided that we should ask you here."

"But my Little Flower (my name for her brought a small smile), I know that you, like everyone, have been touched by this war and have little to spare for extra guests. How could you invite us?"

She thought a moment, lifted her chin and looked me right in the eye, then answered, "We used all of the money you gave me today for the flowers."

"But, how could you know we would come?"

She shrugged and said, "When I told my sister how you looked at me, she knew that you would come. She has had experience with soldiers."

During this I was aware of much whispering and giggling going on between older sister and Schmidt.

We were interrupted by their mother bringing meals to our table. I don't remember much about the meal, only about the delicate way Little Flower Girl daintily dipped meat out of the large communal plate, and how she demurely licked off her fingers. As the last of the table was cleared by her ghost form of a mother. Schmidt gave me a casual kick and said: "Herr Leutnant, I have never known you to go so long without a cigarette."

I took the hint and asked Little Flower Girl to lead me to where I could get a cigarette. She started to tell me just to smoke there, but a kick from her sister quickly made her say, "Please follow me to the garden."

As we entered into a small interior garden she began to giggle.

"Do you suppose we were not wanted there?" she managed to get out between giggles.

I started to get out a cigarette when she said, "Here, you have a piece of meat on your face; it may ruin the flavor of your cigarette." She reached up and gently brushed the corner of my lips. I quickly took her hand, held it in place, and then softly kissed her fingers. She pulled her hand and mine back to her face and stroked her cheek with the back of my hand. Soon we were embracing and kissing. I know it is not delicate to talk of such things, but I must tell you that girl was a tigress. What fire! The fear, sorrow, and hate of war disappeared for a few hours in the arms of a little flower girl.

The next morning Schmidt and I emptied our wallets in payment for flowers that we promised we would pick up later with our Schwimmwagen. We never tried to find our way back, but hit the road back toward our unit. Schmidt only made one comment as we drove along. Just before I fell asleep he said, mostly to himself, "I have never enjoyed buying flowers so much."

Now you may think poorly of me for taking advantage of a hungry young girl, but I have told you this so you can better understand war. I was just doing what warriors do. When one can escape the misery of killing, and seeing one's own killed, he must take it. And please don't think badly of the girls. They were doing what all people must do in war—whatever it takes to survive.

I am not sure if it was that one incident of bombing an obvious hospital or not, but I do know that things changed on the field of battle. There is no real way for one person to know who escalates the hostility in combat, but I can testify that the next few weeks were ones of bitter battles. Shortly after I returned to my unit we were thrown into a big offensive. It was the biggest I was to witness. Our role was mostly on the periphery of the major fighting which took place between armored units. One incident about two weeks after the bombing of the hospital very much sticks in my mind.

We were dug in on a ridge overlooking a rather large plain. From our position we had just watched a rather large engagement between our tanks and the Englander. The English seemed to have the upper hand and we could only watch as our panzers fell back into a range of hills leaving many of their number behind. The entire battle lasted only about forty-five minutes in the early dawn light. As was the custom, as soon as the battle subsided the English ambulances were seen coming out onto the plain. Also two small transport airplanes landed. The English would use these when conditions were right to pick up the more seriously wounded. What was strange is that the German medics did not appear. Word reached us to be prepared to commence fire with our Granatwerfer and 37-mm field guns when the support artillery opened up. Just as the English ambulance assembled around the planes to transfer wounded and prepare to convoy back to their aid stations our artillery rained down on them. My unit's heavy weapons joined in. Most of the ambulances never left the field. I remember thinking, "That will serve you bloody blighters right." Never again did I see or hear of the medical units from either side receiving immunity from hostile action.

CHAPTER FOUR

TAKING COMMAND

The offensive drive that took place right after my rest period did not last long. We literally, as you say, "ran out of gas." Had Montgomery been more aggressive we would have been in serious trouble. Remember, earlier I had told you that I and my men were personally fighting for petrol, tea, and water. Never was that more true than at that time. Every liter of petrol we could scrounge from a captured or disabled enemy machine (we also were not above pilfering some from larger German units), meant that we had that much chance of surviving an English offensive. Montgomery never seemed to realize what bad condition we were in. Rommel was a master of moving his units in such a manner that it seemed we were positioning for another major strike when what we were really doing was slowly falling back closer to the supply areas. When we stopped and dug in it was not to restage, but rather to wait for enough fuel to fall back the next leg. My unit was probably one of the most active. This was because we could move further and faster on less petrol than the heavier units. We also were masters of the quick strike. We would dart in, secure fuel any way we could, and dart out.

Our patrols and strikes were to keep the English thinking that we were reconnoitering for an offensive strike. We were not to engage in any actions that would appear too aggressive. Such action might seem to the enemy to be a delaying tactic and would give away Rommel's retreating movement. Instead our strikes had to have the appearance that we were just looking around, and occasionally taking a chance at capturing supplies just out of devilment, not necessity. This was a very dangerous game. Since we were masquerading as scout units we had to keep our patrols small. Normally, when scouting every effort is made not to be seen, but we had to be seen to have the enemy know that they were being reconnoitered. We had to "accidentally" get ourselves into firefights so that we could gain the necessary petrol to keep up the ploy.

It was on one of these forays that Hauptmann Werner met a terrible fate. It was not unusual for a patrol to be gone several days. However, the

35

Hauptmann usually did not stay out long, as it was not his duty to be out on patrol in the first place. He used to go just to break the tension and boredom swings that come with having to sit back and wait as others carry out the action. I would be especially anxious for him to come back from these little "picnic outings", as he used to call them. I would be in command when he was gone. I did not feel qualified for, and as an Ober Leutnant was actual not truly authorized, to be in full command of a company. Luckily our radio contact with higher command was always a bit shaky and I could therefore fake a bad connection when I felt that higher command wanted some report or confirmation that I didn't know how to respond to. When a messenger from higher command would show up I would just have to cover for the Hauptmann and do my best to respond. I was therefore very nervous about his delayed return. He was often late, but the day came when his patrol was long overdue. At first I didn't even fathom that he might not come back, but by the fourth day we knew he must be in trouble. I sent out two other teams to see if they could locate him. Two days later one team returned with Werner. He and his driver were the only ones still alive from his patrol. He was near death himself. He recovered enough to write some notes which, with the driver's story, let us know what happened. He could not speak due to having had his tongue cut out, nor see well having been blinded by the bright sun.

It happened on the third day out. They had maneuvered in toward an oasis to see if they could catch a small enemy unit watering. It was too small of a cistern to supply a large unit so was a perfect place to find a unit small enough from which to "appropriate" some petrol. They had come upon it on the evening of the second day and the Hauptmann had decided to delay his return until the next morning. They did not realize that the cistern was also being watched by an enemy patrol. As dawn came and went the Hauptmann sent the other Schwimmwagen in his patrol to the oasis to get water as he provided cover. Just as the men began to fill their canvas water bags a small armored vehicle appeared on the opposite side of the oasis and poured deadly fire at them. Seeing this, Warner ordered his driver to charge toward the enemy vehicle while the gunner opened fire. Surprisingly, the armored vehicle backed off over the hill. The Hauptmann had his driver swerve back toward his stricken comrades. However, he was not to reach them as the enemy vehicle reappeared with two others and commenced to create a rain of hot death around his vehicle. Hauptmann Werner had no choice but to leave the others and try to save his own team. They made it to the shelter of the hill, but not before they were hit several times and his gunner was killed and the loader was seriously wounded. They knew they could outrun the slower armored vehicles so they headed for safe territory. Just as he felt that they could slow down and perhaps even stop and tend to the loader, the driver grimly informed him that the Schwimmwagen was beginning to overheat rapidly. It must have taken a round in a vital place. Soon the motor locked up and they skidded to a halt. He was sure that the enemy would not follow, knowing that they could not hope to catch his faster vehicle. Therefore he decided to stay put until dark and stabilize his wounded soldiers.

This proved to be a mistake as they were surrounded and captured the next morning. What followed I am not sure. I only know that they were horribly tortured. The patrol I sent out reported that the loader had been shot in the back of the head. The driver had been left for dead. They found him mangled and badly sliced up and scarred with cigarette burns. Hauptmann Werner had also been badly cut up, burned, had his tongue cut out, and left naked tied to the hood of his vehicle to fry in the hot sun. He had somehow managed to stay alive throughout the agonizing day. He was only able to recognize the coming of night by the temperature; by the end of the day he was blinded by the sun. Early the next morning my patrol found him. After we treated him he regained his sight only enough to eventually scribble some notes for me. We evacuated him but he was not to survive the trip back to a hospital. The driver was conscious when he came in and I was able to question him. I asked him if Moroccans had done this evil deed and was shocked at his answer. It was not Moroccans, but the English. By this time my hate for the English had grown so that I felt no guilt at killing them, but not to a point where I was able to fathom this cruelty by people I had lived among. However, as far as the torture of my friend and commander pushed me over the chasm of hatred, I was not prepared for what followed.

37

About a week had passed since the loss of Hauptmann Werner. I, now having been placed in command of the company, had the outfit on the move constantly. I was learning the good and bad of command. One positive is that I no longer was out on forays into enemy territory. I had to stay back and try my best to fill Werner's big boots. A major negative is that I was no longer out on forays in enemy territory. As crazy as it seems, it was less nerve-racking to be out doing than awaiting the hoped-for return of men one ordered out on patrols and strikes. Word had spread about the torture of Werner. It brought back stories, or perhaps rumors, of other atrocities. We all wondered what the reaction of our command would be. The German command was not known for docile responses. I, unfortunately, was soon to learn what their reaction was to be.

One of my patrols had brought in three prisoners. All three had been slightly wounded and were not in good enough shape to travel. Orders had just come for us to relocate several kilometers to our rear. I radioed for instructions as to where the prisoners were to be delivered. I found it strange when a short message to stand by and await higher orders came through. Dusk was nearly on us and I knew that the opportune time to relocate was beginning to wane. I did not seek further orders though since that was not something a company commander did readily, especially an acting commander. Soon my radio operator brought me the awaited orders. From the ashen look on his face I could tell that as he had decoded them he must have realized they were out of the ordinary. I read and reread the message several times.

• Any English prisoners are to be disposed of by use of flame thrower. Do not bury.

• Remains are to be left where enemy can recover them.

• Upon carrying out these orders relocate to area 7B.

I looked back at the face of my radioman and now understood his expression. I instructed him to send the following message:

• Must relocate immediately.

• Sending prisoners to your AOL [area of location].

As the radioman coded the message I ordered the company to prepare to move out. The message was answered in short order.

38

- Follow orders as given.
- Do not move until in compliance.

Upon reading this concise message I just sat and stared out into the gathering darkness. Hate the English as I did, this seemed beyond my ability. At last I made my decision and had the following message sent.

- Prisoners will be shot as ordered.

I quickly ordered Oberfeldwebel Schmidt to gather the prisoners and a machine gun crew. Before my execution squad was assembled a final message came through from group HQ.

- Carry out orders exactly as given.
- If unable to comply, relieve yourself and immediately report to this AOL.

The meaning was quite clear. I had no choice. I gave Schmidt the orders. A shallow pit was dug and the prisoners were ordered to lie down in it. They realized that they were probably to be shot. One youngster fell on his knees and began to cry. The other two stood and glared defiantly at me. I ordered them to lie down. They remained standing, one coming to attention. I could feel the tears of frustration beginning to well up in my eyes. I yelled for the guards to knock them down, which was carried out. This broke the resolve of even the bravest of these three brave men and they laid face down with their hands over the back of their heads. I had ordered my two flamethrower operators to make sure that they aimed for the heads to lessen the time of agony. I nodded to Schmidt and looked away as he gave the final order. There was nearly no sound other than the loud whoosh of the burning fuel. There was a slight cry of astonishment but the following intake of breath must have instantly stifled any amount of pain-filled protest. I did not even look at the bodies as I stumbled away. I did not care that the men saw me in such a distraught condition. The bodies were left in place as I knew the English would soon be there to investigate our departed position. I notified the HQ of my compliance and departure. Nothing was ever said to me by my commander about this incident. I have never told another person about this horrible, disgraceful incident. I tell all this to you now so that you can know the true dishonor, cruelty, and hate of war.

CHAPTER FIVE

MEETING AMERICANS

Our tactics suddenly changed as word came that the Americans had entered the war and had landed in French Morocco. It was now clear that we were outmanned and the numerous enemy seemed to have unlimited petrol resources. We were repositioned to a more static role in Tunisia. I am not sure why we were not moved further west to directly support the French in their struggle to repel the Englander and Amerikaner out of Algeria and French Morocco. The French definitely were not up to the task, physically or mentally. As Casablanca and Tangier fell and then Algiers, we moved up and took positions just out of the town of Djedeida west of Tunis.

Then came days of waiting. It was one of the longer spells of sitting in place. My position was at the head of a small alluvial fan that spilled out of a canyon that led to a good route through the small hills. After my R&R in Tripoli I began to relax a little more with my troops. Getting to know Schmidt better had made me realize that my training at officer school had not been totally correct. I had been taught a strict code that forbade any informal relation between officers and enlisted men. This might have been an effective discipline tool in situations where one could fraternize with many other officers. However, sitting out in the wilds of Northern Africa there were few other officers to fraternize with. I had only two young officers left and they were often out on patrol or involved in other activities. If I were not to engage in small conversation with my men I would have been totally isolated. Perhaps this would have caused some question to develop among the men as to my character, but I felt it would only distance me so far from them that I would not be an effective commander.

Good leadership or not, I enjoyed getting to know my men. If nothing else, it eased my growing tension as we waited for the Americans, a new enemy. Our anticipation grew with the days of waiting. To my surprise I found out that one of my men was an American citizen. One afternoon during our quiet time Oberfeldwebel Schmidt came to me and asked to speak in private. His grave manner put me on alert. We had not received any mail of late so I knew it was not a family matter. It could only be that he had a serious problem with one of his platoon. It had to be serious because Schmidt was not the type of noncommissioned officer who wanted officers to get involved with business within the company. Schmidt and I still had a bond between us stemming from the Tripoli experience. Because of that I was patient in letting him get to the point. After some small talk he suddenly began to talk about the Americans.

"Do you think it is true that the Amerikaner have really joined the Englander?" he asked.

"Yes, Otto." I by now dared to use his first name in private conversation. "I don't think there is much doubt about that. Why do you ask? Can't you fight Amerikaner?" I said in jest.

"I don't fight anyone." He continued seriously, "I just kill people who seem to want to kill me. I suppose they will bleed like anyone else. It is just that I was wondering what would happen to a soldier who perhaps had ties to America."

"That could be tough. Didn't you tell me about some of the Polish-born soldiers being transferred to other units before you marched into Poland in '39?"

"Yes, but they were only sent to the French border. I think they later were made NCOs among the Polish volunteer brigade. I don't think there will be an American brigade, do you?"

"No probably not. Are you trying to tell me that you are an Ami, Otto?"

This jab still did not cause him to change his serious face. I began to believe that perhaps he just might have ties to America. I decided to be patient. At last after a long silence he began again.

"I don't think it would be a problem for a good soldier, especially if he really felt in his heart that he was really a German. No, I think a good soldier would fight whoever he opposed."

Again a long silence ensued. I was sure if I waited him out he would get to the point of his wanting to see me. Besides, conversation in the desert used to take a long time. One didn't want to talk too fast because once everything was said the boredom would set back in. Therefore, I just sat and lit

41

up another cigarette. I offered one to Schmidt.

"No thank you, Herr Oberleutant. I can only stand about two of those Italian lung burners an hour. Do you think if we meet the Amis they will have decent cigarettes? Those French weeds I got off of that dead Brit last week were worse than even this Italian crap."

"I would think anything would be better than what we have had the last couple of months. One should carry these Italian smokes though. Just think of the sweet revenge you will have, Otto, when some Brit or Ami searches your cold bones and finds only this junk. He probably wouldn't bother to kill another German."

At least this finally brought a brief smile to his face as he contemplated the moment. It didn't even seem to faze him that I had inferred he would die in battle. We all, by that time, just assumed that would be the end of each and every one of us. Schmidt's smile quickly faded. Again after a suitable pause, he began again in his serious tone.

"Do you think if one knew that one of the troops was American it should be reported? To higher I mean."

"I would assume they already know. They have everyone's record. I, however, would like to know if there could be a chance one of my soldiers might not perform as expected."

Otto suddenly got to his feet and looked me right in the eye. I also rose knowing that friend Schmidt had suddenly, once again, become Oberfeldwebel Schmidt. He formally announced to me. "Sir I feel it is my duty to report that Oberjaeger Beckmann believes he might be a citizen of the United States of America."

Oberjaeger Beckmann was well known to me. He was from Ober Schlesien and had been in my platoon from the beginning. He had confided to Schmidt in a conversation about their lives that he had been born in the American state of Wisconsin. His father had immigrated there and farmed for a short while before returning to Germany. While the family was in America, Beckmann and his sister were born. Beckmann had been only five years old when his family returned to Germany. He had no memory of his birthplace nor did he speak any English.

This indeed provided a problem for me. I was not so much worried about Beckmann as I was about the reaction of my superiors if they learned that I knew I had a foreign national in my unit and had done nothing about it. After a lengthy deliberation I instructed Schmidt to make sure that no one else knew about this and that he should watch Beckmann a little closer, especially if we were to meet the Americans. That meeting was not long in coming.

The day after my conversation with Schmidt dawned clear and hot as any other day. That morning, just like many preceding it, was quiet and without contact from the enemy. I stood down the troops for breakfast and then did my morning rounds. All was in order. I was especially pleased with the fine location of the two 88-mm antiaircraft pieces that had just been assigned to bolster our defense. These pieces, though designed as antiaircraft weapons, were proving to be great tank killers. Since up to that time my company only had as its heaviest weapons the three small 37-mm mountain howitzers, this addition was a great comfort. After my walk around I settled for my usual quiet time to read, write, and take a nap through the heat of the day. About 1100 hours, my driver came rushing in and shook me out of my stupor.

"Sir, you had best come up to the command center [a fancy name for my dugout at the rear center of our position]," he said.

"Can't you just bring the message here?" I inquired, thinking that the only break in the afternoon quiet would have to come from the radio.

"No sir, it is not a message. There is an enemy force approaching."

"Good God! Jaeger, after all of this time don't you know what mirages look like?'

"But sir, this is no mirage. There is a large dust cloud coming directly at us."

"This had better not be a dust devil sighting Jaeger. All right, let's go look."

It didn't take me long to realize that this, indeed, was not a dust devil or a small windstorm. Out of the shimmering heat a dust cloud that could only be kicked up by approaching vehicles was getting more noticeable. I sent out runners to put the company on battle alert; even though I could not believe any force would be so dumb as to attack us in midday. I called to my area control to prepare for artillery support. From their reaction it was clear that they thought I had flipped out.

Soon the enemy force was close enough as to leave no doubt that this was not a mirage. At first I felt that it must just be a lost convoy that was stumbling onto my position. However, about 5 kilometers out they paused and then began to spread out into a battle line. I passed the word to hold fire. No one was to give away our exact position until I gave the order. We had not had any of the normal recon or softening-up probes that preceded a large attack. Therefore I felt that the enemy had no real way of knowing the exact conformation of our positions.

The oncoming force began to move forward. At first they did this in short hide and dart tactics. However, since they encountered no resistance they seemed to lose interest in that tactic and were soon just advancing in a line. I was confident in our camouflage, being that we had been in position for so long. As I told you earlier, the desert has a way of turning everything the color of the surrounding environment if one stays in place very long.

At about 2 km out they began to fire sporadically. Their rounds fell short of us and in no perceptible pattern. It was obvious that they did not know exactly where we were and were just firing in hopes of causing return fire so that they could locate our position. I had the men maintain our no-fire discipline. By then we could make out the exact makeup of our opposition. It was a lightly armored heavy infantry unit. There were six light tanks of a type that we had not encountered yet. They were distinctive for the petrol drum appearing fuel tanks they had on their rather high turrets. It was only later that we learned that these were Stuart tanks which some-times carried an extra fuel supply. Behind them were some blocky looking half-tracks and then a line of mid-sized lorries, seemingly full of men. There was no sign of troops on foot, which seemed extremely strange. The advance suddenly stopped and just sat in place. A small vehicle, which we learned later to be a jeep, came rushing up to the center tank. The tank commander seemed to have a heated conversation with the officer in the jeep, since much arm waving could be distinguished by my observer in his spotting scope. The jeep drove back behind the tank as it suddenly lurched forward at a faster pace. The narrowing width of the alluvial fan had caused the line to compress until the tanks were almost side by side. As they came to within just less that 1 kilometer out I gave the order to open fire.

In the total bedlam that broke out a startling thing happened, the enemy advance just stopped in place. Seasoned troops react instantly to enemy fire. They either immediately increase the rate of their advance or they initiate their escape maneuver. These characters just seemed to freeze. This allowed my artillery spotter to adjust fire and bring the concentrated volleys right down on them. At the same time the 88s were smashing the tanks in place. The infantry troops had hastily bailed out of their lorries, but were not putting up any sort of organized resistance. The remaining half-tracks finally began to move, or I should say scatter. There was obviously no preset escape plan. I even saw two of them collide in their panic. The ground troops did finally rally and headed to the most prevalent streambed in the alluvial fan. This was a most unfortunate move on their part because the bed was aligned running almost directly away from our position. One of the machine gun crews in Oberfeldwebel Schmidt's platoon quickly repositioned itself at the head end of the streambed and racked the entire bed with murderous fire. The last of the half-tracks were picked off by the 88s and 37-mm mountain guns.

In less than fifteen minutes it was over. The sound of firing just petered out. The last noise was that of our artillery pounding the battlefield as it took awhile for our spotter to get them to cease fire. Just as it ceased a flight of enemy aircraft flew in on a strafing run. Since the area was shrouded in smoke and dust, and we were no longer announcing our position with outgoing fire, little damage was done.

An eerie silence descended on the battlefield. There was no cheering, no cries of anguish, nothing—just stunned silence. We awaited the anticipated follow-up of a large force. Nothing came. I called for the 2nd Platoon to send a squad into the kill zone. We all watched over cocked weapons as they descended from our position down into the fan. Upon their signal of all clear I called for the 3rd Platoon to hold position and the rest of us filtered out into the carnage. To my knowledge not one enemy soldier left that battlefield that day. I lost one killed and five wounded.

My men began to see what vehicles were salvageable and what

supplies they could find. Two of the lorries had been abandoned and were in perfect shape. Everything else was rubbish.

I was called over to a smashed jeep where the body of an officer was found. It was that of a captain. I searched the body for papers and cigarettes. I paused to light up a Lucky Strike. I have liked them ever since.[3] It was then that I confirmed that they were Americans. I found a wallet on the body. Upon opening it I got a shock. The name on the identification card was German. Hans Tobbermann had lived in Milwaukee, Wisconsin.[4] Also in the wallet was a picture of him, a woman that I assume was his wife, and two young children. After all of this time of killing Englishmen I suddenly had a chill run through me as I thought to myself: "By God I have killed a man."[5]

After the battle I was told by Oberfeldwebel Schmidt that the machine-gun crew that had so quickly relocated to the head of the draw and eliminated the last of the American infantrymen was led by Oberjaeger Beckmann. He indeed was a loyal German soldier.

Having had our position compromised we were ordered to relocate that night. On our move the two American trucks soon ran out of petrol and we learned a lesson. Only take the fuel out of Amerikaner vehicles, don't try to requisition them; they are fuel burners.

One other thing I should mention about our first meeting with the Americans. We were all impressed with their haircuts. Every soldier, even the captain, had very short hair. This spawned a rumor. The Americans we killed on that unnamed battleground were not real American troops as evidenced by their haircuts. They were really prisoners released from Sing Sing prison just to be sent as sacrificial lambs to expose our positions and use up our ammunition. It even came down through official channels not to get too confident, because the real American troops were far more vicious and better armed than the British.[6]

Our first clash with the Americans triggered a new offensive that advanced our lines westward clear to the Kasserine Pass. There we took up strong defensive positions once again. It was from there, after several bloody clashes with the Americans, that my company was pulled back to the rear for the second time; the first since I had taken command.

CHAPTER SIX

AIRBORNE ASSAULT

Rumors abounded as we moved east away from Kasserine Pass. Everyone knew the importance of Kasserine. If the Americans broke through, the Afrika Korps would be in an even tighter vise. We could be crushed between the Americans in the west and the British Eighth Army in the east. The prevailing rumor was that we would be air evacuated to Italy or France as the first of a large withdrawal from Africa. Other rumors had us being air dropped into Algeria behind the Americans, or in to Egypt to destroy the English supply line. In any case we were happy. First, even to think about leaving the dust and constant skirmishes of the battle for Tunisia. Second, the idea of an air assault was thrilling. After all, we were airborne trained and had always felt a bit elitist. At last the day came. We were rallied at a small airfield near Tunis. I was not long in receiving orders.

The next night after getting there I was called to group HQ and given my next assignment. I don't know what I expected group HQ to be like, but I can say for sure that I was quite disappointed. It turned out to be a small poorly lit bunker. There was a bustle of activity within. It seemed like the entire western area was under siege. The Americans were trying desperately to break through the Kasserine Pass area to Stax, on the coast. If they did that they would beat the English who were coming west along the coast from Medenine. The major laughingly said to me, "You see, Hauptmann," I had been promoted to the rank of captain shortly before that, "if we would just step out of the way the Amerikaner and the Englander would get in a fight over who would get to pick our last bones." That was the first time I had heard any of my superiors acknowledge that the Afrika Korps could be defeated. The rumors were not too far off the truth in what was my next challenge. I was to lead an airborne mission. However, it was not to be a part of a large new offensive.

I was to take a group of twelve handpicked men and make a night drop near a small English airfield in Libya. I was to locate and destroy a bridge that crossed a steep gorge which separated the airstrip from the area

47

where the ammunition was stored. I was also ordered to try to blow up as much of the ammo as possible. The orders specified that we were then to head out into the desert to the north and link up with an Italian patrol. They would filter us back to friendly territory.

Upon returning to my company I called in my acting executive officer, Leuntant Roter, and briefed him on what to do in my absence. I then had Oberfeldwebel Schmidt gather eleven of the more experienced men, including himself, and briefed them on our mission. All were very excited. The only negative expressed was the doubt that the Italians would get there in time, since they were known to be a bit nonchalant when it came to time. However, I reminded the men that the Italians had better knowledge of the area than anyone, having been in it longer. Without any time to practice as a unit we were off. Despite the lack of preparation I felt confident. I had joined the Luftwaffe to become an airborne soldier and had not made one jump after training. This is what I had envisioned my life as a soldier to be; not sitting in a hole in the desert awaiting the biting flies and pesky Brits.

The engines of the small two-motor Henkel HE100L droned loud as we caught air shortly after dark. We were loaded six to a plane. I commanded one group and Schmidt the second group. I was to drop near the airstrip and proceed to the bridge. Schmidt was set to drop with his stick across the gorge to attack the ammo dump. It was not until I was in the air that the gravity of the situation struck me. I had been too busy getting our gear organized to give much thought to the danger of the mission. I suddenly was very afraid. I tried to light a cigarette but couldn't seem to hold the lighter (a nice Zippo taken off an American) still. Oberjaeger Beckmann, who was sitting on the bench next to me finally lit it for me.

"Are you a bit cold sir?" he said.

"I wish that was it," I admitted.

He leaned over to me and whispered, "Don't worry sir, we have been wondering when you would slow down enough to realize that this is not a school outing we were going on." To this I could only grin and give him a sharp elbow.

The ride seemed to take forever. I began to wonder if I would be able to stand up when the jump site was reached. My main concern was whether or not I could keep from pissing my pants. I tried to remember if I had relieved myself before boarding the noisy crate. As long as the trip seemed, it suddenly felt as if we had only been airborne for minutes when the copilot pulled back the curtain and signaled to me to get ready. I stood up, shuffled to the bomb door, and pulled it open. The HE100L was not designed for dropping airborne troops. It was a bomber. When we jumped from it we slid down through a hatch into a tube that was just big enough for a man outfitted to jump to fit through. This caused a problem, especially in night jumps. Since it slowed our exit the jump stick would be scattered more than if we could have quickly exited through a door. When I looked down through the hatch for some reason I expected to see lights. In all of my training jumps I had enjoyed the sight of campfires and lamps scattered across the Bavarian landscape around Grafenwoer where we were trained. Instead I was greeted with total darkness. We were jumping at only 500 meters. Just as we approached the jump site flashes of bright light blinked on and off ahead of us. I knew that was from the bombing run that preceded us. The noise of the bombers and the actual bomb drop was to be a diversion for our jump. Hopefully the English would think that our planes were just cover for the bombers. My soldiers were on their feet and hooked to the static line. Upon the signal from the copilot I stepped back and my five men quickly exited. As the last flashed by I quickly stepped over the hatch, hooked up, and stepped down the tube.

I had nearly forgotten the thrill of hitting the silk. Those moments between leaving the plane and feeling the snap tug of the lines are sheer joy. I have since envied the sky divers of today with their long free falls. At 500 meters one is not in the air long. All too soon the earth smacked me hard as I rolled over a rock. The wind was knocked out of me, but I still got up quickly and got control of my chute. Luckily there was no wind and I knew that we should be near to target. It was only after I got to my feet that I realized that there had been no firing. We seemed to be on the ground undetected.

I accounted for all five men and then directed everyone to lay still and be alert for a patrol that could be trying to locate us. We soon became aware that we were quite close to the airfield. We could hear the men on the field running about yelling to each other about the air raid. They seemed to be rolling planes out of scattered bunkers back toward the airstrip. They were probably getting them ready for a dawn mission. It was soon clear that neither we, nor Schmidt's group, had been detected. I motioned the men and we began to crawl parallel to the airstrip in order hopefully to intersect the gorge. There was very little cover and our progress was painfully slow. Just as I was beginning to panic I came to the edge of the gorge. It dropped off steeply. We had not brought ropes and the descent was not easy. In fact several times one or another of us slipped and rolled down the slope, or fell over a small cliff. Each time my breathing would stop and I would await the hail of bullets that must come from the bridge guards. However, only eerie silence greeted our fearful ears. Once we were partway down in the gorge even the sounds from the airfield disappeared. We reached the bottom and found it dry and sand covered. It made for a very quiet path toward the bridge. I started the men along it when my heart suddenly stopped. "How ignorant!" The thought flashed through my brain. "The stream bottom is no doubt mined," I reasoned. I quickly instructed the men to proceed up the side of the gorge where we could advance with less chance of hitting a mine. Great idea, but it did not work. We could not move without great effort and noise on the slope. We had no choice but to get back in the bottom of the wadi. I spread out the men and advanced very slowly. Our only hope was that the wadi would not be mined because any minefield would wash out during a rainstorm. With each step that we advanced along the bed I expected to hear the "whump" of a mine extinguishing the life of my point man.

Either the wadi was not mined or we had been damn lucky. Whatever, we soon were nearly directly under the bridge. There we laid very still hoping to make out the position of the guards. At last a cough gave away the position of a guard standing on the airfield end of the bridge. He seemed to be watching some activity toward the field.

As I was trying to devise a plan to take him out, a call came from about 30 or 40 meters toward the field, "Hey Jack, do you think you could give us a hand here? This damn thing won't even turn over." The guard headed out to his friend without even looking back at the bridge. The stage was clear.

Leaving two men to watch, and cover if necessary, the rest of us scurried up the bridge supports and began to place charges. Suddenly the sound of an engine starter began. "Err-err-err" it began to growl.

"Damn dust must have gotten into the carb," someone muttered.

"Naw, it's probably just a little crud in the distributor. Pull the cap off will you?" our delinquent guard replied.

We continued as fast as we could without alerting the want-to-be mechanics. The bridge was just a poorly constructed pole structure that wasn't going to take a lot to collapse. We were soon down and moving back upstream. Just as we hit the wadibed we heard the lorrie engine again turn over and this time catch. Its noise, as it cleared its flooded cylinders, allowed us to beat a hasty departure stringing the charging wire as we went. After we got a couple of hundred meters away we climbed the ammunition dump side of the canyon. Upon reaching the top and catching our breath I touched off the charge.

Despite being the one who blew the charge, the sudden shattering of the quiet night caused my heart to leap. I can only imagine what chaos it caused among the enemy. Shortly after the bridge blast I heard the "whump" of a mine exploding followed by the "pop pop pop" of an Englander machine gun and the fast chatter of an MG34 Leichtes Maschinengewehr as Schmidt's force hit the opposite side of the ammo area. We began to advance from our side, sporadically firing and making as much noise as possible. I heard the roar of aircraft coughing to life. Before long the airfield was full of the noise of spitfires taxiing out of their bunkers and rolling down the runway. It appeared that the entire force was evacuating the airfield. They must have thought that they were under a major attack. We soon ran into some strong resistance and two of my men went down. I called out the signal to break off and we headed back toward the hills to the north, our planned rendezvous point with Schmidt's squad. As I turned to run, a grenade or a mortar round went off to my right and knocked me flat. At first I thought that I had been hit, but then realized that just the concussion had flattened me. I then heard a cry for help in the direction of the blast and knew that one of my men had not been so lucky. I crawled over to him, but was too late. He was, as far as I could tell, dead. Three men, half my group,

51

gone in just the time it takes for me to tell this. I did the only honorable thing: I got the hell out of there as fast as my legs could carry me.

"Well at least we got the bridge," I thought to myself. "That should slow down the operation of the field for a few days." Just as we reached the drop point a series of blasts shook the ground. We looked back to see the hill on the opposite end of the bridge from the airstrip erupt into the air. Schmidt must have been successful. The three of us awaited his squad. The time began to fly by and no men from the other team appeared. Soon it would begin to get light. We had to move out. Just as we started to leave we heard a noise behind us. Someone was coming. We hit the dirt and trained our weapons in that direction. Shortly two of Schmidt's men appeared.

"Where are the others?" I asked. "We were hit hard," the soldier answered. "I think Mann and Haeffer bought it, and Friedrich was hit. The Oberfeldwebel is bringing him."

Three more down. A large rock grew in the pit of my stomach. Soon Schmidt came in half-carrying Unteroffizier Frohling. Schmidt seemed beat so I ordered Rohl and Tannenberg to carry Frohling and we headed north toward our pickup point. I took the lead and Schmidt, as usual, took up the rear. Just as it got light I called a halt and spread out the men to watch our back trail. At first I didn't realize that Schmidt was not with us. Then it dawned on me that no one was asking me for a cigarette.

I left the men in place and hastily headed back on our trail. I found him about a kilometer back. At first I thought he was dead so I quickly took cover and scanned the area for his killers. At last I felt the area was clear and crawled over to him. As I rolled him over he groaned and it was then that I realized that his shoulder was nearly torn away.

"My God man! Why didn't you say something?"

"There was nothing that could be done, sir. We had to get out of there quick."

"What happened back there, Otto?"

"Things went well at first. We were in place, undetected, well before you blew the bridge. We headed in as you ordered. Then Haeffer stepped on a mine. Before we could recover they had us pretty well pinned down. We were receiving fire from a machine-gun nest on the hill, but Rohl put it out of commission pretty fast with his M34. Then they began laying down some mortar rounds. That is what got me. However, when you hit the other side they seemed to panic and headed for the airfield. They blew up the ammo. The place was bigger than we thought. There was at least one big ammo bunker built into that hill. Sir, you have to get out of here. Surely they will figure out that it was not a big attack."

"Just as soon as I get you ready to move, Otto."

I was working hard to stop the bleeding. The bones were all shattered and hanging out. I wasn't sure if any of the shoulder was still attached. All I had to work with were our two medical kits. I started to give him morphine and he stopped me.

"No son, you will need that." (It was only later when I thought about it that I realized the way he had addressed me.)

"Otto, we must get you out of here. Can you walk?"

"No, I am afraid this is it for me. You must get the rest out of here. Leave me; I will be all right."

"But you can't stay here, old friend; you will bleed to death."

"Yes, I suppose so, but I will do the same even faster if I move, and I will only slow you down. Besides the Englander will find me soon. Now move along."

I knew he was right, but how can you leave a friend? At last I lit a cigarette and placed it between his lips. I put a pack of Luckies in his pocket.

"Hell, I won't be needing so many now that you are not along to conjure cigarettes off of me. Say hello to the flower girl for me if you see her first."

I started to leave. He grabbed my pant leg, looked up with a grin, and said, "Erich, you are all right you know, even if you are a damn officer. And don't worry. I have always wanted to see Cairo and now maybe I will." He gave me a half salute. I saluted and took off at a run back to the men.

We headed out, despite it being full light, for our pickup point. By the next morning we were there. That day we were to be retrieved by an Italian motor patrol. They did not show up. In fact, they never did show up. We waited three more days before I decided we should move out. Our water was running low despite strict rationing. Friedrich, who had a nasty leg wound, was by now delirious. I knew that he would not last long. I decided to head for the coast.

At first we moved only with great stealth, trying to keep out of sight as much as possible. However, by mid-morning we just walked along oblivious to the terrain and to our exposure. In the afternoon we found some shade under a large rock outcropping. I decided that we should only travel at night because of the heat.

As we prepared to move out that evening it was discovered that Friedrich was dead. We halfheartedly covered the body with stones and moved on. About midnight the wind began to blow from the north and we could not walk directly into the blowing sand. We started to walk at 45-degree angles to it, tacking every so often hoping to stay on a northerly course. Soon a full desert dust storm was blowing and we huddled together to wait it out. The storm blew all the next day. Our water was depleted. I knew that we could not just sit there, so I got everyone moving. At first we stayed together pretty well but as we got tired each man just kept walking and soon we became separated. As soon as I realized that no one was following me I tried to go back and gather everyone, but in the storm I could find no one. I immediately sat down knowing that in the morning we could regroup.

CHAPTER SEVEN

MY WAR ENDS

As it got light the storm abated some, but there was still very poor visibility. I wandered about for perhaps an hour and could find no one. Never in my life had I been so alone. At first I must admit that I just sank to my knees and cried. I did not have the strength to do that long. Luckily my compass still functioned so I set a new northern course and set out. About midday I realized that the wind had quit and I could see again. As it got hot I laid down in a small wadi and tried to forget my thirst and my sorrow.

I heard a plane coming from the east and at first started to hide myself better. Then I realized how stupid that was and jumped up. The plane was a bit to the south and a bit high, but I began to wave my arms and yell anyway. As it droned on I slowly lowered my arms and cussed the SOB who would fly around and not even care who might be down there in trouble. It was then that I realized that someone else was yelling at the plane. There, not more that 100 meters from me stood Oberjaeger Beckmann. At first we just stood looking at each other and then we ran together and almost were to embrace when Beckmann recognized me and suddenly came to attention and saluted. I started to salute back, then said, "The hell with that Beckmann," as I held out my hand to shake his. "I am sure glad to see you. Where are the others?" I asked.

He only shook his head and replied, "I lost everyone some time last night, sir. You all just sort of disappeared." After that we just sat for awhile and each enjoyed the fact that he was no longer all alone.

Beckmann looked at me very seriously and said, "Sir, I have to confess to you that when I found myself all alone I just sort of panicked. I convinced myself that I would now die here in this pile of dirt. But now I sure feel better, with you knowing where we are and all."

I remember these words well because they struck me hard. There I was, lost as all hell, no food, no water, and this kid was telling me he felt better because I was going to lead him out of this wilderness. I wanted to grab

55

him and scream, "Who the hell do you think I am, Moses?" However, I just reached over and patted his knee and tried bravely to say, " Don't worry Oberjaeger, we will make it out of this overdone sandbox."

Two more days went by and still no relief. By this time we were both a mess. I felt as if my skin were stretched so tight over my face that at any minute it would just rip apart. Unfortunately, I knew that this feeling was not far from the truth. When I looked at Beckmann I saw a mirror of what I must look like. His eyes were nearly swollen shut. His nose and cheeks were a mass of sores and his lips seemed to be coming apart. Still, from what little I could see of his eyes, I saw trust. This gave me the courage to move on.

I knew the end was nearing when I caught Beckmann urinating into his hand and trying, through his swollen lips, to drink the urine. At first I was revolted. Soon, however, I noticed that it did not seem to affect him so I also tried it. The first salty pungent sip caused me to gag, but I forced myself to calm my stomach and tried again. It may have given my body one more chance to capture the last drop of life-giving moisture out of its own secreted waste, but at the same time it filled me with a shame that I can not describe. We plodded on.

I believe it was the next day—but I can not be sure, as time became lost in a haze of heat, dust, and a retreat so deeply into my inner thoughts that I was able to shut out most of the pain—that when we were just finishing a night's march in the cool of the early dawn, we heard the sound of laboring engines. At first we thought them to be very far away. Then we realized that they must be just on the other side of a small rise in front of us. We made a mad desperate dash for the top of the hill. As we got close enough to see over the crest a small patrol of six vehicles came into view. Beckmann began to yell and wave his arms over his head. I knocked him down. I had recognized them as English.

"My God, Sir, are you crazy?" Beckmann pleaded. "If we don't catch them we will die."

"Don't you remember Hauptmann Werner? Is that the way you want to die?

"But we don't have any water. I won't live much longer."

"Think Juergen, the Englanders stay close to the coast. It can't be far." (I don't think it ever occurred to me what I had planned to do when we got to the coast. It just seemed in my mind the point of safety.)

By now the patrol was passing in front of us. They obviously had not spotted us. Beckmann curled up and began to sob quietly. Second thoughts began to race through my brain. I even stood up. But it was too late. The patrol was moving away from us. I sat down again and dejectedly put my head into my hands. I suddenly felt Juergen shaking me and saying, "Sir, sir I'm sorry. Of course you are right. Those Englander Schweine would only have fun finishing us off." I wished that I could feel better in knowing that at least one of us was sure I did the right thing.

We rose and started to move on. I decided to follow the track the enemy patrol had made hoping it might lead to an oasis. Just before we were going to have to lay up against the heat for the day I heard the metallic clank of metal on metal ahead of us. We crept forward to find the English patrol camouflaging a temporary position also to hole up for the day. We ducked back down behind a small hillock. "Perhaps they will leave a bit of food behind. We will wait," I told Beckmann.

We could hear the bastards washing and throwing their wastewater on the sand. We clearly heard the sound of empty tins being thrown out as they gluttonously ate their rations. Soon, all was quiet as they settled down for a midday nap. I heard Beckmann straining and sort of grunting. I looked over to see him on his knees, penis in one hand, straining to produce a drop of moisture into the other. "Quiet, damn it," I growled.

He looked at me with panic in his eyes and gasped, "I have nothing left."

This desperate moment was the needed impetus for me to overcome my hate, fear, and last resolve. I came to my feet and said to Beckmann, "Come, at least perhaps we will die with the taste of water in our mouths." Juergen only shook his head, rose to his feet, and followed me. I left my pistol and papers there in the dust. Juergen had long lost his weapon. We staggered toward the English camp. We were clear in among the vehicles before I realized there were no guards posted. We just stood there and looked at the prone bodies of England's finest. I must admit that it did not even occur to me to try to make an offensive move. At last one bloke looked up at me seemingly not even recognizing me as an enemy. I raised my arms over my head and sank to my knees. Beckmann followed suit.

The English private just looked bewildered. Then he jumped to his feet and desperately looked for his rifle. In his panic he fell over his buddy who came quickly awake and cussed his clumsy companion. The first private finally secured his rifle, aimed it at us, and tried to point at us with his head. The other fellow at last noticed us and jumped up bellowing, "What the bloody hell?" Soon the whole camp was awake and we were surrounded with locked and loaded weapons. At first all questions were only directed at each other.

"Where in bloody hell did these buggers come from?"

"Who in the fuck was on guard?"

"How did you get their friggin' guns away from them Jack?"

"Damn! Are there any more?"

At last a captain showed up and ordered everyone to take up defensive positions. All of them started to scramble and just leave us there alone kneeling in the dust. At the last moment a sergeant looked back and yelled, "Christ, Wilson! Get your ass back here and watch these two. Goodman you had better get over here and help him." We again were under the cold watchful eyes of a couple of muzzles.

At least an hour passed as the English awaited the expected onslaught of an imagined bloodthirsty crew of our fellow Nazis. Two different teams were at last sent out to scout the surrounding hills. Through all of this we kneeled in the hot sun trying to keep our hands over our heads. If one of us started to weaken and lower our hands a threatening look or gesture let us know that to do so was to invite a lethal pill of lead. With a loud expelling of breath Juergen passed out and fell face first into the dirt. I started to move to help him, but it was quickly understood that he could just lie there. Finally, the scouts returned and reported to the captain. He came over to stand in front of me and ask, "How many more are with you?"

I thought it best to play dumb and just look up at him, trying not to let my face look threatening in any way. He began to pantomime his question. In return, I tried to let him know that there was just the two of us

58

as I said over and over, "Allein, allein.

The captain at last gestured for me to check out Beckmann. I rolled him over and found him still alive. The sergeant said, "Captain, by the looks of the blokes they have been out in this bloody sun a long time. In fact I think that emblem on that officer's blouse is for the Luftwaffe. They must be downed airmen."

The captain turned to one of the guards and said, "Wilson, give the poor blighters a drink."

The somewhat chubby private snapped back, "No bloody Nazi Hun is going to drink out of my canteen."

The sergeant cut in, "Damn it, Wilson; do what you're told. At least get one of those empty ration tins and give them some water."

Wilson grudgingly went and retrieved a thrown tin and filled it with water. He carried it over to me very cautiously as if I would jump up and try to strangle him at any moment. I took the tin and said, "Dankeschoen." I slowly let some water drip onto Beckmann's lips. He opened his mouth a bit and I poured some of the life-giving moisture into it. At first he gagged a bit trying to swallow with his swollen tongue, which was so large it almost filled his mouth. His eyes fluttered open and he tried to focus on my face. As he recognized me and the tin he tried to grab it. I pulled it away and said (still using only Deutsch), "Easy Juergen, you must take this slow." I let him sip the rest of the tin of water. As he finished I motioned the guard to fill it.

"Bloody damn greedy he is now," the guard muttered.

"Wilson, you fat pig, give the man some more. They obviously have been without for a long time," the sergeant barked.

My tin was refilled. I slowly took a sip, also gagging because of my swollen tongue. I had been dreaming of this moment for days. I had imagined the soothing, refreshing flow of pleasure as cool water slid down my throat. But such was not the case. The water seemed to have to force its way down my gullet. It hit with a crash that caused my stomach to spasm and writhe. Still I desperately wanted more, but I knew it probably would not be best for me. Also, I did not want to beg to my enemy. They would have enough pleasure killing me with out me adding to it by begging. Despite my foreboding, when Wilson indicated that he would refill the tin,

I held it out eagerly and gave it to Beckmann. I continued to let the sneering English private refill it several more times.

Beckmann and I seemed to take to captivity quite well. As soon as we settled in the shade of a camouflaged lorrie we both fell sound asleep. I woke to the sound of the English captain and his sergeant having a discussion on the other side of the lorrie.

"Damn it, Sergeant, I know that a few of the blokes have a fierce hate for Huns, and with reason, but we can't do that."

"I suppose you're right, sir, but it will be a bloody nuisance to haul them along."

"Besides, Sergeant, if you are right and they are fliers they might have some good information on the location of fields."

"Well, we had better make up our minds soon, sir. We have to be moving out in an hour or so."

"Very well, Sergeant. Get the men up and let them have tea before we move on. I will try to communicate with our guests one more time. If I don't think they can provide us with any info I will have to decide what to do. But just remember, I am still in command here, so you let the men know that they had better not try to act on their own."

"Wilco, sir."

I heard the sergeant move out as the captain strolled around the lorrie. The private guarding us snapped to attention. "At ease," the captain said. "Give us a little space but watch the buggers as I try to find out who the hell they are." The private backed off a few paces but I could tell that any quick move on my part would be foolish. Beckmann remained unconscious.

To my surprise the captain crouched down right beside me. I could tell that he was working hard on what to say. Finally he just said, "Name," then after a short pause, "der Name?"

I responded with my name and rank.

"Good then, Herr Hauptmann, we may get somewhere," he said. He reached into his breast pocket and took out a pack of American cigarettes. He offered me one. I made a decision that just could have saved my life. I answered him in English.

"Thanks, it was nice of the Yanks to join the war so we could all

60

have better cigarettes," I said in a tone that I hoped would be friendly.

Though the captain only smiled, the guard burst out, "Well I'll be. The bugger speaks the King's English."

"And that you do Captain, where did you learn it?" the officer said.

"I spent a year in Southampton in '34 studying. I am an English teacher. At least I was before this wonderful chance to vacation in Africa."

"You realize you've got your arse in a jam, don't you. It seems some of my lads are not to anxious to share their water."

I only nodded.

He continued, "I've got a tough decision to make. If I don't think you and you partner there can provide us with some information, I just might not be able to convince my lads to let you ride along on our Sunday drive."

"Now captain, you don't appear to be a soft leader. Your men will do as you order, I am sure." I hoped I sounded much more confident than I felt.

"That I will give you. I won't bullshit you; the decision is mine. So what will it be?"

"If you're asking me to spill my war secrets out here on the sand, Captain, I guess you had better get your blokes to load their rifles. I don't have any to give, and if I did you know that I am a German officer and probably wouldn't do that." I waited for a response. None came. So I continued, "I was on patrol and was to link up with some Italians and they never showed." I knew I had goofed up, I should have told him we were lost fliers.

"What is the Luftwaffe doing walking around, you guys run out of planes?"

"I am not a flier. I command an air defense unit. We were just getting a break from our routine duty."

"Just two of you?"

"No, I had a full section, but we got separated in a big dust storm a while back."

"Yeah, we were pinned down too. What was your mission?"

"Just a routine patrol."

61

"Now Captain, you and I know that is horse shit. No one is this far out in nowhere on a routine patrol, especially a Luftwaffe unit. Where are your vehicles?"

"We only had enough petrol to get back to our rendezvous point."

"Now let's start again, before my cigarette and patience run out. What were you up to."

"All right, we were looking for temporary base sites."

"So you are telling me that you blighters are about to go on a big offense?"

I took my cigarette and deliberately looked at its length.

"It looks like we are running out of time Captain, so I will spill my big secret. Field Marshal Rommel would like to kick Monty's ass right out of Africa." I took a last draw on my cigarette and flicked it away.

"Thanks, Captain. Now I will tell you my secret. I think you crash landed out here, and I need to know where you took off from. We will talk again in the morning and then I had better get some answers." With that he stood up and walked away briskly.

Soon, to my surprise, we were given some tea and canned cakes. To the English soldiers this tea may have been a long shot from their familiar afternoon tradition, but to me it was a high tea worth remembering. It brought back flashes of an earlier time when I had sat with my English hosts as a friend, not as a despised enemy.

Within an hour we were loaded into the back of a lorrie with two guards and were on our way. I slept most of the night. Once I awoke to hear the driver talking to his assistant driver. I was leaning on the canvas that divided the cab from the cargo area.

"Freddie told me that these blokes claim not to be the buggers we are looking for."

"Yeah, he told me the Hun officer told the captain that they were out on patrol."

"Sure, a patrol to overrun the Bir Haheim Airfield."

"No, Fred says the cap found out they were friggin' air crewmen."

"I'll be damned; I was sure we got some of the bloody bunch that blew up that airfield. So what the hell is he dragging them along for?"

62

"Hell! Jock overheard him tell the sarge that he felt the bloody bastards can tell HQ where some of the Hun airfields are, but you know the cap He is a bit of a soft one he is. He won't let anyone splatter those bastards' blood over the sand."

"Aye, I'm afraid your right, mate."

"Well if you bloody well ask me, I think we are damn lucky not to have found the bastards that hit the airfield. From what I heard it was more than a patrol."

"Righto ya are about that. I heard the whole place was destroyed in the matter of about an hour."

They fell silent and I drifted back to my exhausted sleep.

I did not wake until I felt the vehicle stop and heard the sound of many soldiers. We were obviously in a bivouac area. I heard an authoritative voice bark out, "Stand back lads. We have a load of ravin' Nazis to dump. I don't want you camp girls to get hurt." His taunt was greeted by jeers and yells.

"Get the bastards out here, Sarg, and we will show the buggers who is boss."

"Camp girls, ya say? You children should be more respectful of your superiors. Let's see your bloody cargo."

As Beckmann and I jumped down from the truck the crowd that had gathered stepped back quickly. Then they rather hesitantly stepped forward and glared out at us. One finally said, "Rather pathetic lookin' blokes ain't they, Sarge?" We were led over to a tent and shoved inside. We didn't see anyone, other than the face of a guard occasionally checking on us, for the rest of the night.

The next morning the captain who had captured us dropped in and said, "Well, I am not sure why I brought your sorry asses in, but you had better not play tough guys. We have no reason to let you drink up our water."

I only looked at him and tried to sort out my reactions. Part of me wanted to say "Bugger off," while the rest of me wanted to thank him for saving us from the desert. Before I said either, he spun around and was gone. We spent the day without even being interrogated. That evening we were once again loaded into a lorrie and spent the night bumping through the desert. I was not so exhausted as the night before and had plenty of time to think.

One would think that I would have bravely been sitting there planning my escape. Instead I mostly was thinking of my time in England. I thought, "Wouldn't it be ironic if I was now headed for a POW camp near Southampton?" Would any of my old school mates come and visit? Wouldn't it be grand to have Janie show up. The memories of the times I spent with that pretty little maid kept me from sitting there and stewing over my fate. I, who had tasted the pleasure of a roll in a spring meadow with a lively young English maiden, now would probably experience my last roll to earth with an English bullet in my skull.

We found ourselves at our next destination somewhere around 0300 hours. We were rather roughly deposited out of the truck, separated, and shoved into barbed wire enclosures. I could make out a tent so I walked over to it to see if I could find a cot. Inside I could barely make out the forms of men sprawled out on the ground; there were no cots. I couldn't see any open area so I went back outside and just sat in the dust. I knew that my real time as a prisoner was just beginning.

At dawn the men from the tent began to filter out. None of them even seemed to notice me. I, however, noticed that they were all officers. There must have been about a dozen of us all together. At last a colonel came over. At first I just sat there, but then realized that he was standing over me and glaring. I jumped to my feet and came to attention.

I saluted him and said the obligatory, "Guten Morgen, Herr Oberst."

He returned the salute and told me, "Hauptmann we may be in a rather unusual situation here, but we are still in the German military."

"Yes, sir!" I acknowledged.

"The only way we can resist these bastards is to keep a tight military bearing. Is that understood Hauptmann?"

"Yes, sir!"

"I am Oberst Beck and I am the senior officer here. If you have any questions or problems you come to me."

"Yes, sir!"

Before I could ask any questions, such as where were we, he spun on his heel and walked away.

Soon we were lined up, double-timed to a latrine area, allowed to take care of our morning needs, and wash our hands and faces. From there we were hustled through a food line and were handed a piece of bread and an apple. Luckily I still had my M1931 mess kit strapped around my waist along with my Feldflesche (canteen) and therefore had a cup to get the offered tea. As I sat down, a Wehrmacht captain sat next to me. He quietly said, "I see you met our honorable leader. I hope when we leave here they take the old ass somewhere else."

"You mean we may be getting out of here?" I asked.

"Yes, this is just a gathering point. Be ready to be interviewed though, and I must warn you they get a bit rough especially with you being Luftwaffe."

"Great, just what I need to get my day off right, but thank you very much for the warning, Hauptmann."

"The name is Reibolt. Also, you had better ask about getting yourself some medical attention. You seem to have been sunbathing a bit too long."

I had forgotten the condition my face must have been in. We finished our meal in silence.

Right after the meal I heard my name called out. I went over to the gate and was quickly taken out of the compound and marched over to another area. I was taken into a tent. Upon entering I found myself standing before a table manned by a big burly Englander sergeant. He was reading some kind of report and ignoring me. At last he looked up, stood up, and came around the table. He said nothing as he walked slowly around me. I kept my eyes straight forward. There were two guards in the tent with us standing right behind me.

At last he said as he stood behind me, "I have been informed that you are a downed pilot. Where did you take off from?"

I chose to say nothing.

He repeated in a much more demanding tone, "Where did you take off from?"

65

I answered in German, "Ich bin Kein Pilot."

I suddenly felt the crash of a hard object on the back of my head. A flash of red seemed to envelop me as I fell to my knees. I tried hard to refocus. I thought for a moment that I would pass out. I took a deep breath and tried to get control. My mind was in a panic and I wasn't sure that I could keep from urinating on myself. At last I got control and repeated, Ich bin Kein Pilot." A sudden pain slammed into my back between my shoulder blades and I crumpled down onto my face. It was several seconds before I could even draw a breath. At last I gasped and got back to my knees. I kept my eyes downcast and saw his boots as he walked back around in front of me.

"Now Captain, perhaps we should start again, and don't try to be cute. I know you speak English. Where is your airfield?"

I answered cautiously in English, "I am not a pilot."

He slapped me across the face. He then reached down and lifted up my face. He held a sock full of what I presume was sand and swung it before my eyes. "Do you want more of this, Captain? You don't seem to understand how this works. Here are the rules. I ask you questions and you answer them with the truth. Now where did you take off from?"

I decided to change tactics by answering with my name and rank. I don't think I got it all out when suddenly the lights went out. I can't say that I remember his sock clobbering the side of my head, but the lump and bruise that were there later told the deed. I don't know how long I lay there unconscious.

As I became aware of the world again and got it to quit spinning, I realized that I was again lying face down. A different voice broke through the fog. "Captain, when you feel like it would you please sit up in the chair." I looked around and saw that there was now a chair in front of the table. After a bit I slowly got up and sat in it. Only then did I look across the table at an English major. I couldn't help looking around the room for the friendly sergeant. "I think the sarge went for a bit of a walk," the major said in a friendly tone. "He seemed to be a bit aggravated with you, Captain. Didn't you two get along?" I heard a guard behind me snicker. The major offered me a cigarette. It was the last thing I wanted, but I took it anyway.

"Sometimes, the sergeant gets a bit carried away, Captain, but please remember he is just doing his job. It seems that you don't realize that all you have to do is answer a few questions and you can go back to your mates. Why don't you just tell me where you were flying from, and what your target was before the sergeant comes back?"

"I am unable to answer you, Major, because I am not a flier.

"Yes, I know. I have here a report that you were on patrol. But frankly, Captain, I have a problem with that. I have been in Africa for some time and don't remember any report of the Luftwaffe driving around, way behind the lines at that, to drop your shit on us. You don't deny that you are an officer in the Luftwaffe, do you?"

I nodded in consent, but said nothing more. He suddenly got very angry but still did not yell. He sort of stage whispered between clenched teeth, "The Luftwaffe does not go on patrols. Perhaps you were not the pilot. But, Captain, unless you want to suffer some more of the sergeant's direct method of questioning you had best tell me where the bloody flight you were on came from and where it was heading."

I chose to remain silent.

He got to his feet so quickly that his chair fell over and he walked to the door saying, "Very well, you stupid Hun, the sergeant can have you."

I sat there in silence for perhaps fifteen minutes. The longer I waited the more I began to panic. What shall I say or not say? Would they believe me anyway? How long can a man hold out if they choose to get real tough? Such questions popped through my mind. I began to remember the condition Hauptmann Werner had been in when they brought him out of the desert. At last I heard someone enter. I figured it to be the sergeant. I knew it to be him when I felt another blow to the back of my head.

As I spun to the ground I heard him say, "I only allow my friends to sit in that chair. So friend, have you decided to talk or not?"

I said nothing, but started to get to my knees. I was put back down with an excruciating kick to the ribs.

I am not sure how long my "interrogation" with the friendly sergeant went on. I do know that soon I began not to feel the blows as much. I just remember thinking that it was important to keep trying to get to my knees just to defy the bastard. I finally found that I could not move and was going in and out of consciousness. My last memory was lying there in the dirt trying to control my breathing so the sergeant would think that I was unconscious. I heard another person enter the tent. The new guy asked the sergeant, "Haven't you done enough, Sergeant?"

"Well, Lieutenant," the sergeant replied, "that is up to the major to say isn't it?"

"What do you expect him to tell us, Sergeant?"

"I need to find more about the location of Hun bases, sir."
I could tell the officer was bending over me, even though I did not dare to open my eyes.

"It is quite possible that he doesn't know, Sergeant."

"Yes, perhaps he isn't a pilot, but he is an air officer."

"Luftwaffe yes, Sergeant, but don't you recognize that insignia on his collar? He is a paratrooper."

"Well, I'll be, so the bloody bastard still must have jumped out of an airplane."

"Yes, perhaps, but the only report we have on paratroopers is that the only unit in North Africa is an infantry unit, and it is clear over in Algeria. Why don't you let him be tonight. Perhaps we will find out why paratroopers are over here when he is in better condition in the morning? That is if he does recover. It looks like you have really done a bloody job on him."

I don't remember being dragged or carried back to the officer's compound.

My next memory was of the sound of shelling not far from camp, maybe five or six kilometers. I awoke to find myself lying outside the tent. Someone had bathed my face and covered me with a blanket. Suddenly there was lots of activity. A large lorrie pulled up to the gate and the guards began to yell at us to get in to the back. I tried to stand, but could not. I seemed to hurt everywhere. The Hauptmann that had talked to me the day before came over and helped me to my feet. He half carried me to the lorrie where other officers helped me climb aboard. As soon as we were all aboard, along with several guards, the lorrie took off in a rush. I was painfully bounced about as I lay on the floor. I don't remember much of that trip. I do think we were under way two days, if not three. My first clear memory is that of being in a hospital.

As the fog that had set in during the beating in the tent began to clear, I was surprised to realize that I was in a reasonably clean hospital ward. At first I was only aware of the smell of antiseptic and laundry soap, then of the fact that I was warm and lying on a real mattress. For a moment I thought that I was dead and this was what heaven was to be. Next, I became aware of the moans, cries, and curses of other men. I think it was some time before I realized that these curses and the conversations I began to comprehend were in both English and Deutsch. It was quite a shock to find myself in a ward with both English and German soldiers.

Before long I was visited by a German doctor. He had with him an English lance corporal who took notes, and a German orderly. "Well Hauptmann, welcome to El Alamein," the doctor said. "You seem to have taken the scenic tour to get here. Are you able to understand me today?"

"Yes, Herr Doktor," I replied.

The doctor turned to the lance corporal and said, "Before we can assess the extent of this man's injuries we need to get him hydrated again. Keep him on a saline drip and try to get as much fluid down him as possible." Without a further look or word to me he moved on down the line to the next German soldier two beds down the row. It was only then that I became aware of the tube connected to a needle in my arm. Soon the German orderly returned with some cool tea for me to drink.

The next day the doctor returned and determined that I had several broken ribs, possibly a bruised kidney, and a rather bad concussion. He also ordered some salve to be put on the sun blisters on my face. I began to feel the effects of my conversation with the ignorant bastard of a sergeant back in the desert POW camp. Each breath I took was very painful, as was each time I urinated; which I did often due to the large quantity of liquids they were forcing through me.

I had been there about a week when the doctor, on his rounds, declared. "You are lucky Hauptmann you are mended well enough to make the next cruise ship. If you had not gained strength so fast you would have missed this boat and would have to spend time in the cattle yard."

After he left I asked the orderly, when he came by, "What did the doctor mean by 'spending time in the cattle yard?'"

He replied, "If you are able to get up, Herr Hauptmann, I will show you."

He helped me out of bed and over to a window. I looked down on an astonishing scene. The hospital was on a small hill overlooking a flat covered with large pens surrounded with barbed wire. Instead of cattle, the pens were full of men. I could tell that they were mostly German; however, in one pen there were Italian soldiers. There did not seem to be any tents or other shelters for them. The orderly said, "Sir, as soon as you are well enough to move you will be sent to the cattle pens."

"But the doctor said something about a boat," I said.

"The rumor is," he replied as he helped me back into the bed, "that many of us will be loaded up on a transport that is due in."

"Where will it take us?"

He shook his head. "I have no idea, Herr Hauptmann, but I know that it can not be worse than here. The English are low on supplies and therefore have very little food to keep this big a mob fed. The men out in the pens barely get enough to survive on."

"But I have been fed well here."

"Yes, sir, but that is because there are English soldiers here in this unit and we only have one kitchen for all."

Later that day I noticed the English soldier who was in the bed next to me was trying to get a cigarette out of the cigarette pack on the stand between our beds. He was having great difficulty because his hands and face where all swathed in bandages. I painfully got up and got one out for him and put it between his lips. I asked him, "Where is your lighter?"

"In the drawer there, mate. Say, I thought you were a bloody Hun."

"That I am, soldier, but I still know how to work an English lighter."

"Well, thanks, it is just that you surprised me with your English, and you speak it bloody well at that. Take one of those bloomin' weeds for yourself if you've got a mind to."

70

We carried on a bit more conversation and then lapsed into silence. I have no idea what he was thinking, but I don't doubt it was much the same as I was. Just a few days ago I was out in the desert trying my best to kill him, or blokes just like him, and now we were lying in adjoining comfortable beds, sharing a smoke and casual conversation. This was one strange world.

A couple of nights later a transport arrived and I was able to get up and make my way to the wharf where I was loaded aboard. No longer was I in a comfortable bed. I now found myself in a dark damp hold filled tightly with canvass bunks slung five deep.

72

Section II

TRANSPORTED TO THE LAND OF THE ENEMY

CHAPTER ONE

THE CRUISE

We were hustled aboard the ship so fast that we didn't even notice its nationality. It was not until we were under way that the word spread through the hold that we were aboard an American vessel. We all began to speculate as to our destination. It had always been assumed that if captured one would be sent to chop down trees in Canada. It was a common joke for a soldier to say as he watched an approaching enemy force, "I can smell the sweet scent of pine trees already." A companion would say back, "The only thing you will smell is the dry African dirt we throw over your face if you don't keep your damn head down." This type of banter firmly imbedded in the Afrika Korps soldier's mind that he had three choices: one could die; one could spend the remainder of the war freezing one's ass off in the Canadian north woods; or one could kill every English soldier before he got you. Therefore, as we sat in the dark damp hold of a ship transporting us to captivity, it was natural that we settled on the fact that we were headed to Canada. After the first demoralizing realization that it may be many years before I ever see my home again, there was sort of a sense of relief. Of course, I did not dare share such sentiment with anyone else. It would have been very unpatriotic to feel anything but shame at being a prisoner of war, even if it meant getting out of Africa.

At first we were all just mixed up in the ship's holds without consideration of rank or physical condition. However, soon a leadership structure began to emerge and an officer area and a wounded area were designated. Feldwebel were designated as block leaders and junior officers were given areas of responsibility. Later the senior officers were moved to another area in the ship. I, being one of the better English speakers, was given the responsibility as a liaison, should the opportunity present itself. My personal bunk area was right near the back of the stern, or aft hold. This was considered the best area because of its proximity to the aft latrine and to the passageway to the aft deck. Not having ever been to sea, I was unaware that it was a poor place to be during rough seas.

Before the night was over, we were under way. I am sure the convoy we were a part of did not want to spend much time at anchor for fear of air raids. To our surprise there were no guards in the hold with us.

Shortly after we were under way an announcement was made over a loudspeaker system in very good German, "Welcome to our cruise ship, gentlemen. We will be traversing the beautiful Mediterranean for the next couple of days, so lie back and enjoy it. If any of you would prefer being shark food rather than enjoying our hospitality, just try getting to the deck area without being invited and our guards will accommodate you. We will be traveling through waters sometimes patrolled by your U-boat fleet. Though few of these pesky bastards still survive in these waters it is possible that one could attack us. In case we are torpedoed, be advised that we do not have enough life preservers or lifeboats to accommodate you. Therefore, I would advise no one to make any noise designed to deliberately attract an attack. If caught doing so, drastic steps of retaliation will be taken. Further instructions will be given as appropriate. Have a good night."

Our first night was spent rather quietly as each individual laid in his bunk and thought about his predicament, and perhaps began to worry about being drowned in the hold of a ship sunk by our own navy. Most of the men soon fell asleep. For those who had been in the pens rather than the hospital, as a few of us were, this was their first night in a bed of any kind for some time.

I was awakened by the lights coming on. No announcements were made and no guards came through arousing us. At first everyone remained in their bunks and there was very little talking. I assume everyone else, like I, was just lying there in anticipation of what would happen next. Eventually a few soldiers got up and headed for the latrine. Some were heard to loudly exclaim, "Well, I'll be damned! Look at this, real shitters." Soon there also rose the cry, "There is actually hot water in the showers." With that there was a bustle of activity as soldiers crowded into the latrine and shower area. Loud laughter and joking were heard as the showers became packed with soldiers. I joined the melee. The latrine was rather large and had on one side a row of stainless steel urinals each large enough to accommodate four or five men at a time, standing shoulder to shoulder, and a long covered trough with at least twenty nice wooden toilet seats. On the other side the walls were hung with copper sinks and polished stainless-steel mirrors. The floor was all in white tile. It was a more opulent bathroom facility than many of the soldiers had ever seen. The shower area was a large room, perhaps 3 meters by 6 meters, with showerheads along both of the long walls. It also had a white tile floor. By the time I got to the shower it was packed and everyone was fighting to get under the water. There were even dispensers of liquid soap in holders along the wall. No one even seemed to consider the fact that most had no clean clothes to put on, or even towels to dry off with. It was just a treat to wash the old sweat and dirt off. I realized that I had been very lucky to have been in the hospital. I was very clean compared to the rest of them so I stayed in the showers only long enough to get a bit of hot water spray on me.

Soon cries of anger rang from the shower room. The hot water had run out and those latecomers where cussing the greedy bastards who had used it up. I was afraid that a riot would break out. Oberst Fischer, the ranking officer in our section (he had not been moved to new officers' quarters yet), soon took charge and at least kept total pandemonium from breaking out.

The loudspeakers again came to life. "Attention in the holds! Attention in the holds! If noise discipline is broken again, the water will be turned off in the latrines. This is the only time this warning will be issued. In ten minutes you are to be in line at the fore hatchway to receive your morning rations. Later today you will receive a personal issue of clean clothing, towels, and bedding. That is all." Everyone struggled back into their clothes despite still being wet. A mob began to collect at the fore end of the hold. Oberst Fischer quickly called all the officers together and gave orders to get the men organized by section and to line up by section. This was carried out with little problem. It was good to see that even in these circumstances the German soldier was well disciplined.

It was discovered that there were some Italian troops mixed in. They were collected in one section and given an area as much to themselves as possible.

An American sailor appeared at the top of the hatchway and hollered down in fair German, "Will the officers please come forward." We all stepped forward following Oberst Fischer. The American sailor instructed us to make sure that NCOs were instructed to take charge of the troops in the bay, then to follow him. We were led up a long passageway. We soon came through a distribution line. There we picked up trays, a spoon (no knives or forks were given out), and a tin cup. We were then given a ladle full of wheat mush, some greenish substance we discovered tasted like eggs (dehydrated eggs), a piece of ham, and two slices of toast. Best of all we were given a cup of hot, real coffee. The ham was of good quality, though of a different cure than most of the officers were used to. I recognized it as the sugar brine cured ham I knew in England. The real surprise was the bread. It was our first encounter with the white fluff you Americans call bread. We fell upon the food, despite its strangeness, with eager appetites. It was the first meal of any quantity most of the men had enjoyed for some time.

As we were finishing our meal, an American naval officer came into the room. As he spoke in Deutsch we recognized him as the voice over the loudspeaker. "Good morning, gentlemen. I am Lieutenant Meier of the United States Navy. I wish I could have met you under better circumstances, but let me make it perfectly clear that strict discipline will be maintained on this ship. You are to take back to your men that they will be accorded every courtesy of the Geneva Convention rules for prisoners of war. However, they must remember that is what they are, prisoners of war. We have limited supplies of food, clothing, and water. You are to see that your men do not waste anything. If supplies run low it will be they who will suffer. I have a list of the duties that are to be taken care of by your own men. Please note that a group will be assigned as kitchen helpers. We understand that you have Italian soldiers among you. Our head cook is of Italian descent and has asked that these men be assigned to him so that he can better communicate with them."

Oberst Fischer stood up and asked the lieutenant, "Where are you taking us?"

"You will be placed in interment camps where you will remain until the end of the war."

"Yes, I understand that, but where are these camps?"

"That is not information I can give out, Sir." (We were impressed at his military courtesy, despite our POW status.)

"How long will we be aboard this vessel?"

"Until we get where we are going, Herr Oberst."

"I demand you give us some information as to our destination."

"I will say this only one time. The rest of you had better take note of what I am saying. You are in no position to demand anything. If you develop an arrogant attitude about this, that is the attitude you will get back. Now unless you have an important problem please sit down, Herr Oberst."

Oberst Fischer stood for a second glaring at the Lieutenant, then sat down with a flourish. The lieutenant began to leave, then hesitated and came back to ask, "Do you have an officer who speaks English?" I started to raise my hand then thought better of it. The oberst looked at me and nodded, so I stood up. The lieutenant addressed me in English, "Very good, Captain. Our ship's doctor does not speak German and will need you to work with him as a translator. You will be asked to report to him later. What is your name?" He wrote my name in a notepad and left.

The Oberst just sat there with a tight lip and a glare on his face. He was obviously furious at having been so lightly dispensed with by a junior ranking officer. At last he exclaimed, "Ha, I have heard the Amerikaner were a cocky bunch, but it surprises me that they don't acknowledge superior rank when confronted by it. Very well, we will have to carry on the best we can. Be sure the men don't become seduced by this show of luxury. They must be reminded that this is the enemy and they are just giving us this showy treatment to break our loyalty; and that will not happen under my command. Is that clear?"

We all jumped to our feet at attention and, in unison, sounded off, "Jawohl Herr Oberst!"

Soon after returning to the aft hold, we witnessed just what the Oberst had warned of. Among all of the groups of men the conversation was concerned with the fine meal they had just had, and jokes about the American's baby-soft toilet paper. It seems that more than one finger had broken through. I heard one man remark, "These Americans are so soft they even pamper their butt holes." To counteract the persuasive pampering by our captors, Oberst Fischer sent those officers who had an assigned area to their places to call the men together to give them a lecture about the dangers of falling into the seductive hands of the enemy. Unfortunately, the next turn of events negated the effectiveness of these talks. The loudspeaker interrupted the ongoing meetings with directions to again line up to receive supplies.

I joined the first group to go through the supply line. First, I received a wool blanket, a towel, and a cloth laundry bag. Next, I was given a paper bag with a red cross on it (later, I found it contained a small bar of soap, a washcloth, a toothbrush, and a note in German about our rights as prisoners of war). After that we filed by some tables with clothes on them. We were issued two pairs of underwear, three pairs of socks, one pair of fatigue pants and one shirt that had POW stenciled on it. At the end of the line an American sailor looked at our footwear. Those whose boots were totally worn out were given a pair of boots the sailor called "boondockers." The boots were the only item that, when issued, the prisoner had a choice of size. This was a bit difficult since American sizes made no sense to us.

When we returned to the aft hold we were instructed to put the new clothing on and pile our clothing at the end of the hold. The men, including me, started to comply, but the Oberst stopped us. With a red face he hollered at us, "Don't you see what they are doing, men? They are taking away your identity as German soldiers; remain in your uniforms." The men just stood there and whispered to each other trying to figure out what to do. Oberst Fischer again railed at the troops, "Yes we are no longer able to serve das Vaterland by fighting our enemy with weapons, but that does not mean we should not remain soldiers. How could you face your loved ones dressed in the clothes of a common American worker? They might not be able to see us standing here in this floating dungeon, but we must act as if their eyes and those of der Fuehrer are watching us." His speech had the intended result and a cheer went up as soldier after soldier came forward and threw his issued clothes onto the pile. I noticed that no one gave up his paper sack, towel, boots, or blanket.

The ruckus was interrupted by the loudspeaker, this time in English, "Attention on board. Attention on board, a U-boat alert is under way. I repeat, a U-boat alert is under way. All hands report to battle stations." Then, in German, the American lieutenant came on and warned us, "You will cease the noise in your areas at once. If there is not complete silence drastic steps will be taken."

At first there was a lot of murmuring as the men tried to find out what was happening. Then they fell silent. I could see fear on the faces around me as each man looked at the small dark space we were trapped in. I knew they were thinking the same as I, "What a terrible place and way to die." The silence was suddenly broken by the tapping of metal upon metal. Someone had smuggled a tin cup back from the dining area and was tapping it on the hull. Obviously, he wanted to attract the U-boat. An argument broke out as others tried to stop him, warning that if torpedoed all of us would drown. However, others argued that it was our duty as soldiers to help sink this vessel even if it meant our lives. Besides, we were in the Mediterranean Sea and the Americans would stay near the coast they most controlled. We could swim to safety. Two other cup smugglers joined in the tapping, and the rest of us fell silent. Soon a squad of armed guards burst into the hold led by a huge NCO. They cleared a corridor back to the tappers who were seized and rather brutally beaten. They were dragged out of the hold, and several armed guards remained at the aft and fore hatchway entrances with their weapons at the ready. All of us prisoners retired to our bunks and laid there waiting, sweating, and bracing for the impact of a torpedo.

The alert must have lasted about four hours before a klaxon horn sounded and we were sure that the vigil was standing down from full alert. Soon the German-speaking lieutenant entered the bay with several more armed guards. We learned later that these guards were Marines and no one should mess with them, even the American sailors. The lieutenant walked over to the pile of clothes that still lay there. He carefully looked at them, nudged some of them with his toe and then asked, in a near whisper, "What is the meaning of this?"

Oberst Fischer came forward and in a quiet but forceful voice said, "We are soldiers of the Third Reich and will as such remain in our uniforms."

The lieutenant turned a bit red, started to speak, then turned his back on Fischer and spoke loudly to the prisoners. "Very well. If it is the

80

German way to look and smell like swine, I suppose it is your right. Just be aware that when you act like decent human beings you will be treated as such." With that he spun on his heel, saluted the Oberst, and marched right past him, almost brushing against him as he went out.

The guards were rotated and we knew that they were going to eat, but we were not fed. About an hour later the lieutenant returned and ordered all of the officers to gather their gear and follow him. We were being separated from the rest of the prisoners. We were soon settled into a large cabin. The Oberst and the two Majors were taken elsewhere. The rest of us settled in and spent a hungry and sleepless night. In the morning we had to line up to use the one small toilet room and share two sinks. There was no shower facility.

I fully expected we would go hungry the next morning. I was, I must say, pleasantly surprised when we were taken to the dining room for a hearty breakfast. There we were served by Italian soldiers dressed in the American issue and acting very chipper. From their attitude toward us, however, it was clear that they no longer considered us their superior officers. The lines between allies and enemy were becoming blurred.

Shortly after lunch I was called out of the officers' bay. I was taken to a small office area which I found was the operations area for the guard detail. There I met the German-speaking lieutenant, Lieutenant Meier. Lieutenant Meier spoke to me in English in a very haughty manner.

"Captain, I understand that you have been chosen as the officer to assist our ship doctor."

"That is correct."

"Are you familiar with medical terminology?"

"I have no medical training, if that is what you mean."

"Well, then, how do you suppose you can translate what the doctor says?"

"I am not exactly uneducated, Lieutenant, and most medical language does come from Latin or German."

"It would behoove you not to get smart mouthed around me, Captain. I may be of German family background, but I am not a Nazi sympathizer, and I am in charge here. Is that clear?"

81

I quickly knew where I stood with that young man. He, I suppose, had to act tough toward prisoners so that none of the other Americans would think his German blood was ruling his national allegiance. Therefore I just answered, "Clear enough."

He suddenly became busy on his desk and seemingly forgot I was even standing there before him. At last he looked up and said, "Well, I guess you will just have to do." He addressed the guard who had brought me to his office, "James, take this man to the dispensary and introduce him to Dr. Levins."

Dr. Levins was not what one would call a man of military bearing. He was a short, rather soft-looking, pudgy man of perhaps forty, though he looked much older. I suppose it was his premature graying hair in conjunction with the thick glasses he wore perched on the end of his rather large Jewish nose. The sailor escorting me didn't salute the doctor, which I found strange. He just said to him, "Doc here is the Kraut the Luey promised you for a translator. You want me to stick around and watch him?"

The doctor just waved him off with, "Thanks, James, I don't think he will cut my throat." He extended his hand to me and said as he gave it a hearty shake, "You still want the job here, Captain, knowing I'm ein Jude?"

"I didn't know I was here for a job," I answered, "and furthermore, why should I care if you are Jewish?"

The doctor looked me right in the eye for a moment then said softly, "Sorry, shall I start again, Captain? My name is Doc Levins, and I need a person to help me with ill POW'. Would you be interested?"

"Yes, Herr Doktor, I would be pleased to do so. It may make the men feel better to have a Deutche Hauptmann to translate their medical problems."

"Good. We can get started as soon as you clean up. Didn't they give you any clean clothes?"

"Well, yes they did, but our colonel has ordered us to stay in our uniforms."

"That is understandable, but it does pose a problem. No offense, Captain, but what remains of that uniform you are wearing not only stinks, but I am sure that it is unsanitary. Perhaps you would consider changing to a POW uniform long enough for us to clean yours."

"Stinks huh?" I sniffed my underarm. "I do believe you are right Herr Doktor. A change would be the only sanitary solution," I relented with relief. I needed an excuse to ignore the Oberst's orders. The thought of having clean clothes was very appealing.

That is how I came to be the ship doctor's shadow. It was to lead me to a whole new understanding of my enemy.

CHAPTER TWO

WORKING WITH THE ENEMY

When I returned to the officers' quarters dressed in clean POW garb I got some strange looks, but no one came right out and asked me why, or accused me of treason. In fact, I am sure I saw several of the other officers smell their own uniforms. Later that evening we had another U-boat alert. This time one of the ships in the convoy was actually torpedoed. We could hear and feel the shock of the explosion. I later heard that the ship that was hit went down very quickly. We all lay in our bunks with mixed feelings. Part of me felt glad that our forces were still actively fighting the enemy. The other part of me was full of fear. Would the U-boat Kommander recognize this ship as a POW ship? No. More than likely we looked like a normal troop ship and would therefore be an inviting target. Shortly after the U-boat raid we heard the ship slow and come to a stop. We assumed that it was taking on survivors.

The next morning when I got to the dispensary, it was a beehive of activity. Every available space was filled with survivors of the torpedoed ship. As I came in, the chief corpsman looked up and ordered. "Good, we can use the help. We have been at it all night. Get some fresh water and keep pouring as much liquid down these poor bastards as you can." I didn't even hesitate in starting to carry out his order. Somehow, in the midst of all that pain and suffering, nationality and rank were not an issue. The majority of the injured were burn victims. As I looked down into their pain-filled eyes I didn't see Americans. I didn't recognize the faces of the enemy. I just saw young men frightened and in shock. Only once did I hear a wounded sailor ask one of the corpsmen, "What the hell is a Kraut doing in here?"

That evening we reached the Straits of Gibraltar. All of the Americans took turns running up on to the deck to see the famous rock, despite the fact that the ship was in full alert. I was not allowed on deck, and was sent back to quarters to be locked down with the rest of the POWs. For perhaps the next eight hours I was locked into those tight quarters with my fellow, by this time very ripe, junior officers. They still had not changed uniforms and had no access to showers. Soon we felt the increasing roll of the ship as we reached the open Atlantic.

When I was at last allowed to report to the dispensary we were well out to sea. When I came into the dispensary the doctor met me and said, "Well, Captain, it's about time you earn your living. I hope you have a strong stomach." Actually, I was feeling a bit queasy. We headed belowdecks. Our first stop was the bow compartment. As we came down the hatchway into the area we were nearly overpowered with the stench of vomit. I had to stop a minute and fight to get my own stomach under control. What a mess. There were probably two or three hundred prisoners in that confined area. The bow compartment was not as big as the aft area and was not as high. The bunks in that area were only four high. I noticed that the men had changed to POW garb and seemed to be clean. Everyone seemed to be just lying in their bunks in various stages of dying. The floor was a pool of vomit. The doctor began to retch a bit himself and quickly led our party back out of the area. In fact, we went clear up to the deck. No one seemed to realize that I was a POW. The doctor led me over to the rail and offered me a cigarette.

"Same damn thing happened on the way over here. First day out the poor bastards in the holds found out they weren't cut out to be sailors."

"What can we do for the poor fellows?"

"First, Captain, I want you to go down there and kick butts out of those bunks. They have to get moving. Get them to clean up themselves and the place. I'll get some buckets and mops brought down."

"What did you do to get the American troops over this first seasickness on the way here, Herr Doktor?"

"We got them up on deck exercising and getting some fresh salt air in their lungs."

"Can we not do the same for those poor blighters down in that sewer pit?"

"You forget, my dear Captain, that those men are prisoners."

"Strange, I saw only men down in that stinking hole, doctor, and damn sick men at that."

The doctor looked at me, took several last puffs on his cigarette,

85

threw it into the sea and as he walked off said, "OK! I will see what I can do."

I descended back into the hold. There I called the NCOs together and mapped out a plan to get the men up and cleaning the place. I gave strict orders that no man was to be left lying in a bunk. If they could not move, two buddies were to be assigned to haul them into the shower and keep them under cold water until they felt like helping in the cleanup. As the troops were, in some cases, dragged out of their bunks with a cacophony of protests, word came to me that when the area was clean the men were to be allowed on deck on a rotating basis. The doctor had evidently gotten to the ship's commander. The word of this cheered up the lot, and they began to attack the cleanup.

The worst problem was the jail, or as you Americans call it, the brig. The ship's brig was in the tip of the bow. I was not allowed to go in there, but what I could see from the door was that it was very cramped and lacked ventilation. There were a couple of American guards in there, but they also looked   a little green. I did get them to rouse the prisoners and get them mopping out the place.

I proceeded to the next hold compartment. There were two other compartments between the bow and aft hold compartments. I was greeted with the same stench in the next two, though perhaps not so bad. Toward the center of the ship the roll did not seem so bad.

When I got to the aft compartment I nearly lost my stomach again. This was the only hold where the men were still in their old uniforms. Not only was the stench of vomit overpowering, it was now mixed with the sour sweat of several hundred unwashed bodies. I found out that the showers had been shut down right after the incident with the clothes. I found few men who could even get out of their bunks. More than one man was lying in his own excrement as he could not, or at least felt he could not, even get up to go to the latrine. This added stench was almost too much to take. I asked for permission to use the fire hoses. Shortly after that request went out I was called to deck. There I was met by a party of American naval officers. With them was Oberst Fischer (dressed in a clean uniform, though not POW garb. A man of about fifty, dressed no different from his companions, with a half-smoked cigar in his teeth, stepped forward.

"You the Kraut officer who wants to break out fire gear?"

By now I was aware that "Kraut" was the slang American term for Germans.

"Yes, sir," I answered, as I came to attention and saluted, assuming him to be the ship's commander. My salute seemed to surprise him and he gave a return wave of his hand that may or may not have been a salute.

"The last I heard, Captain, I was the man in charge of this rusty bucket. I do believe that makes it my responsible to call for fire gear. You got a fire?"

"No, sir!"

"Then what the hell do you need fire hoses for?"

"To perhaps save lives, sir. If you could see or better yet smell that pit down there you could see why something drastic has to be done."

"Well, Captain, you've got some balls; I'll give you that. Well, lead on and we'll take a look."

We didn't even get to the hold before most of the party bolted back up to the deck. The commander, to his credit, accompanied me all the way to the hold. He stood there not saying a word, then signaled me back to the deck. As we got there, I heard him take a deep breath of fresh air. I realized why he hadn't spoken to me. He must have held his breath the whole time.

"Why in the hell are those men still in those filthy clothes?" he sputtered.

I explained to him that they had been ordered to do so.

"What dumb, uncaring son of a bitch ordered them to stay filthy?" he yelled.

I noticed Oberst Fischer start to slide back behind the American party. I took a deep breath and said, "Our colonel," as I gestured toward him.

The commander spun around and barked at my colonel. "Is that right, Hans?" The use of his first name was not lost on me.

Fischer stepped forward, came to attention, and said in a firm voice, "Yes, commander, I felt that my men need to retain their military bearing."

The commander turned a bit red, took the cigar out of his mouth for the first time, and said in a near whisper, "You get your sorry ass down there in that mess and tell me if they have 'retained their military bearing.' Then you help this captain get the place cleaned up. Use hoses or whatever else it takes to clean out that shit hole. Do you understand me, Colonel?" With that, he headed back for the bridge followed by his entourage.

Oberst Fischer, after informing me that "this would go in his report about my insolence," joined me as we went back to the hold and got the cleaning going in earnest. Shortly, it was discovered that the showers had been turned back on. This set off a near riot as men swarmed to that small room ripping off filthy clothes as they went. Taking a shower in a room with a slick tile floor aboard a rolling ship is quite a task. The drill went something like this: slide through the shower on the slick floor tile to get wet, then try to avoid the naked bodies stacking up with a FLAP, FLAP, FLAP on the wall of the shower room; quickly step back and soap up as you slide back and SLAUP, SLAUP, SLAUP, as soapy bodies stacked on the other end; step forward and slide back under the showerheads to rinse off, FLAP FLAP FLAP. I don't need to tell you the comments, protests, and threats that accompanied this activity. I don't believe any of the strange threats made about what would happen if someone bent over were ever carried out. In Hitler's army homosexuality was not tolerated.[7]

A further riot, but also a rather comical one, broke out as the men got to the pile of POW clothes and tried to sort through it to find uniform parts that fit. Finally we just got them to take the proper components and sort them out among their friends. This worked fairly well, even though the end result was a mob of men, all in ill-fitting uniforms. As the area began to resemble a living area rather than a pig sty, troops were let up on to the deck where they were made to walk around in a couple of circles so each got a chance to be near the rail. Also, to the delight of the men, at one point in the circle they were handed a cigarette and at another point a cup of hot coffee—real coffee (if one can call the weak American variety "real coffee").

Thus began a daily routine. I would join the doctor on his morning rounds of the hold compartments, and the officer staterooms to assist him in examining any soldiers who were unable to rouse themselves for the twice daily exercise times on deck. I was able to get the other officers to the showers. Many of the men never did get over their seasickness. Some we had to take to the dispensary to put them on IVs for short periods of time because they became so dehydrated.

In the afternoons I assisted in the dispensary. The highlight of the day was a long coffee hour with the doctor or with the rest of the American dispensary staff. I at first had a hard time understanding their various accents. Most of them were from New England, with a couple of Mid-westerners mixed in. They called me simply Erich (or I should say Eric, since the German "ch" seemed to be too difficult), or when joking or irritated "Captain Kraut." I especially enjoyed my time with Doctor Levins.

Doctor Levins was a highly educated man who had traveled widely. He had spent time in Germany after World War I and was quite familiar with Berlin. He had even been to Potsdam to visit Sanssouci. Most of the time we talked about such places as if he would someday revisit them with me. A special treat when having coffee with "Doc", as he finally had me call him (I found out that he detested my use of Herr Doktor), was that often we put some "sugar" in our coffee. "Sugar" was a very nice Jamaican rum.

I didn't see the dark side of my relationship with Doc Levins until one night a guard came to my quarters and awoke me with orders to report to the dispensary. I thought it must have been an emergency with one of the German soldiers. When I got to the dispensary I was told to report to the doctor in his personal quarters which were right next to the dispensary. I knocked and was bade to enter. The doctor was sitting at his desk, which was a fold-out table that he could write on while sitting on his bunk. His quarters were quite confined. The furnishings in the room consisted of a fold-down bunk, a wall and footlocker, a small fold-out table (the desk), a sink, and a commode. He motioned for me to sit on the footlocker. I sat and waited for him to speak. He just sat there reading a letter and drinking rum, straight. The room was nearly saturated by the smoke from the cigarettes he lit one after another. At last he turned toward me and I could see his eyes were red and teary and his face was a beet red. He spoke to me in a very drunk voice.

"You think you are pretty damn smug don't you Herr Hauptmann? Here you sit and drink my rum, and enjoy your ride to America. You don't think I know what you damn Nazis are up to? You butchering bastards will answer for this, you know." As he growled these words with true hate in his voice, he waved the letter he had in his hand before me.

I tried to interrupt him, but he shouted over my mild protest, "It's true what my wife wrote me, you know? I have read these letters over many times since we left Africa and I know they say the truth. Don't dare deny it you verdammter Nazi."

I again tried to interrupt, but he continued. He fumbled through a small box he had on his desk and retrieved a small photograph. He waved it in front of my nose.

"Look at them; look at them if you dare, Herr Hauptmann. That is my uncle and his family. Why did you swine take them? Where are they? As if I don't know."

As he yelled this he came to his feet and, short though he was, looked immense in that small cabin as he stood over me. At last he sank to his bunk, poured another shot of rum, downed it, poured another, and sat there in silence. After perhaps fifteen minutes he looked over at me as if discovering me for the first time. He finally pointed a finger at me and said, "Get the hell out of my quarters you gawd damn Nazi." I went back to my quarters.

The next morning I reported back to the dispensary with some trepidation. I found everything quite normal. In fact, Doc seemed his normal self to me. We went through morning rounds as if nothing unusual had happened. However, in the afternoon as we stopped to have our coffee, Doc asked me to join him in his quarters. I reluctantly followed him. He sat on his bunk with me in my usual place on the footlocker. We chatted amicably as we waited for the orderly to bring the coffee. After it was delivered he asked me to shut the door. I did so. We sat there in an awkward silence for a while until he cleared his throat and said, "Erich I wonder if you have thought about what we talked about last night?"

"I am not sure what we really talked about, Doctor."

"You were here last night. Were you not?"

"Yes, but I can't say as we talked. You seemed to have something on your mind, but I am not sure that I could figure out what it was."

"Are you aware of what is happening to the Jews in Germany?"

"Yes, Doc, I am aware that the Nazi party has officially announced its opposition to Jews."

"Opposition you call it? Wouldn't hate be a better word?"

"I won't deny that."

"You do know, don't you, that the Jews are being arrested?"

"I have heard that in Potsdam some Jews are being relocated. My mother wrote me about her neighbors."

"Did she say why they were being, as you say, 'relocated'?"

"She said that she was told by the authorities that they were being relocated for their own safety."

"Safety from what, for God's sake?"

"Some of the youth in Germany have taken Hitler's words to mean that the Jews should be forced out of the country and had begun to vandalize their property."

"Didn't you hear of the atrocities of Kristall Nacht in Berlin?"

"Why yes, I read about the Jewish riots and how it was put down by the Berliners."

"Is that what you were told, that the Jews rioted? The truth is, their shops were burned, and many were beaten without provocation or resistance."

I could only shake my head. He went on.

"I visited my uncle in '34. He is my father's older brother. He and his wife have a clock shop in Charlottenburg, or I should say had. He is a kind man and very proud of being German. He used to kid me about my saying that I was German. He would laugh and say, 'German, why you can only say ten words in Deutsch and even speak them like you have your mouth full of Knoedel.' He seemed to be loved by all of his customers and neighbors. But, do you know what those fine people did? They stood by without any attempt at assistance and let a mob of young punks, Brownshirts I believe they were called, break in to his shop in the middle of the day and smash all of his clocks and take all of his tools. If that was not bad enough, now my wife has heard from some Jews who were able to find their way out of Germany that he and his whole family have been arrested.

91

No one knows where they have been taken. Do you?"

"No, of course not, Doctor, but my mother wrote me that she thinks her neighbors have been relocated to special Jewish villages in the East. Perhaps your uncle was taken there."

"Either you are a liar or very naïve, Erich. You don't publicly beat and humiliate people and take away all of their belongings to relocate them. No, I believe what my wife has heard is correct. She writes that there is some proof, though even our government denies it, that the Nazis are taking Jews and other so-called undesirables to death camps."

"Death camps?"

"Yes, camps where they are worked to death or perhaps slaughtered as they get there. No one knows for sure."

"I don't know what you want me to say, Doctor. I can only assure you that I think that that is a rumor started by people who want the Americans to hate all Germans. I assure you that I know nothing of such a program in Germany, and would certainly not support it if I did hear of it."

The doctor wiped tears out of his eyes, lit yet another cigarette, and drank his coffee in silence. At last he rose and spoke in a firm voice, "Erich, I assure you that I believe this terrible thing is really happening. However, I am also convinced that you probably don't know anything about it, and I choose to believe you that you are not the type of man who would condone it. Now let's get back to work."

Nothing more was said about this subject, but many is the time over the next couple of years that I thought about this conversation. You may be interested to know that when I at last got back to my home I asked my mother and some other people about this and they too were without any knowledge of such camps. It was much later, through my brother who had been in the East, and later through actual film footage, that I was to learn that there really had been such places.

CHAPTER THREE

THE STORM

Life aboard ship became a rather boring routine. I certainly don't see how people enjoy long cruises, even as a tourist rather than a prisoner. Even if they are on a luxury ship. A ship is only so big. I certainly have had no desire to go on another cruise.[8] There are some events that broke my normal routine that you may find interesting.

One day, probably the third day out into the open ocean, while I was with Doctor Levins on his rounds an announcement came over the speaker. "Attention in the holds. Starting today, in shifts of fifty men, you will be allowed to view a movie. The compartment leaders are to have these men selected and ready to be escorted to the ship's theater. This morning we will start in the forebay at 1030 hours. The mid-forebay will be ready at 1430 hours. That is all." This created some excitement in the bow hold where we were at the time. Not only was it to be a break from the routine, but also many had never seen a Hollywood movie. Even then there was an infatuation among Germans for American movies. Everyone crowded around the sergeant's area asking to be picked. It was decided that everyone should have an equal chance (except for the top sergeants, of course, since it was their right by position to go, a fact of military life that no one argued with). A deck of cards was produced and everyone rotated through and picked a card. Those not having face cards were eliminated. This process continued until the appropriate number were designated as the lucky ones who could go. I must admit that I also pulled rank and placed myself in charge.

At the chosen time we were escorted up through an interior passageway and into the theater. The "theater" turned out to be a large stateroom were the Americans did training and exercise during inclement weather. We were all instructed to sit on the tile floor. Naturally, as the OIC (officer in charge), I sat down right in front of the screen. The screen was really a bedsheet from the dispensary tacked to the wall. It took some yelling pushing and threats to get everyone squeezed into the room. At last, the movie came on. To our surprise, the first thing to come on was a film clip in German. A very distinguished American officer, speaking a clear Hoch Deutsch,[9] came on and welcomed us as "guests" of the American people. He went on to say how unfortunate it was that the great people of Germany and the United States of America were involved in this terrible conflict. He then went into a lecture given as if by a father to innocent but naughty boys. He spoke about the need for the whole world to rally against the criminal policies of the Nazi party. Several soldiers tried to stand up and protest. However, it was almost impossible to get to one's feet in that packed room. Also, several armed guards appeared along with Lieutenant Meier who proceeded to holler threats until the protesters sat down. I don't remember much more about this piece of propaganda.

The next two film clips were newsreels, in English. There were a lot of hoots and yells as the film showed American troops landing in Africa. When the newsreels showed Montgomery (that was the first time I actually saw what he looked like), the audience really raised a ruckus. I was one of the few in the crowd who could understand English, and I was rather shocked to learn that the Allies were so successful. My view of the war was much different. One would have gotten the impression from watching those pieces of news that the war would be over in a matter of months.

The one section of the newsreels that the POWs did enjoy was the part showing American football. It was most everyone's, including my, first look at this strange sport. We couldn't figure out what was going on, but when they showed some very nasty tackles, we all laughed and cheered. The close-up of some girls in short skirts (I think you call them cheerleaders) jumping up and down caused quite a stir, and some rather rude, but funny, comments.

At last the feature movie came on. It was also in English. I can't even remember what the film was, but I do remember that it was a very old film-strip that had been run too many times and was very filckery and full of scratches. By this time the room had become very hot and the floor very hard. We were, by then, used to the roll of the ship, but sitting on that hard slick floor it was very noticeable. We all would slide back and forth crunching even tighter together. The air became even more stale. Our diet had made all

94

of us a bit gaseous and the odor of flatus became overpowering. Most of the men fell asleep and everyone was leaning on everyone else. It is no wonder that I cannot remember the movie.

At last the movie ended and the lights came on. As the groaning group filed out of the bay many bodies were left lying about. At first we thought them to be sleepers, but soon found that they had passed out. Several had to be taken to the dispensary where smelling salts brought them around.

Not only was this "entertainment" time enjoyed by men from all of the bays, it was repeated several more times. The same movie. The men chosen to go were still picked by a draw of cards, but it was now the lucky ones who got to stay back. The NCOs (and certain officers like me) decided not to use their rank, thus allowing other soldiers to have the privilege.

On about the eleventh day at sea the convoy went through a rather large storm. Since we were traveling east in the storm path between Africa and the Caribbean we were in very rough seas for several days. On the advice of Doc Levins I tried to keep eating hearty meals. It did keep me from becoming as ill as the majority of POWs aboard. Doc and I were kept busy in the holds trying to ferret out the sickest prisoners for treatment. Most just had to endure since there were so limited facilities aboard ship to treat the sick and injured. Several men in the bow were injured by falling out of bunks or crashing against bulkheads on the way to the latrine. It was almost impossible to move around in the bow as it slammed up and down in the waves. The sickest lot were the poor blokes in the aft hold. Not only were they more subject to the slamming up and down (though not as bad as the bow) than those at midships, but also could not sleep due to the noise of the screws. They had become accustomed to the STRUM, STRUM, STRUM of the propellers, but now it was STRUM, STRUM, WAP, WAP, STRUM, STRUM, WAP, WAP, WAP as the stern came out of the water so far the blades of the props would slap the surface. Due to the choppiness of the sea, the rhythm was not even consistent.

The worst was during the third day of the storm. During the night the rough seas had backed up the bilge flooding the aft latrine. When we went down on our rounds to the aft hold the smell of raw sewage almost drove us back out. Probably 80 percent of the men were very ill. A cleanup crew was busy at work trying to swab out the mess in the latrine. It was at least 20 centimeters deep in sewage. The crew were armed with buckets. The drill went something like this: As the ship rolled and the sewage slopped to one side, jump into the latrine, run for the bulkhead, and climb as high as possible to avoid the tide coming in (the sewage slopping back your way), reach down, and fill your bucket. As the tide went back out run for the hatchway and hand your bucket to the bucket brigade to the deck. Wait until the next favorable tide and repeat the process. If one miscalculated, one's boots were filled with soggy toilet tissue or unmentionable gunk. God help the clumsy fellows who slipped and fell. I was very pleased to be an officer on that day and not one of the poor fellows actually filling buckets. I definitely shall never forget the face of one tall skinny young boy from Bavaria. His face was actually green. I have never seen such agony in the face of a man on his feet still working. When I said something to him he just grinned and said, "When I get home, sir, I won't even go out in a rowboat. Can you imagine that I almost volunteered for the navy?"

The storm at last abated and we went back to our routines.

CHAPTER FOUR

OTTO'S FATE

Strange that you should ask about Oberfeldwebel Schmidt. I was going to tell you about him this evening. I had thought a lot about Otto while aboard ship. I had come to the conclusion that he had died a hero's death keeping the British from following us into the desert. I was determined to put him in for a medal when I returned to Germany. Somehow I naturally felt I would return to my homeland as a soldier of a triumphant army. Now would be a good place in my recollections to let you know what happened to him after I left him lying there alone and wounded, for he did not die in that godforsaken place.[10]

At dawn, as the morning sun's rays took away the cool breeze of the African desert night, Otto fought to not lose consciousness. The pain in his shoulder was starting to intensify. Up to now it had only been a slight throbbing under a blanket of numbness. He knew that he must stay alert. Surely the British would follow the raiders now that it was light enough not to stumble into an ambush. He must delay them long enough to allow his men to gain some travel time. Otto had always considered them "his" men. To Otto the presence of an officer was a bit of a nuisance; it's only redeeming value was to give higher officers someone to blame for the unit's shortcomings. Besides that, I think he had started to look at me as a guardian would his ward. He also knew that if he passed out he may never awaken. He could not see his wound. He could not turn his head to see his shoulder. He had, however, seen my face when I had bound the wound and had said my farewell. What he was sure of was that it was very serious.

As he lay there, in order to stay conscious, he tried to remember how it had happened. He had always expected to be downed in combat. After so many years the event was inevitable. He had thought it would happen differently. He had imagined himself charging the enemy at the head of his men when a blinding flash of pain would slam through his body, throwing him off of his feet. He would jump up, continuing to encourage his men to annihilate the bastards despite his overwhelming pain. Only when the enemy machine-gun nest was overrun would he sink into a comforting final darkness. But that is not the way it had happened.

They had been pulling back from the attack on the ammo area. The actual attack had been swift and short-lived. The Englander had been caught off guard. At first there had been little resistance. When the explosions had demolished the bridge, the English soldiers left on the ammo area side of the gorge seemed to be without leadership. There had been much yelling and running around as if in panic. His first actual sight of the area was in that brief flash of light from the explosions. He was surprised not to see piles of supplies and ammo. It was only after that brief look that he had realized the ammo was stored in bunkers or caves in the small hills about 200 meters from the gorge. Realizing that they could not destroy the caves, he had ordered his squad to withdraw as soon as the enemy began to organize and put up a resistance. It was an even bigger shock when he heard the explosions of the bunkers as the British, for some reason, began to destroy the caves. Mortar rounds began to impact near him and he remembered diving for cover. As he lay in a depression a Jaeger jumped right on top of him. Just as he did the Jaeger had let out a quick breath, almost like a cough. Even as Otto screamed at the idiot to get off him, the Jaeger had continued to lie like a dead weight on him. At last Otto lunged up to his feet thrusting the young boy off of him. The boy rolled off onto his back and laid still. Only then did Otto realize that he was dead. While kneeling over retrieving his dead soldier's identification tag he felt a blow to his neck. He thought he had been hit by a flying rock from the bunker explosions or a nearby exploding mortar round. There was no blinding red-hot searing pain. Just the initial shock of the impact, bright flashes of light like New Year's Eve sparklers, followed by a fuzzy numbness. At first he couldn't seem to organize his thoughts and just got to his knees and tried to remember where he was, or what he was doing. Then he remembered the situation he was in and jumped up and ran back in the direction he had instructed his men to go. As he ran he shifted his machine pistol from his right hand to his left. For some reason the left hand didn't hold on and the weapon dropped. He ran back to pick it up, but as he reached down his hand didn't seem to work. He snatched up the weapon with his right hand and ran on. As he caught up with his men, he got them to take up temporary fighting positions. As they lay there waiting for the enemy to follow he checked out the extent of the damage the rock had done. He reached up with his right hand. He was shocked to realize that he could not feel it touching his left shoulder. His hand came away covered with blood. He felt his shoulder again. Only then did he realize that a big portion of his shoulder was missing. So it had not been a rock, but a mortar fragment. It had entered near the base of his neck and exited out his back just above the point of his left shoulder. The whole area was still numb. He moved the men out once more. Unteroffzer Frohling was also wounded and Schmidt half carried him until they joined up with the rest of the group, despite his own condition. Later, as they ran through the dark he could not keep up. He finally took up a temporary fighting position, and decided to await his fate. That is where I found him, bound the wound, said my farewells, and left him.

For several hours Otto was able to stay alert, but as the heat grew he began to go in and out of consciousness. At last he slipped totally under. When at last he regained consciousness it was almost dark. Otto knew that he would not make the night if he were to remain immobile. He thought about trying to catch up with his men, but then reasoned that that was not an option. They would be many kilometers from his location by that time. He decided the best, and perhaps only, option was to go back and surrender.

It took him nearly all night to stagger back to the airfield. He lost count of the times he stumbled and fell. As he neared the site of the battle he was impressed with the lack of noise. As he entered the actual ammo site no British were to be found. From the flickering light of a few remaining fires he could see that the area had been hastily abandoned. He went to the bridge and found it totally destroyed. He started to descend into the gorge to get to the airfield side but stumbled and tumbled partway down. He again lost consciousness.

He awoke to voices calling each other from one side of the gorge to the other. He realized that they were in English. He wanted to call out, but could not seem to rise out of the fog he felt himself in. The next thing he knew he was on a stretcher being placed aboard a small plane. He was aware that his was one of several stretchers aboard the aircraft. He again slipped under as the plane bumped down the runway on takeoff.

The jarring of the plane landing brought him back to awareness. He was taken from the plane to a waiting lorrie by men who seemed to be talking an Arabic dialect. He next awoke lying on a bed in a dimly lit room. He could make out several other beds in the room. He heard three men come in, but could not understand them because they spoke English.

"Here are the blokes that just came in, sir; they were prepped by the Gyps [Egyptians] last night. We were too busy to do any triage."

"Are they more of Monty's boys?"

"No, Sir; they are airmen flown in from a small air station that was overrun night before last."

Otto could hear them working their way toward him. As they visited each bed, orders were given and Egyptians came in and picked up some of the men and rushed them out. The man Otto figured was the doctor did not spend much time at the bed next to his. After a brief exam the man's face was covered up with the blanket he had over him. Otto knew that he was dead.

The doctor came to his bed and said, "Good, this one is awake. How are you doing soldier?"

Naturally, Otto did not answer because he had no idea what the man had said.

"Well," the doctor continued, "Let's see what is up with you."

The blanket was pulled back. The doctor spotted the wound in his shoulder and went right to work examining it. One of the men with the doctor pulled the blanket down the rest of the way and started to look for other wounds.

He suddenly stood up straight and Otto heard him almost yell, "What the bloody hell? This bastard is a blinking Hun."

The doctor and the other man with him stepped away a bit to let the light from a small window over the bed illuminate Otto better. Though Otto could not understand them he knew that his being a German had been detected. All he could think of doing was to give them his name and rank. The three just stood there like he was some sort of freak or something.

At last the doctor said, "He is not going anywhere with that wound; we'll worry about him later. Let's help these other blokes." As they moved

100

to the next bed Otto figured the doctor must have told them just to let him die.

Soon Otto was the only one left in the room. No one came in. After several hours of fitful sleep he awoke to find himself still alone. The shoulder was beginning to emit a dull pain. He had a strong craving for a cigarette. He also needed to piss really bad. He attempted to get up to find a latrine. As he rolled to a sitting position the room began to spin. He tried to lie back down but fell forward instead. The fall seemed to take minutes. Everything was happening in slow motion. He did not remember hitting the floor. He awoke to a blinding pain in his shoulder as someone lifted him to the bed. He became aware of two men, he figured to be Egyptian, changing the dressing on his wound. He passed out again.

When he awoke it was dark. He remembered trying to get out of the bed to go to the latrine. He wondered why he no longer had the urge to urinate. It was then that he realized that he had soiled himself. For the first time since being wounded he realized the situation he was in. Tears came to his eyes and he felt ashamed that he was so weak. He had never been an aggressive or particularly brave young man, but the years of war had hardened him and he had long ago ceased to be concerned about his own future. He, like all old veterans, just learned to live one day at a time until that bullet or artillery round with his name on it came out of nowhere to end it all. Now he laid in the enemy's grip, unable even to get up to relieve himself.

When morning came an English orderly, accompanied by an Egyptian, came in and brought him some warm tea and some bread. Later in the day he was moved to another building where he found himself in the company of several other wounded soldiers. By now the pain in his shoulder was excruciating. He was to remain there several days until transportation to a POW camp was organized. At the camp he was left in a tent lying on a pad on the ground. He could feel the bedbugs he had picked up in the English hospital above the throbs of pain coming from his shoulder. No one came to look after his wound or change the dressing. Twice a day someone did bring a thin beef broth and some bread.

After three or four days, he was somewhat unaware of time, a German doctor came by and examined him. The doctor was very upset. He angrily growled at the orderly with him, "How damn long has this man been lying here? My God, he stinks. Could you not have at least cleaned him up? Let's get him up to the hospital right away." Otto was moved once again. This time to a rather nice hospital. There he was stripped and scrubbed and a new dressing was applied. That evening he was operated on and the rotten destroyed flesh was removed. The next day the doctor came by and explained to him that not much could be done to repair the damage since the hospital was not equipped very well; also, the doctor said that he did not feel competent to do the type of reconstruction that was necessary. One major relief was that painkillers were available. Otto began getting healthy doses of morphine.

After a couple of weeks at the hospital Otto was placed aboard a ship and transported to England. He didn't remember much about the trip because he was so heavily sedated. Once in England he underwent a series of seven or eight operations under the care of a German army doctor who had been well known before the war for his orthopedic surgery.

Soon he was up and around. He gained limited use of his shoulder and arm, much to his and the doctor's surprise and delight. While in the hospital, he found himself in wards right along with English and American soldiers. There he quickly began to learn English and was rather shocked to find he liked most of his former enemies, especially the Yanks, as the "Limeys" called them. They also seemed to like him. Only a few were bitter and avoided contact with him. He soon found himself working in the hospital kitchen plying his former trade as a baker. The hospital staff especially liked the Stollen he made during the Christmas holidays. In fact they liked his work so well that even after he was moved to a nearby POW camp he was given a pass to come back to the hospital and bake.

Otto, as I, believed that we would never see each other again, though both of us were to wonder what fate had brought the other, and each swore to himself to look the other up, or the family of the other, some distant day should we ever get back to Germany.

CHAPTER FIVE

LAST DAYS ABOARD SHIP

Life aboard ship remained routine. By now, after the storm, there was little to do in the dispensary. Most of the men had gotten over their seasickness and not so many were losing their balance and breaking a bone in their falls. We prisoners were allowed to be on deck through much of the day until we entered Caribbean waters.

As we entered the blue-green water of the Caribbean our progress was slowed as the convoy began to increase the rate of their zigzag. U-boat alerts were also increased. There was also a noticeable mood shift among the POWs. A rumor was spread that we were just a few miles off the coast of South America. It was also rumored that anyone reaching South American shores would be granted political asylum. New schemes for escape began to emerge. Problems really escalated when two men actually found a way through the guards and reached deck. They were spotted trying to get a life raft out of the emergency locker and, when challenged, jumped overboard. The ship's commander refused to turn about and try to recover them.

Soon afterward the announcement was made by Lieutenant Meier that we were in waters that were very shark infested. This we did not doubt since we had all seen sharks following the ship feeding on garbage thrown off the fantail. Lieutenant Meier also warned us that the marines on guard had been warned not to let any more unauthorized POWs on deck (as he put it) "alive". The commander's refusal to attempt a rescue of the men who went overboard caused a near riot. I too was very upset. This was exacerbated by my overhearing two sailors in the dispensary joking about how much sharks liked to eat "kraut". I didn't need to remind myself that I was among the enemy.

As we cruised within sight of Cuba it became clear that our destination was not Canada, but the Gulf Coast of the United States. When I asked Doc Levins about this he said only, "I hope you like chili beans." His answer did not make a lot of sense to me at the time. Soon we were off a flat coast with long beaches and mangrove swamps. The day before spotting land

103

we had gone through a large oil slick and lots of debris. A ship had obviously been torpedoed in the last day or so. Therefore the sight of land was doubly welcome. We were soon all confined to quarters.

Not long after being confined a riot broke out in the forebay. A group of men had charged the hatch guard and attempted to get to the deck. It seems that the rumor was rampant in the hold compartments that the ship was off the coast of Mexico, and many of the men saw it as the last opportunity to escape. Several men had been wounded and two were dead. I was called to the dispensary under heavy guard to assist with the treatment of the wounded. I found the mood there very heavy and could feel the distrust and hate, even toward me, by the dispensary staff. There was no amiable coffee break with Doc Levins that afternoon.

Later that evening, right before lights out, I was again called to the dispensary. Once there I was instructed to report to the doctor's quarters. The memory of our last late-night conversation caused me to be hesitant to knock on his door. My fears were confirmed as soon as I entered his quarters and smelled the rum and cigarette smoke. As the time before, he motioned me to sit on the foot locker. I did so. He sat there and continued to write at his desk, pausing to drink another shot of rum. At last he leaned back and looked with bleary eyes at me. After several minutes he spoke, "Let's hope to hell he lives through the night."

I waited a few seconds for him to clarify who 'he' was. When no explanation came I asked, "Who lives through the night?"

"The poor bastard marine who was severely beaten by your men today."

"You don't think I had anything to do with that, do you?"

"It is our own fault, I guess. We have treated you Krauts a bit too casually. But, I still do not understand why they did it."

"The men are soldiers, Doctor. They feel it is their duty to try to escape."

"Escape! To where, for God's sake? If they did get overboard and to land, where the hell would they have gone?"

"I believe they thought the land we see is Mexico."

"Mexico? Don't the ignorant bastards know Texas when they

see it?"

"Texas? So that is where we are. No, Doctor, I don't think any of them have ever seen Texas, or perhaps even heard of it."

"Well, no matter, except that I warn you that if that marine dies, I shudder to think what the rest of the marines are liable to do. In any case that is not why I called you up here. First, let me make it clear that I hate even the word Nazi, to say nothing of the atrocities you people have brought upon the world. However, you have personally behaved yourself and have performed the duties asked of you aboard this ship. Therefore, I have written a letter you may take with you expressing this. Perhaps it will come in handy for you."

He handed me an envelope, and I thanked him and started to leave. He reached out and took my arm and sort of pulled me back down to the footlocker. We sat there in silence for awhile and he at last sort of coughed and said, "I know that your being a prisoner and my being Jewish has been difficult for you, but . . ."

I interrupted. "I again reiterate, Doc, I have no animosity toward you."

"Perhaps that is so; but Erich, I have been subjected to prejudice my whole life and know that you as a German have a built-in disgust for all Jews. But, I will say that you do not let it surface; that is admirable. That as it may be, I have a favor to ask you."

"What can I do for you, Doctor?"

"Do you remember what I told you about my uncle and his family? I have written his name and the address of his shop and home in Charlottenburg. You will perhaps get back to Germany before I. Would you try to find what has happened to him and his family? He has a wife and two girls. If you find any information would you write me? I have also included my name and address."

I took the paper from him and guaranteed him that I would try. I started to leave. As I got to the hatchway he stopped me and shook my hand. "Perhaps we shall meet again in peace my friend. Then you can buy the rum," he said as we departed.

The next day we were confined to our compartments, but could tell

105

the ship was at anchor. We were ordered to pack our belongings and be prepared to depart from the ship early the next morning.

Right after breakfast the ship maneuvered into a docking at a long wharf. Soon afterward we went down the gangplanks to stand upon the homeland of our enemy. I can't say that I have ever felt so alone and doubtful about my future. Even my moment of surrender was not like that empty feeling I had upon getting off that ship. When I had surrendered there had been a feeling of relief, but not so standing in a loose formation on that dilapidated wharf in Texas. The men around me stood in silence. No doubt they also were feeling the despair of the moment.

When all of the POWs were on the ground we were marched off the quay and in to a small street. I was shocked at how many of us there were. Onboard I had seen everyone in the course of my rounds with the doctor, but never in one body. As we started to march, or perhaps walk is a more appropriate term, I realized that I had lost my land legs. I was wobbling and staggering, trying to get my body to quit adjusting to the pitch and roll of the sea. Everyone else was also having the same difficulty. The streets were lined with onlookers. Evidently word had been passed that we were to be unloaded that morning. I was to learn later that we were the first German prisoners of war who had been unloaded in that port. We never were told what city it was. Soon the guards alongside us goaded us into a trot, what you American soldiers call double-time. This was most difficult for our sea legs. Men started to stumble and fall only to be yelled at and threatened until they got back up and moved with the group. The people on the street began to laugh and jeer at us. I expected to feel the sting of rocks pelting us, but nothing came. They did not need to throw material things to hurt us; their jeers, laughs, and insults were enough. I could feel the heat in my cheeks as I was humiliated and angered at the same time. I reached the height of my hate for the enemy at that time. They had caught us unaware and unprepared. Had we known what was in store for us we would have formed up properly and marched as proud soldiers through the streets no matter what the guards would have done to us.

Mercifully the distance we had to go was not far. Soon we came to a long line of trucks and buses. We were quickly hustled aboard them

106

and were on our way. We traveled through a land of very large fields, with few trees. There were nice farmsteads scattered through the fields. Occasionally we came through small towns. We were all impressed at how poor the towns looked. Was this really America? Perhaps we were in Mexico. Most of the people we saw were dark skinned. Many of their homes were poor wooden shacks with goats and chickens in the yards. However, parts of the town were quite nice with large houses, though still of wood, with lawns and trees. There seemed to be a large disparity between rich and poor. In many ways there was a resemblance between the farmlands around Tunis and this landscape. After about four hours we were at my first home in America. A new interesting, adventurous phase of my life was about to begin.

108

Section III
PRISONER OF WAR

CHAPTER ONE

WELCOME TO AMERICA

After about four hours of travel in a basically northeast direction our convoy pulled into a large barbed-wire enclosed area with wooden guard towers every hundred meters or so. At one end I could see rows of long single-story wooden buildings. At the other end stood rows of large tents. In between was a large open area. Several large buildings stood in the middle. At the entrance a few large, nice houses with new lawns and young trees stood outside the fence. At the entrance to the main compound a guard-house blocked the exit. To the rear of the enclosed area was another area of single-story buildings, much like the ones on the opposite end of the compound from the tented area. I deduced that it must be the garrison area for the guards. Next to it stood the motor pool area.

The entire area looked the same as any new military training area anywhere in the world. My only impression as I stiffly climbed down out of the truck was of the humidity and the dust. How could it be so humid and have the air full of dust at the same time? The result was an instant grimy feeling as the dust clung to my wet skin.

I didn't have much time to contemplate my new surroundings. For one thing, I was trying to overcome a wave of fear and apprehension that was threatening to take over my entire thought process. I felt more fear at that moment as to what my fate as a prisoner of war would be than at any time up to then, including my capture and loading onto the transport ship. How long would I be held in this inhospitable environment—in this stark, flat, treeless cage? The other fear was reminiscent of my first days as a soldier. Just as a new soldier, I had been stripped of my former identity. I stood mentally naked before a power yet unknown to me. I had no way to protect myself or to hide myself from this power.

My contemplation was cut short as the people in charge exercised their power by yelling and threatening us as we scrambled to form some sort of a formation. As in my recruit days I felt the confusion of being a nonperson trying to figure out just what these strange men, who obviously held my future well-being in their hands, wanted of me. I could only imagine the fear the men with me who could not understand English felt. I was able to

110

comprehend that some of the shouting was out of the frustration the guards were experiencing because they could not get their new charges to do what they were asking, or ordering, them to do. They tried to compensate for the lack of understanding by yelling even louder and more fiercely. Despite the confusion we eventually were in a ragged formation. We were all mixed up without regard to rank.

Once we prisoners were lined up, the noise and the dust settled, and we just stood there waiting. I was in the front rank and thus had a clear view of the other end of the compound. A large crowd of men, obviously prisoners, had assembled to gawk at the spectacle of a new shipment of inmates. I could see them elbowing one another pointing in our direction as they animatedly talked among themselves. Though I could not hear them, I could well imagine their jokes and jibes. Why is it men, no matter what the circumstances, feel superior if they see others about to go through what they have already experienced, even if it is unpleasant?

I wanted to believe that surely they were expressing sympathy for their fellow German Kameraden. However, I knew that it was more than likely their mirth came from witnessing the fate of strangers experiencing the confusion and mental anguish they themselves had survived. We stood and stared at the line of guards who watched over us with weapons at the ready. They seemed to show no fear as they glared back at us. They obviously viewed us as presenting no threat, but also as people for whom they had contempt.

After at least a half-hour of our standing there in silence, a small formation of men came through the main gate and marched, rather sharply I noted, to our front center. I understood the delay. It was a deliberate ploy designed to further establish the captor's power over the captive. We were not to get the idea that these men were at our beck and call. They were not here to serve us. The noncommissioned officer in charge of the guards saluted the officer in the front of the group, spun around in a very precise about-face, and double-timed back to the line of guards. An officer stepped forward. I could see a silver emblem on his lapel, but could not make out what it was. Another soldier, with two stripes on his sleeves, stepped up beside him. The officer spoke out in a loud clear voice. He spoke in English with a strange but understandable dialect.

"I suppose I am required to welcome you to this camp." The corporal (I was to learn the rank insignia later) translated in a German that was very good, though somewhat old fashioned. I was to learn that many of the Deutsch speakers in America had learned German through their families who had been in America for sometimes several generations. They used phrases and words not used in modern Germany for many years. Those translators who had learned their German in school spoke a strange combination of High German mixed with a conglomerate of dialects. Obviously, each of their instructors had influenced them with that instructor's particular dialect despite the fact that they were supposedly learning Hoch Deutsch (high German).

The officer's "welcoming" speech continued. "However, I want it to be made perfectly clear that you are not particularly welcome here on our soil. Had I been in command of the troops who faced you in battle you would have been part of the soil of Africa rather than garbage brought to rot on American soil. Let it be clear to you that you are not guests in this country, and definitely not here in Hearne Camp (that was our first hint as to our location). You are prisoners. You were soldiers who took up arms to support a madman in his quest to dominate the world. Perhaps you felt that you could share in some of that power over the people you stomped under your hobnailed boots as you marched across their homelands. I am here to tell you that your stomping days are over. You are now nothing but a group of cowards who chose to raise your hands rather than fight to the death. Despite my disrespect of what you symbolize I will see that you are treated humanely in this camp until the day I can ship you back, with your tails between your legs, to try to survive in whatever may be left, which I personally hope is not much, of your ravished and defeated homeland. Let it also be clear that I will not tolerate rebellious behavior nor attempts to escape. Both will be punished swiftly and harshly. While here you will be assigned work details which I expect you to carry out in as efficient a manner as if they were the orders of your own commander. We are not giving you these tasks as punishment, but rather to keep you engaged at useful activities in order to help you through this necessary time of

112

incarceration. I personally will not be communicating with you on a regular basis, but will expect that you will listen and obey those men I have placed over you as if I personally had given you the orders. In fact, if any of you and I are to again have a personal chat it will no doubt be an occasion you will regret."

With those cheery words of encouragement, he spun on his heel and marched smartly back out of the compound. No one said a word to us, or moved a muscle, until the gate slammed behind him. Then a sergeant with many stripes stepped forward and smiled at us as if we were all part of a big joke. He at last spoke. "I suppose all of you are feeling very cheerful right now. Colonel Whitmore has a way of making new prisoners feel welcome. I do want to assure you, however, that he means what he says. My name is First Sergeant Blake. I am the noncommissioned officer in charge of this dust bowl. I am afraid that America was not very prepared for accepting prisoners of war. Our entrance into this scrape was a bit sudden, thanks to your cowardly Jap friends. Consequently, this camp is not ready to receive all of you. As you can see, we don't even have buildings for you as of yet. However, we soon will have them. That will be your first task here. Starting tomorrow you will build your own accommodations. How long you stay in the discomfort of the tent city you see behind you is up to you. If you choose to refuse to cooperate, or dawdle in the building, then enjoy the pleasure of tenting in the dust. When I release you from this formation you can find yourselves a tent, none are assigned other that those at the far end near the entrance. Those are for the officers.

In one half-hour report back to this area, in formation, prepared to march to the latrines and the wash area, then on to the chow line. Officers stay in place. All others are dismissed."

After the enlisted men went to settle their gear in the tents I looked around at my fellow officers. Most I knew already from our boat ride over. It was surprising how few of us there were. My eyes met those of Oberst Fischer. His glare made it perfectly clear that he had not forgotten, nor forgiven me, for the incident on the ship.

First Sergeant Blake again addressed us, "It will be our policy here to allow you to maintain your normal rank structure. As long as order and discipline are kept, camp orders will come through you. Who is the ranking officer?" Oberst Fischer stepped forward. "Very good, sir," First Sergeant Blake continued. "As soon as we reassemble, you and your adjutant will be escorted to lunch with Colonel Whitmore. Each section will have one of my NCOs as its liaison. There will be three companies designated within your group which will become the 2nd Battalion. Company designations will be by alphabet starting with A as in Able, or should I say Adolf (at that he had quite a laugh with the other guards). Starting tomorrow morning you will fall in, in proper formation. By then have your company commanders designated. That will be all. Dismissed!"

We then retired to the officer area and settled into tents. I found a six-man tent with five other officers I knew well. Two of us were captains, the other four lieutenants. Within the hour we were called out to be marched to mess.

We soon found that the buildings in the center of the compound were the mess. We were taken to the latrines at the far end of the compound and then on to eat. Upon leaving the mess hall we went through a line and were issued fold-up canvas cots and a blanket.

That evening Oberst Fischer called us together and designated company commanders. It did not surprise me to find that I was not given a command. I was sure that it was a deliberate slight for my comments on the ship. As the meeting was concluded, Oberst Fischer ordered me to stay back. I thought to myself, "Here it comes." To my surprise, after the others left for their tents the Oberst slumped down on to his cot and proceeded to take his boots off. After a sigh that was a mixture of relief at getting his boots off and frustration, he addressed me in a calm and civil manner.

"Hauptmann, I have to admit I have some leftover harsh feelings about you; however, on thinking it over I may have been a bit arrogant about our situation on the ship. You were thinking of the welfare of the men. You just chose a damn disrespectful way of going about it. My English is lousy and I need someone I can rely on for a liaison and interpreter. Are you willing to give it another try?" I assured him I was. "Very good, Herr Hauptmann, then report to the front of the formation tomorrow as a part of my staff."

114

I retired to my tent a bit bewildered. As I entered, I seemed to interrupt a clandestine meeting in progress. As I walked into the tent the place grew suddenly quiet. The five officers in the room looked at me and then at each other as if waiting for one of their group to approach me. At last Hauptmann Ekels, a panzer officer spoke up. "Erich, what do you think of the security of this place?" I knew right away what the drift of the meeting was: escape.

"I was not overly impressed, " I answered. "It seems to be a bit lax." Hauptmann Ekels looked at the others and they nodded. He turned back to me.

"Would you be interested in joining a few of us to get out of here?"

"And just where would you go?"

"We figure that if we could get to the coast we could find a boat and get to Mexico. It is supposed to be neutral, isn't it?"

"That might work, if one of you could speak the language a bit more proficiently."

"We have been thinking about that. Oberleutnant Midler here speaks a little Spanish, and I, as you know, speak a little English, but we could use a better English speaker. Are you interested?"

I did not have to think about that for long before I answered. "I am not thrilled about the prospects of years in this hole; count me in. However, let's not be too hasty. Let's look the situation over for a few days and then start on a plan."

They all seemed in agreement so we settled down to a restless night on our hard cots in the steamy heat of an East Texas summer night. I didn't think I would ever miss the rocking of that old troop ship, but it sure beat the accommodations of my new place in that luxury Texas hotel.

The next morning found us up in formation early for roll call and a plate of a strange gruel the cooks called grits. If you thought that went over well with the prisoners, think again. However, at least we ate it. On the other hand some of the guards who took a plate really raised a fuss as a few dumped it right on the floor. Some of them sputtered about "more of that redneck slop," and the rest about what stupid creatures the Kraut cooks were that they couldn't even cook decent grits. The coffee was weak, but good,

115

and the bread was white fluff, which we later learned was the preferred bread in America.

After dinner we again received some clothing. This consisted of another couple of sets of underwear, several pairs of socks, and obsolete or repaired American uniforms. These uniforms were all stenciled to identify one as a prisoner. The trousers had a large "P" on the front of the right leg and a "W" on the front of the left leg. The shirt had a "POW", or just "PW", stenciled on the back between the shoulder blades. We were informed that those who still had serviceable German uniforms could still wear them. Badges and insignias were permitted. Most of those with their own uniforms at first chose to wear them exclusively. However, they soon learned that it was best to save their German uniforms for selected days. I had only a shabby excuse for a German officer's uniform, but I still proudly wore it on holidays and other special occasions. As most of the other prisoners, I was careful to wear my German clothing if I knew a photographer may be about. I feared what would happen to me upon returning to Germany if a photo of me in American clothing were to be seen there.

The camp commander didn't let us stay idle long. We were divided into groups and put to work building wooden barracks, latrines, and a mess hall. I was assigned to an old American sergeant to serve as his interpreter. That is when my troubles began.

Sergeant Jones was probably a good enough fellow. He was probably just a little intimidated by Germans is all; at least, I wanted to think that. One thing is for sure, there was one German he decided to dislike a lot: me. It didn't take our relationship long to get off to a rousing start. His very first order to the men in my party was something like, "Y'all Kraut fellars gonna be totin' this here marterial o'er to that thar gang of fellars o'er yonder."

When no one moved, he looked to me and said, "Cap'n, ain't you posed to tell these fellars in Kraut lingo what I done said?"

I could only respond with, "Excuse me?"

"Scuse ya fer what? he inquired.

"Pardon me, Sergeant, but I did not understand you," I said cautiously.

He then must have thought I was either deaf or perhaps a little dumb because he began to talk very slowly and very loud. "Y'ALL . . . TELL . . . Y'ALL'S . . . FELLARS . . . TA . . . TOTE . . . THIS . . . HERE . . . MARTERIAL . . . O'ER . . . YONDER . . . Y'ALL HEAR?"

"I do hear you," I assured him. "I just don't understand your English very well."

"WHAT Y'ALL DON'T UNERSTAN?" he hollered again.

"Well for one, what is 'mar-terial'?" I asked.

"Marterial is stuff, y'all know. Lak this here pile of marterial here," he said as he kicked some boards.

"Oh material!" I said as I realized that it really was a dialect of English he was speaking. That was a mistake.

"Oh! So y'all is some sort of wise ass," he growled as he squinted his pig eyes at me and stuck out his chin.

I tried to respond in a calm voice, "Pardon me, Sergeant, I have studied only in England and thus only understand English."

He turned quite red and yelled right in my face, "ANGLISH! SO NOW SOME DUMB ASS KRAUT IS GONNA TELL ME AH CAIN'T SPEAK NO ANGLISH? WEEL AH TELL YA SUMIN Y'ALL BES UNERSTAN. Y'ALL IS GONNA BE GAWD DAMN SOARRY Y'ALL EVER MET THIS HERE'N AMERICAN THAT CAIN'T SPEAK ANGLISH SO THAT YO DUMB ASS KRAUT BRAIN CAIN'T FIGUR IT OUT. Y'ALL HEAR?"

Needless to say the quality of my life suddenly took a nose dive. I spent the next several days on the run carrying the heaviest loads that good Sergeant Jones could find.

After the second day of this treatment I called the tent group together and started to lay out some serious plans for escape. We figured that the best way was to build a ladder that we would hide in the construction area. This proved to be no problem since so much activity was going on in the area where the new barracks were going up that the guards didn't keep very good track of what everyone was doing. Our plan was to use the ladder to go over the fence on a dark night. We would wear our German uniforms so we would not be considered spies. We planned to go over right into the guards' barracks area since we felt that would be the place they least expected a

117

breakout attempt. Once in the guard area we would take a jeep or truck and drive nonchalantly out of the compound. If we were detected in this drive we would head south at a fast clip until we were out of sight of the camp and then head north. We figured they would assume we would head for Mexico. Instead we planned to head to Kansas City, which we figured it was somewhere to the north. We chose Kansas City because we knew it was a Wild West town. We knew that from the movies. There we would get cowboy clothes and try to work our way west, then south to Mexico. Now as I look back on the plan I know how naive we were. Perhaps the best word is dumb rather than naive. We had no idea that many American movies bear no resemblance to the truth. Also we had no real concept how big America really is. I suppose, even if I had known that, our plans wouldn't have changed much. I was desperate to get away from the nasty Sergeant Jones.

After about a week I had had enough of his nasty comments and orders. He started yelling at me to "get ma lazy Kraut ass in gear" and I just sat down and refused to obey his abusive orders. I found myself in solitary confinement.

Solitary confinement was not all that bad. I was put in a small one-room hut with no windows and no furniture other than a mattress on the floor. Actually the mattress was much more comfortable than the canvas cot I was using as a bed in my assigned tent. Twice a day I was taken out for exercise and a chance to go to the latrine to empty the pail I had in the hut. I usually did not use the pail, preferring some discomfort in waiting over the discomfort of sitting is that small space among my own stink. I also was allowed to go to the mess hall, but only to pick up my meals. I took my food back to my "private room" to eat. It was during this stay that three important events happened. First, I met Corporal White. Corporal White was the day time guard assigned to take me to the mess hall and to exercise. Corporal White was from New Hampshire and spoke, in my way of thinking, a very understandable dialect of English. At first I did not dare to speak any English for fear of causing the same reaction Sergeant Jones displayed. Then one day I had a bit of a stomach problem and was forced to reveal to Corporal White that I could speak English by asking to go to the latrine.

"Well I'll be damned," he exclaimed, "why didn't you let me know you spoke English? It sure would have made it easier on me."

"I was afraid you would not be able to understand my English."

"Why, hell yes I can understand it. In fact, it is damn refreshing to hear the English language spoken without this damn Texas drawl, or worse yet by these ignorant Deep South bastards."

"You mean like Sergeant Jones?"

"Oh, that's right. You are in here because of a run-in with the old redneck bastard himself. I suppose you would have had a hard time understanding him. I only catch about half of what he says."

"I sure didn't mean to rile him. What really worries me is that I have no idea what I will do when I have to go back and work under him."

"Yes, you are right to worry. Sergeant Jones doesn't forget a grudge. As a matter of fact, I am on this duty because of a run-in with him over a comment I made about the South."

"Well, what's wrong with this duty? It seems you have it easy baby-sitting me."

"If all the POWs in solitary were like you this would be a good job. But the hard-core Nazis they put in here are big trouble, and a bit dangerous to be around. Say, you are not one of those Nazi fellows are you?"

Strangely enough, I think Corporal White was the first one to actually ask me that question. I later realized that most Americans just assumed that all Germans were members of the National Socialist Party. I didn't answer for a minute since I had to really think about it for a moment myself. I was not a party member, but I must admit at the time I still had leanings to many of the teachings of the party. I thought it best that I just answer, "No, I am not." Later I would have to wrestle with this question in my own mind.

After that first ice was broken, Corporal White and I became somewhat friends, at least as close to it as we could come with me being a prisoner and him a guard. While I was in solitary for that month he would come over some evenings when he was off duty and sit on a stool outside my hut and talk to me through the wall. He had been a history teacher before America entered the war so we had that in common. He had never been to Europe and had lots of questions for me. I, for my part, didn't have a lot of curiosity about America at the time and I asked him questions mostly about his family

119

and about the school system in America. Since he was at the time the only friendly American I knew (I can't say that Dr. Levins had been all that friendly even though in his sober moments we had enjoyed some nice talks), I didn't consider him an enemy as I did the other guards, especially Sergeant Jones.

While in solitary, another unpleasant event happened. Three of my tent mates decided to escape. The morning after they had escaped I was taken over to the camp commander's office and interrogated as to what their plans may have been. Naturally I denied having any knowledge of their planning an escape. It didn't really matter, though, since they had been gone only two days when a truck drove up to the confinement hut area where I was being held, and unloaded them under heavy guard. Hauptmann Eikels and Oberleutnant Heimer were put into the hut next to mine. Since there was only about a meter distance between the huts, I was able to talk to them through the wall when it got dark. They bitterly related the story of their short taste of freedom to me.

They had been told by Sergeant Jones that I would probably never come back. He told them that if I ever got out of solitary he would make sure I would be sent to the maximum security POW camp up in a place called Oklahoma. Since we had been in camp we were constantly threatened with being sent to Oklahoma, where we were told we would really experience hard labor. Sergeant Jones quickly switched the hostility he had shown me to my tent mates. He felt it his duty to "cleanse thar Natzi souls fur thar own good." Life began to be too miserable for them to take the chance that I might rejoin them, so they decided to leave without me.

They chose a cloudy night when the wind was blowing the dust enough that the guards would tend to stay on the lee side of buildings to keep out of it. One by one they ran across the yard to the construction site where the ladder had been cleverly placed as part of a scaffolding set up to build a brick chimney on what was to be a laundry building. From there they stole over to the fence separating the POW compound from the guard area. We had been right in our assessment that that section of the fence would be the least guarded. So far so good. Their big concern when they got there was that the light from the guards' barracks window cast a bit of light on that section of the fence. However, the large floodlights that were located around

120

the compound were arranged so as not to disturb the guards and were shaded so that they would only cast their light out toward the center of the POW area, thus leaving a small area of the fence in shadow. The three fugitives laid down next to the fence to get a breather, survey the area, and plan their next move. Corporal White later told me that they even found a cigarette butt there, so the three must have been there some time. The shadow must have made them feel rather secure. They scaled over the fence with the use of the ladder. They pulled it over with them as we had planned. The three quietly walked from the fence to the guard barracks so as not to invite attention to themselves. Once at the barracks they ducked behind it and leaned the ladder up against the wall. There they sat against the building listening to the radio inside and the off-duty guards talking to each other. When it was evident that the guards were not aware that anything was amiss they moved quietly out to the motor pool. Just as they were about to move into the area, thinking that no guards were on that side of the motor pool, a flash of a match lighting a cigarette stopped them. They then saw the guard hunkered down behind a jeep so as to hide the glow of his cigarette from the gate area where his superior probably was. The guard did not tarry over his smoke long, snuffed it out, field stripped it, and resumed his rounds. As soon as he was about 50 meters away, the three POWs crawled into the motor pool and under a jeep. They worked their way toward the gate until they located a light truck not too far from the gate. Though none of them was familiar with American trucks, Eikels was familiar with many types of motor vehicles. He had been raised on a farm and also had experience with French and captured British equipment.

They started the truck, turned on the headlights, and drove toward the gate at an orderly pace. Their plan was to get close and hopefully partially blind the gate guards with their headlights, then accelerate through the gate. As they got near the gate they were surprised that there seemed to be only one guard at the gate and there was no barrier. The guard was standing there with his rifle on his shoulder and one hand shading his eyes so he could see who was driving the truck. As they drew up beside him he yelled at them, "What the hell do you think you're doing going to town at this time of night? First Shirt will have your ass!" Hauptmann Eikels pulled up beside

121

him and stopped. The guard walked up to the window to peer inside. At that moment Eikels swung the door open knocking the guard flat and hit the accelerator. As far as they knew, not a shot was fired as they sped away. This turned out to be true as the new recruit at the gate got so flustered he couldn't get off a shot when he got back to his feet.

As soon as they were a distance away from the camp they turned onto a larger road and turned off the headlights. They were pleased to see that due to the fences on each side of the road they could tell where the roadway was, thus allowing them to travel at a fairly fast speed. Before too long they were confident enough to turn their lights back on and increase their speed even more. They turned onto new roads several times not caring where they were or what direction they were going. What mattered was that they were putting distance between themselves and the camp. As dawn approached they came to a small river and were able to hide the truck in a small thicket of trees.

During the day they took turns on watch. They were surprised at the lack of traffic over the bridge they could see from their hideout. Among the few vehicles they did see, none were military vehicles; that worried them. They had assumed that the roads would be full of military vehicles that they could blend in with. After all, wasn't America at war also? Due to the lack of military traffic they decided to travel only at night.

At dusk they started out again. As they headed out they were shocked to notice that they were almost out of fuel. None of them had, as I had experienced, fought against American troops in Africa and did not know that American vehicles were very inefficient. They were beginning to panic as they drove along and failed to come to a town. They were learning that America was either much larger than they imagined or a lot less populated. At last they came upon a small store at a crossroads that had two gas pumps in front. They were pleased to see that the lights were on and someone was there.

As they pulled up an old man hobbled out of the store, spit a wad of tobacco on the ground, and said, "Howdy fellars. Y'all lost or just skippin' out fur a beer?"

Heimer was at the wheel and was not sure what the man had said so he replied in his best English. "Good morning, Mr. Store Manager. Can we have some petrol?"

The store manager cocked his head and said, "Y'all must be one of those New Angland fellars. I shore don't know fur sure what you want. If'n you are lost, Huntsville is back that way." He pointed off to the east.

Heimer realized that he had a problem so he just pointed at the nearest gas pump and said, "Please."

"Oh! I see, why didn't y'all say so? I guess y'all army fellars don't need no ration cards. How much y'all need?"

Again Heimer, not to sure what the old man had asked, pointed at the pump and said "Please?"

"Well shit, y'all yanks don't talk much do you?" With that he proceeded to pump petrol, or as you call it, gas into the tank. When he had put in 5 gallons, he stopped and came back to the window saying, "Sorry, fellars, that is all I can give y'all. That will be one dollah." He held out his hand.

Heimer realized what the old man wanted and said, "Thank you," rolled up his window, and drove off leaving the old man shouting and cussing in his wake. They could see from the gauge that the old man had not put in much fuel. After about an hour they came to a small town. It seemed to be settled for the night and the only activity was at a small building they took to be a Gasthaus. They drove around the small town until they spotted a petrol pump. They waited some time before they decided to try to steal some petrol. Unfortunately, they found a lock on the pump. They found a tool bag in the truck and, using the tire tool, were able to try to break the lock without creating too much of a noise. They quickly proceeded to fill the tank. It was then that they realized it was an electric pump and the electricity was not turned on. They ended up driving out of town with a near-empty tank. As they knew they were nearing the bottom of their tank they spotted a farm with a nice barn. Seeing no other alternatives they decided to hide out in the barn.

As dawn again came they were pleased to see a fuel tank on a stand in the farmyard. Closer inspection revealed that it even had gasoline in it. They realized that they would not be able to stay undetected in the barn, so they might as well chance it. They boldly pulled up to the pump and started to fill their tank. Soon an old man ran out of the house in his long underwear and started to shout at them. "What the hell do y'all think you'er doin'?" Eikels kept letting the gas flow out of the gravity tank and yelled back.

"No problem, Mr. Farmer, we are with the army."

"No problem, like hell. Y'all get out of here."

Ekels decided to try a bluff. He walked right up to the farmer and glared at him. "I said this is for the army. Go back in the house, farmer."

The bluff seemed to work as the farmer spun on his heel and went back inside. Ekels laughed and said to the others as he continued to fill the tank, "It is good to see that Americans are like Germans and obey authority."

The other two got out of the truck and stood between the truck and the house to show the farmer he had better not mess with them. To their surprise the farmer, accompanied by a teenager who they assumed was his son, stepped out onto the porch. They were both carrying shotguns. Being unfamiliar with your American love for guns, they had not considered that private citizens, especially such poor ones, might have guns. They soon found themselves sitting in the dust before the porch with hands on the top of their heads waiting for the farmer's son to bring the deputy sheriff from town. Thus ended their bid for freedom. All of them were quite humbled and disgusted with themselves. Their first capture had taken a larger, better-equipped army. This capture had taken a skinny old farmer and his son.

Not long after their return to the Hearne POW camp the three escapees were transferred to the maximum security camp in Oklahoma. I was never to see them again. They had, however, done me a favor before they left by telling the camp commander that I had in no way been involved in the planning or preparation for their escape. This I was to find out through my new friend, Corporal White.

The third incident that occurred during my stay in solitary was the reunion with Oberjaeger Beckmann—the same Oberjaeger Juergen Beckmann who had been captured with me back in North Africa. Our reunion took place shortly after the transfer of the escapees. One day when Private White escorted me to the mess hall, I was sitting in a small room in the back of the building reserved for solitary confinement soldiers who had

124

been given their privileges back to eat outside of their "private" huts. I heard a POW KP come in with my meal but didn't look up until I heard someone exclaim, "Well, I'll be damned, if it isn't the Hauptmann." As I looked up sharply I saw Beckmann snap to attention and start to salute me. Before he could get his hand up I jumped up, forgetting military protocol, and shook his hand.

"Juergen," I exclaimed, "I wasn't sure if you were here or in Africa. When did you get here?"

"I was one of the first here in Hearne camp. I left Africa while you were in the hospital. In fact I was sure when I last saw you that you wouldn't live to make it out of Africa, — ah, SIR."

"Damn, Juergen, it is sure good to see you. If I ever get out of solitary we must get together. How are you being treated?"

"Great, sir. I must tell you about it, but for now I had better run; I am not supposed to talk to men in solitary."

With that short conversation he went back to his duties. I saw him again much sooner than I thought.

That evening I heard a rapping on my wall. I settled near the wall and rapped back. It was Beckmann. "Juergen, what the hell are you doing? If they catch you, you will be in one of these huts."

"Don't panic, sir. I am a friend of Corporal White's, and he is in the front of the building standing watch."

"How did you get in with the guards so fast, Juergen?"

"Well, sir, remember that I told you that I was born in America?"

"Yes, but won't that get you in more trouble if they find out? They might consider you a traitor and shoot you."

"I thought of that and didn't tell anyone until I figured out who were the German haters and who wasn't. The few who know are making some inquiries for me as to what my status might be. They, in the meantime, have made sure that I get the best duty." That is why I have come here tonight. Rumor is that you are soon to be returned to normal status."

"Great! I am sick of these four walls."

"That's the good news. The bad news is that you are going to go back to Sergeant Jones's section.

"Shit! The bastard will really get me this time."

"You are probably right. That is why I have been making some inquiries. I hope you don't mind that I have been making some plans for you without your permission, sir."

CHAPTER TWO
JOURNEY TO THE WILD WEST

I sat looking out the window as the train station slowly seemed to move out of sight. Perhaps this illusion was because that is the way I wanted it. I wanted Hearne and my time in that steambath to disappear. I wanted to believe that it had just been a bad dream. If it wasn't, then what would become of me? How could I survive long under the humility of being a prisoner under the glaring eye of people such as Sergeant Jones? I tried to remind myself of the reality. I was on a train headed to some place in the American West. How Beckmann had managed to arrange it was still a mystery to me. All I know is that shortly after I was released out of solitary I was transferred to the 1st POW Battalion on the other side of the camp. I was assigned to the same company that Beckmann was a part of—the company slated to be transferred to a new camp at somewhere the guards called "the Far West."

I had some hope for the future. Surely it would be better wherever we were going. It was a good start. The train we were in gave me hope for that. The cars were very new and appointed in a rather luxurious fashion. They were quite different from the railroad cars that I knew in Germany. The big difference was that there were not separate compartments within the car. It sort of reflected my early impression of the Americans. They were a rather uncultured people who still liked the opulence of the high class. At the same time they seemed to be afraid that they might give the impression that the rich lived better than the poor. The railroad car was all one compartment but was as nicely appointed as the first-class compartments aboard a German train. An interesting feature to me was that the seats were hinged and could face frontward or backward, thus allowing two banks of seats to face one another. Again the gregarious nature of the Americans showed through. The other impressive things were the size, the car was much larger than a European passenger car, and there was a nice toilet room on each car, with running water and flushing toilets. Had it not been for the armed guards at each end of the car, I would have felt that I was on holiday.

As we went on our way it was obvious that we were a low-priority

127

train. Every few miles we would pull over and wait as another train passed us from both east and west. Several of the trains were also passenger trains and we could see that most of them were nowhere near as new and nice as ours. Beckmann was soon friends with the guards and was able to keep us informed about things. He had asked the guards why we had such a nice train, being that we were prisoners of war. The answer was that the American Department of War allowed the railroad companies (it surprised us that the rail system in America was private) to arrange the schedules. The POWs were put on first-class trains so that the railroad companies could charge the government more money. It was heartening for us to find out that things in America were just as corrupt as they were in Germany. The thing that really impressed us in a very disheartening way was the sight of so much war machinery on its way east, obviously to be sent to Africa or England to kill our Kameraden. We hoped that this was the only east/west rail line, but Beckmann was to find out that it was only one of many. Surely, we speculated, this was the one that carried all the available war materials.

Besides the freight trains, we saw several trainloads of American troops. They, oddly enough, were aboard trains much older than ours. As these trains would pass, the troops aboard would flock to the windows to gawk at us. Many would hang out the open windows and shout what we figured were curses at us. They didn't seem to do it in a vicious manner, but in a spirit of mirth and superiority. They must have been green troops who had not experienced war and thus were not filled with the hate of the enemy that it brings. Only once did one of these casual contacts with the enemy become ugly. Early the second morning our train pulled into a siding. Another train coming from the west pulled in beside us. It also stopped to wait out faster trains on the main line. We found ourselves eyeball to eyeball with the American troops aboard that train. We could see that they were quite crammed into the old cars. In the center of each car was a mound of duffel bags. At the end of each car was a small coal stove. The seats were not wooden as the third-class trains were in Germany, but they were obviously nowhere near as nice as the ones we had in our cars. At first we just stared across at each other. Then I noticed they became very motivated. They were all animatedly talking among themselves and pointing at us. They had obviously just become aware that we were POWs. Their talk turned to shouts and taunts. Soon the taunts were shouts of anger. Before long an officer jumped off their train and came over to ours. He was met at the foot of the steps up to my car by the captain of the guards on our train. I was close enough to the exit that I could hear the officer from the other train. The captain saluted him so I could tell he was a superior. He started talking to our guard captain in a friendly tone.

"Good evening, captain. I see you have a load of Krauts. Where are you heading?"

"We're hauling these boys out to a camp in New Mexico. Where are you fellas bound for?"

"We're headin' across the pond to round up another bunch of these Nazis, but there seems to have been a mistake here. As you can see they put us in that old relic of a train while these damn Krauts are in these new cars. My colonel has ordered me get us switched around."

"Now, just what do you mean by switched around, Major?"

The major's voice went up a notch. "Don't be coy, Captain. You know damn well what I mean. Let's get with it. We don't have a lot of time." With that he spun around and signaled back to his train. I could see the men on that train start to gather their things.

Our captain almost yelled at the major, "Don't get in a hurry, Major. There is not going to be any switching." His voice made it obvious that he was more than a little nervous.

"Like hell you say!" the major shouted back. "I didn't ask you to switch; I am ordering you to. Do you understand the word 'order,' Captain?"

"I sure and the hell do, Major, and my orders are to take these prisoners, on this train, to New Mexico." The captain shouted back.

Soldiers started to unload off the other train. I could see that they had heard the confrontation and were mad. The major again yelled right in the face of the captain. "You had better get your ass out of my way, Captain, and get those damn lice off that train or I will have my men throw them off." The captain stepped back and signaled to the sergeant standing on the train steps behind him. The sergeant yelled an order and most of the guards on our train jumped to the ground and raised their guns at the ready in a

129

menacing manner. It would have been a great time for some of us prisoners to jump off the train on the other side and make an unnoticed departure, but we all remained with our noses to the window watching the spectacle unfolding between the two bodies of American soldiers.

For a moment I thought that the group from the other train would charge across the short distance to our train. A few started to but were brought up short by the guard sergeant's shouted command and the responding quick shouldering of rifles aimed directly at the threatening invaders. It seemed like ten minutes, but was probably only a minute or two, that the two opposing forces stood in silence and stared each other down. The standoff was broken as the civilian train crews from both trains ran in between the two lines of men.

The oldest of the civilians came over to the major and said, "Easy does it, son. You know damn well that we can't switch trains. The powers above you and me decide who rides in what train. Besides that, even if we did allow you fellows to exchange places we couldn't get the engines changed around. Now we both got schedules to keep and we are behind. Why don't you get back aboard your trains and let us get you where you have got to be before the war is over?"

The major looked back to his train. I saw for the first time another officer standing on the steps of the opposing car. He finally nodded, and the major shouted to his men and waved them back. They climbed aboard muttering and cussing. The train crews ran back to their engines and wasted no time in getting us on our way. As we started to pull out I saw the major give a parting finger gesture that I had learned was the ultimate American insult. Later we heard that the captain had first given him a parting snappy salute. American or not, that captain gained a lot of respect from we Germans.

Our progress was slow. It was obvious that we were a very low-priority train. We stopped in nearly every small town. Had we been in Europe, we would have never gotten anywhere at that rate, but it seems that there are few towns in the southwestern United States. In most of the towns a crowd would gather to stare at us. At a few stops we were allowed to get off, under close watch, to get some exercise. When we were off the trains the local crowds would back off quickly and give us room. At one stop to our surprise a table was set up, manned by a group of ladies. The tables were laden with coffee and sweet cakes (which I later learned were donuts).

At first we didn't understand, but when a lady at the table gestured to me I looked at the closest guard. He shrugged and then nodded so I carefully walked over to the table. A smiling young girl gave me a donut. The next lady, a rather old woman, asked me, "Would you like cream in your coffee?"

I smiled and responded, "Yes please. That is very kind of you."

As she gave me a cup I noticed I was standing at the table all alone. I looked back to the other prisoners and saw that they were all watching me with a look that was a mixture of fear for my safety and envy. "Come on," I yelled in German, "these fine ladies will not hurt you."

I looked back around and saw very confused looks on the faces of the ladies at the table. I stepped aside as some of the POWs formed a line and came to the table. When the old lady asked the first guy in line if he wanted cream in his coffee the Soldat just looked blank. When she asked a second time, I translated. The Soldat smiled and said to the lady, "Ja, bitte, gnaedige Frau."

At this a gasp went up from all of the American women. A rather large, officious lady in the rear said, "My God, these are Germans!" Another woman said, "Oh dear, what should we do?" One lady threw down the towel in her hand and muttered, "Well, I won't serve them." Just when things looked like a panic would set in the young girl who gave me the donut said, "Please ladies, the Lord said to love thine enemy and to minister among the heathens. We can prove to these misguided souls that they are in a land of civilized Christians." She then turned to me and asked, "Are you in charge here?"

"I am an officer, miss."

"Then tell your men to come by and be served."

"Yes, miss, I will be pleased to do so, but please tell your ladies that we too are Christians and appreciate their kindness." I then passed on her request to the men, who began to file by and take the offered coffee and donuts from the now stern-faced ladies.

"Are you really Christians?" the pretty young girl asked.

"For the most part, yes, we were all raised as such."

131

"Then how can you be involved in fighting a war for those terrible men?"

"Just what 'terrible men' are you speaking about?"

"Why those Nazi people led by that madman Hitler."

"We are soldiers, miss. We do our duty for our country, just as your men do."

"But our men don't kill innocent women and children."

I looked her right in the eye and said in a calm voice, "I pray to God that you are right." I wanted to tell her much more, but instead I just smiled at her and said, "Thank you again, and may we all hope this madness of war may soon be over." I spun on my heel and walked back to the train. This incident was to incite a flood of thoughts of home and the safety of my loved ones. Could peace ever come no matter who won when even women like those righteous ladies had so much fear, or perhaps even hate, for people they knew nothing about?

Not at all stops were the locals so gracious. Most of the time a group of young men would gather and derisive yells would be thrown, with the occasional stone, our way. At one stop while we were exercising, I remember a small boy running toward us out of the crowd, stopping short and sticking his tongue out at us before running back to the safety of his gang with a triumphant yell. I remember thinking that I hoped that before he was old enough to become a soldier the war would be over, because his type of personality would lead him to an early grave.

Late at night, on the second night, we changed trains near a large town that Beckmann learned from the guards was Albuquerque, New Mexico. None of us had even heard of it. In a much older, dilapidated train, we headed in a northerly direction. I kept my nose to the window watching the desolate terrain flash by under a bright moon. A tide of emotions flowed back and forth through me. I saw in the faces of those around me the look of quiet fear. It was not the wide-eyed fear with lips stretched so tight that the teeth were exposed that one sometimes found during the bombardment preceding a battle, or the slobbering fear I had seen on the face of one of the English soldiers I had been ordered to execute. It was the piercing-eyed, clenched-teeth look of men facing the unknown. I knew my face wore the same mask. Would I ever see the fatherland again? Were they taking us so far into the wilderness that no one would ever know what became of us? Certainly escape was becoming less and less an option. At the same time another emotion would flood back over me like an incoming tide. I found myself becoming excited. What an adventure! Would anyone believe me when I told them of all that was now happening to me? As I looked at the moonlit wasteland pass by I became aware of someone standing behind me looking over my shoulder. It was Beckmann.

"Sir, does this remind you of our little hike in Afrika before we gave up to the Englander?"

"Yes, I was thinking of that just now. Do you know where we are heading Jurgin?"

"According to that big blond guard named Olsen, we are going to a place called Farmington."

"Are these guards staying with us there?"

"No, sir, they joke among themselves that they are going to leave us near the edge of the earth and then they will go back to civilization."

"Damn, if Hearne is what they refer to as civilization what the hell will we find in this wasteland?"

"I have sure been worried about that, sir. I do know that if Wisconsin, where I was born, looks anything like this I can sure see why my parents came back to Selasia."

"Look at the bright side, Juergen, if the world is really round, as far as we have traveled we must be almost back in das Vaterland." It felt good to laugh at such a joke when we were otherwise so depressed.

That next morning, after a night of travel through some very isolated terrain, we arrived at our destination. We were unloaded into a field and then reloaded onto trucks. We were all so tired we hardly noticed the new guards—that is until we were on the trucks. We then became very aware that they were different; they were Schwaize, Negroes. We had all, of course, seen Negroes in Africa (I had never seen one until I got to Africa), but these were different. In Africa, none of the Africans had been in charge. As we started down the road every head was turned to the rear of the truck where two armed Negro soldiers sat on the end of the benches that ran down the sides

133

of the truck. They did not look at us, but at each other. I could see from the tight jaws that they were both very scared, but trying not to look so. Later I wondered: Had we all yelled together, would they have just dropped their rifles and jumped over the tailgate?

We were transported through a large valley. The land was under agricultural production, but it was easy to see that it had not been long ago that the area was desert. Each farm had a wood construction, usually white, farmhouse (though some were of a mud, which I learned was adobe construction), a barn, and several outbuildings. Occasionally, we passed a small cluster of adobe huts, with a conglomeration of impoverished-looking brown-skinned children. We were not seeing the anticipated cowboys and Indians, but we were not in doubt of the fact that we had arrived at the great American frontier.

CHAPTER THREE

ON THE GREAT AMERICAN FRONTIER

We finally reached our destination. It looked strangely like the last one—a large fenced compound enclosing rows of tents and piles of material to build shelters. As we unloaded and fell into formation (this time in an organized manner), I had more of a feeling of dread than fear. I knew what was before us. The only difference between here and Texas seemed to be the color of the guards. This may not seem a big deal to you. As an American, having been raised in the so-called melting pot of America, you can not know the thoughts that went through my head as I stood in that first formation in New Mexico and looked out on people I had always thought of in the context of being uncivilized natives from the Dark Continent now standing before me armed with loaded rifles. I can only say that I did not look at them as members of the enemy army; they were much more threatening to me than that. I had steeled myself to someday be shot by the enemy. However, I had no idea what these "natives" would do to us.

We were not in formation long before the camp commander and his entourage arrived. He was white as were all of his officers. I don't remember the "welcoming" speech. It was very similar to the one in Hearne, but of a less threatening nature. I do remember him saying, "If you think that you want to escape, you had better stop at my office and get a map, because not even the Indians know the way to civilization from this camp." Somehow I don't think he meant that entirely as a joke.

Not much time was wasted settling in. The next morning we set to building the camp. Having done it once before we were quite organized. Buildings began to appear out of the stacks of material. The Negro guards were much quieter than our last guards. Naturally there were a few with a mean streak, but for the most part they were very quiet. They would just stand back and watch us, giving little instruction, rather than constantly yell at us as had been the case at Camp Hearne. Another big difference was their willingness to pitch in when needed. They seemed to enjoy showing us that they were not just dumb riflemen. They also were anxious to show off their

135

strength. If they helped move a stack of boards or some other building material, they would take the heavy end. Perhaps it was a ploy to make us Germans work harder; if so, it worked. We did put out extra effort and sweat just to show them that we too were strong and knowledgeable about building. Besides the physical structure, other things were being built. Though some of the POWs had been together in Africa and in Texas, there were those of us like myself who were new to the group. The camp began to bond as a unit whose mission was to survive until victory. In our case, "victory" became the day we would set foot on German soil. We did not think in terms of who would win the war, only in terms of "when I get back home." Another relationship was beginning to form: the relationship between us and our guards. In that aspect I had more contact with the guards than most of the other prisoners. I was once again in the role of translator. My closest contact was with a sergeant by the name of Washington. Sergeant Washington was a big man the color of a big Belgian horse I remembered from my summer visits to my uncle's farm. His skin had the same burnt umber tone topped off with an intense black mop of hair, sort of similar to the mane of my uncle's horse. His disposition was the same confident, powerful demeanor of that stallion. To best demonstrate this I need only to tell you his reaction when I later told him about my comparing him to that horse. [Naturally that was several months after we began working together.] When I dared to tell him about my first impression of him, he just burst out laughing and said, "My Gawd, cap'n, I has been told more than once I is as big as a horse, but you is the furst man to ever tells me I looks like one." There was nothing that seemed to bother Sergeant Washington. This was lucky for me because, just as it was with Sergeant Smith in Texas, I had a big problem at first trying to understand the English used by those Negro guards. This was made worse by the fact that they among themselves had difficulty. Some spoke with Southern accents; some were from Harlem in New York City; others were from Chicago; and to round it out a few were from Los Angeles, California, and spoke what the others called "uppity Hollywood." When I would ask them what they meant by some order they gave they would just laugh and do their best to clarify. I had the feeling that they didn't feel I had not understood them because I was German, but rather because I was white.

136

Our camp was built rather quickly without much in the way of negative incidences. Two POWs I didn't know did escape one night, but they were brought back two days later, one having been bitten by a rattlesnake. This pretty much put the fear in all of us about the idea of escaping in that wild rugged land. The two biggest changes in our life came in the way of policy changes by the Americans.

First we were called into a special formation one day and informed we would be paid. We were told the government of the United States would abide by the rules of war and would pay us at the rate of a private in their own army. All prisoners were to get the same level of pay. The officers, we were informed, would receive further reparation on return to our homelands. We then were lined up and taken through the pay line to receive eighteen dollars in script. Most of this was then deducted from our "pay" to pay for laundry and special rations such as soap. I believe I was left with around eight dollars per month. I was not sure how much eighteen dollars was, but later, when we were allowed to go to the camp commissary, it was discovered to be, for the circumstances, a generous sum. In fact, for most of the enlisted soldiers, it was more than they had received from the German government. The negative aspect of the pay was from the viewpoint of the German officers and their ability to command. An important part of leadership in the German army was the aspect of privilege. It was assumed that officers would live better than the enlisted soldiers. It was a fact of life that was never questioned. This separation in living standards created a natural platform for leadership. When this was taken away, the bond of respect was also weakened, thus making it harder for the officers to order the enlisted to perform duties they themselves would not do. This allowed the guards to fill that gap and be the natural leadership. The guards would then "let" those officers who cooperated remain in the leadership loop.

The other significant policy change was the decision to allow POWs to work outside the camp. Whether from a benevolent reason or an economic one based on the lack of labor created by the quick expansion of the American military forces, the decision had been made that POWs would be allowed to volunteer to work on local farms. This policy was announced to us shortly after we had finished building the camp. The policy was read to us by the camp commander at an evening formation. Right after the formation our commander called a meeting of the officers. Oberst Rieter asked all of us what we felt about this development. Most of us felt that it would be good to keep the men occupied and prevent boredom to avoid discipline problems that could cause unneeded friction between us and the Americans. Major Fliederman and Hauptmann Rote were adamantly opposed. They were both very strong party members and had both served as political officers in their respective units.

"Can't you see what these Ami Schwein are trying to do. They are using German sweat to advance the war against the Reich," argued Major Fliederman.

Oberst Rieter countered, "Major, I hardly see how a few of our men working on farms in this desert hole can advance the war against das Vaterland."

"Every bushel of grain produced is more bread for the American army. Every day's work is one that can free an American man to be a soldier. How can you not see that the American's are not using us, Herr Oberst? It is bad enough that you have let these Schwarze lord it over our loyal German soldiers. Now you will let them make us the field slaves they once were and still should be?"

"That is enough, major! Need I remind you that we are still in the Wehrmacht and I am still the ranking officer here."

"Perhaps it is you that should be reminded that we are still in the Wehrmacht and that we still owe allegiance to der Fuehrer."

With that the major, Hauptmann Rote, and several other officers jumped to their feet and saluted with a "Heil Hitler," and stormed out of the building. Naturally, out of habit perhaps more than loyalty the rest of us jumped to our feet and also saluted. After they left a silence fell over the room. Oberst Reiter finally said, "I guess that is all the information I need for now. I will give the camp commander my decision in the morning. Dismissed!" As I started to leave the Oberst stopped me. "Erich what do you think of this policy?"

"I really do not feel qualified to comment on it, sir."

"Perhaps, not as a Hauptmann but, due to the fact that you are the one among us who spends the most time with the guards, you may have a feeling about the motive behind such a policy."

"Sir, I have no concept of the motive, I do know, though, that if the men don't find enough to keep them occupied trouble will develop."

"Thank you for your assistance Erich, I will want you to come with me as a translator when I give the camp commander my decision in the morning. Good night, Hauptmann."

The next morning found us in the camp commander's office. Oberst Reiter asked for some further information as to the tasks the men would be asked to do. It was the intention of the program, the camp commander assured us, not to treat the workers as slave labor, but as normal farmworkers. At any time Oberst Reiter could suspend the program, or an individual volunteer could choose to return to compound duty. The Oberst sat quietly and mulled this over. I knew what he was thinking. This opportunity for the men to be treated with some dignity was a wise way to go. However, such a decision would defy the wishes of the politicos in the compound. To defy the party faithful was a dangerous route. At last he turned to me and asked me to tell the camp commander he would accept the offer on a trial basis if each placement could be monitored by a German officer. I found it strange that he asked me to translate something I knew his English was perfectly capable of speaking. I guess he just wanted someone else in on the defiance of the party.

The arrangements were soon made and I found myself as the German monitor for the program. When we returned to the compound and Oberst Reiter announced his decision to the officers, quite a fracas broke out with Major Fliederman. He and his staunch Nazi group all but called for a mutiny. Later in formation, when Oberst Reiter announced his decision to the men, it was met with a rather positive murmur among the troops. Many came forward later to inquire as to how they could volunteer.

Within the week I found myself headed out of the camp in a jeep accompaning Sergeant Washington, an armed private, and a Caucasian lieutenant. Our destination was to meet with local farmers and arrange for workers. All of the farms were within the small valley where the camp was located. I was very apprehensive. I was not sure how the American civilians

139

would treat me. Most of the negotiations were conducted by the lieutenant, but when the final agreements were made I was introduced and the farmers asked me questions about the men. I was surprised that the questions were not about security or worries about personal safety. What the farmers wanted to know were things about the ability of the men. Questions like: "Are most of the men we will get familiar with farming?" or "Do you have tractors in Germany, or do you just farm with horses?" The questions that most surprised me were ones concerning the welfare of we POWs. They wanted to know if we had proper clothing and what the men would want for midday meal. Could it be that these people were actually concerned about us as men, or were they just worried if we could do the work? Not all of the farmers were so friendly. There were some who made sure that sufficient armed guards were available and were concerned about who would bear the expense of feeding them. All in all the plan for POW labor came together quickly.

Within a week my comrades were being loaded aboard trucks and distributed about the valley. I found myself each day in a jeep with Sergeant Washington and a driver going out with the labor convoy. At first we went as a group and would stop at each farm to drop off workers. After the last was dropped off, Sergeant Washington and the ever-present armed guard would take me back to each farm to observe that each group was being treated right, and that no problems were developing. In the evenings we would again pick up the groups and return to the compound. It soon became clear that this procedure took too much time. Therefore, the idea of going out in one convoy was abandoned and the trucks would disperse on individual routes.

Everything seemed to be going quite smoothly. An unforeseen side benefit was that we prisoners were paid extra for our days spent under the government contracts. Every POW received eighty cents per day plus a ten-cent bonus for extra expenses. This may not seem much to you, but it was a goodly sum to us. This pay was over and above our eighteen dollars I spoke of earlier. The U.S. Army let us establish bank accounts which meant that some of us were able to leave America with nearly $200 in our pockets.[11] From my personal point of view, it seemed like the men were doing

140

quite well. Each day I would report back to the Oberst. He never seemed to show emotion toward the contract arrangement, one way or the other. I could, however, tell he was beginning to show signs of depression. He would only say, "Hauptmann, do not expect tranquillity to last? We are still prisoners and prisons are never peaceful places." Unfortunately he was right. The first problem that developed was on the farms. During the third week one of the trucks hauling workers was stoned by some people on the road leading to the farm they were assigned to. When I found out about it I naturally thought it must be rebellious teenagers from the town. On the next morning two other trucks were stoned at other locations. This time the rock throwers were seen, and they were not teenagers. I naturally told Reiter about it and he subsequently made a protest to the camp commander. The next morning the Lieutenant joined Sergeant Washington and me, and spoke to the farmers about it. They all agreed to look into the matter. That was on a Thursday. That Friday morning several trucks were stoned going to and from the farms. Normally, we worked on Saturday, but Oberst Reiter refused to let the men go out that morning. I think he would have done so no matter what, but his decision may have been strongly influenced by a late meeting with Major Fliederman and Hauptmann Rote. I did not attend the meeting but from my tent I could hear the hollering.

I was with the Oberst when he met with the camp commander that morning. I was aware that this refusal to let the men go out would perhaps cause a very negative reaction by the American commander. I was fully prepared to spend another stint in solidary confinement. To Reiter's credit he did not look or act like anything but a confident, strong German officer as he told the camp commander of his decision. After he gave his decision the American colonel just sat there in silence and stared with a stone face at us. At last he spoke.

"You realize that you aren't some kind of a union boss who can negotiate terms, don't you?"

"Jawohl, Herr Kommandant! I am not a union leader. I am an officer in the Wehrmacht, and as such have a duty to see that my men are treated in a proper manner."

"And I am an officer in the American army in charge of a prisoner-of-war-camp, in which you happen to be a prisoner. Have you forgotten that part Mr. Colonel?"

The Oberst did not answer, but just sat there and stared back at the camp commander. After what seemed an hour, but was probably only 10 or 15 seconds, the American broke the interlocked stare and swung around in his swivel chair to look out the window. He continued to do so for several minutes, with his elbows on the chair arms and his hands held in a praying gesture with his fingertips resting on his chin. At last he swung back around to face us sitting right across the desk from him. His face was in a friendly smile. He at last spoke. "Now look here Colonel Reiter, we are both in a pickle, if your men don't go out to the farms I will be forced to lock this camp down tight, because bored men are trouble. This could be a very long war and this camp could turn into a real shithole for you Germans. For my part I understand your duty to see to the welfare of your men. You have to understand it is also my duty to do so. Also, I assume you understand perfectly well that if I don't live up to the agreement with the farmers they would have the political pressure to make sure my superiors find a nice position for me in Africa. Since I would rather deal with you Germans in a situation where I am the only one carrying a gun I have to do something. Here is what I suggest: Tomorrow your translator, the captain here (he pointed to me), will join Sergeant Washington and go out and talk to the farmers to find out just what is going on. Then we will meet again to decided what the next move is."

Reiter nodded his head and said, "Should not you and I as the respective leaders go out to the community?"

The colonel shook his head and said, "No, sir, I don't think that is a good idea. First of all, you and I being military men may understand your role here; but frankly, to civilians you are just another prisoner." At this Oberst Reiter's face turned a bit red with anger, but he said nothing. The camp commander continued, "Secondly, I don't want anyone in the community to think that we have a problem here. I want them to realize that it is they who have the problem. That is why I don't even plan to send one of my officers out with Sergeant Washington."

142

Reiter's face relaxed a bit, then he looked at me, and then turned back to the American and answered, "As you wish, sir; you have made it clear you are the commander here."

Early the next morning Sergeant Washington, his driver, and I headed out for the farms. As we drove into the first farm, which was also the biggest in the area, we saw a gathering of several of the local farmers. As soon as they spotted us they waved us over. Mr. Brewster, whom I knew as the owner of the farm, came right up to the jeep with a big smile on his face.

"Boy, am I glad to see you fellows," he told Sergeant Washington. "I was afraid that you had abandoned us."

"You did hear that our trucks was bein' stoned didn't ya?"

"Well, yes, and we have found out that it was a bunch of damn wetbacks."

"Wetbacks?"

"Yeah, wetbacks, you know Mexican workers from across the border. The guys that worked on our farms before we got these Germans."

"Yeah, we discussed 'bout them 'fore we started this program; you said that you wouldn't replace any of the locals. You was only to use POWs when other labor wasn't available."

"Well, yes, we did say we wouldn't replace any of the local labor, and we haven't. These wetbacks ain't local. They are not even citizens. Fact is, they are not even legally in this country. We just hire them to do the jobs the locals won't do."

"Then I don't see why they all is stonin' our trucks."

"Well, look here, Sergeant. I think if you will let me talk to the Kraut officer here we can get this thing settled."

Sergeant Washington looked at me and shrugged as he gestured me to go off with Mr. Brewster to talk. The old farmer took me over to the group of men and said, "Fellas, this is the officer that is in charge of the POWs. I think he will be able to square this up and help us get them back in the fields." He turned to me and asked, "What rank are you, young man?"

"I am what you Americans would call a captain."

"Very good; well, here is the deal, Captain. I don't think the nigger

143

sergeant over there can understand the problem here. After all, he probably was just a field hand like these Mexicans before he started strutting around in that uniform. Problem is that you Germans are too damn efficient. Now, don't think we don't appreciate that, but it is causing a problem.

"I don't understand."

"What you must understand, Captain, is that us white men ain't expected to do the menial labor here in this country. If we were to do everything on the farms, these Mexicans would not have any work they were capable of doing, and they would all be starving to death. Therefore, we leave all of the menial tasks that they are smart enough to do so they can have jobs. Now we wouldn't mind your men doing all of the farmwork, but we know that someday this war will be won and you will all be sent back to Germany. If we don't keep the local Mexicans here and keep the wetbacks coming up every season we could be in a real hurt later. You understand, don't you?"

"Excuse my poor English gentlemen, but I seem to be understanding that my men won't be stoned by these wet Mexicans . . ."

"Wetbacks we call them, cuz they swim across the Rio Grande to get here."

"All right, we won't be stoned by the wetbacks if we won't work so hard."

"Well, yes, and no, Captain. We don't want your men just slouching around, but they have to leave some jobs, like hoeing weeds, for the Mexicans."

"How will they know what to do and what not to do?"

"Well, we will have a code phrase. What do you think, fellows?" he asked the other farmers.

One of them volunteered, "How about when we say to one of your workers 'Mexican work', they will know that they aren't to do that."

"What do you think, Captain? Can you teach those words to your men?" Brewster asked me. I assured him that I could. It was soon agreed that I would try to get the men back in the fields the next day if they would get the word out that we were not going to replace the wetbacks.

On the way back to the compound, after I explained the situation

144

to him, Sergeant Washington was very quiet. I could tell he was a bit upset about being left out of the negotiations. At last, I spoke to him. "Please, don't think that I am trying to do your job, Sergeant. I just wanted to get this program going again. It is good for my men." We rode along for some time before he spoke.

"You ain't got no black folk back home do you, Cap'n?"

"No, Sergeant, I had never even seen one of your people until I went to Africa."

"Well, do you have a group of people that ain't the same as the people that run everything?"

"Well, not really, Sergeant. We have poor people, but we are all basically the same. I will say that most people know their place in society and are satisfied with it."

"Then, Cap'n you ain't got no idea what it's like to be a people that ain't people."

"I am not really sure of what you mean, Sergeant."

"That's the problem, Cap'n. Ya see, you don't understand, not because you is German, but 'cuz you is white. Now, Jackson here (he nodded toward his driver) and me we was both raised up in Detroit. There is three kinds of folks live in Detroit. There is the rich folks; they's all white. There is the workin' whites. Then there's us niggas. Now, we worked with the white guys and we even sometimes went to company functions with them. I was even a floor boss at work. I graduated from high school even. You see, it aren't that we is still damn near slave folk like the black folk down in some parts of the South. But, we sure and the hell ain't equal members of society. When a new white guy came to the plant, even if he were an outsider, say from Philly, he didn't get the shitty jobs in the plant. No suh, and after work he could stop in at Sally's pub and have a beer with the good old boys. Now say a black kid from right in Motor City, that there is what we call Detroit, came to work. Why, even if he was the son of one of the old workers at the plant he damn well started at the bottom. You better bet yo butt that he didn't dare stop at Sally's bar after work. Right Jackson?" (Jackson got a good laugh at that.) "You see, we was people just like the white guys, but yet we was not the same kind of people. Now I know you is

145

a nice guy even if you is a damn Kraut, but don't say yo don't understand what I is talkin' about. Why, just take the way that fella Hitler treated Jessie Owens at the Olympics. He weren't about to come down and shake some nigga's hand. Yeah, I knowed that some folks said it was 'cuz Jessie was an American, but you and I knows better. It was 'cuz he weren't people."

I just sat back in my seat and didn't say anything. For one, I had never heard Washington say more than about one sentence in a row. Secondly, I was really not sure of what he was talking about. Yes, I had read that an American runner had won several events at the Berlin Olympics. However this was the first time I had heard that he was a Negro, and certainly had never heard that Hitler had refused to shake one of the winners' hand. I had only read how thrilled the winners had all been to have der Fuehrer come down and honor them. Frankly, I must say at the time I didn't believe what Washington said. He obviously had believed some nasty American propaganda. I finally said, "OK, Sergeant, I am not sure why those farmers wanted to talk to me rather than you. I thought it was because they don't trust the army; that is the same as in Germany, but none the less what do you think you will tell your colonel?"

He looked at me, shook his head, and said, "Like talkin' to a blank wall. Well, I thought you would want to report to the old man."

"No, Sergeant, I may be a white man, but I do understand that I am just a prisoner. It is best that the colonel doesn't even know I talked to the farmers. I just want to get the men back to work."

"Yo shor is the damnedest Nazi I ever heard of. OK, let's get this damn show back on the road."

I didn't realize it at the time, but that little incident formed a bond between Sergeant Washington and me that was to lead me to some new and interesting adventures.

Not only did the work program get back under way it soon expanded, and Sergeant Washington and I were kept busy running around the country making sure that all the men were doing what they were expected to and being treated well. I must say that for the most part they were treated quite well by the farmers. In addition to farmers many men went to work in agricultural industries during the harvest. As the first snow blew, the last chores were completed and we Germans found ourselves locked up in our little compound waiting out the winter.

That first winter in America was a tough one. I had been quite busy, other than my time in solitary while at Hearne, since I had landed in America, but now I experienced the frustration, anger, and shame of being an animal locked in a cage. We officers tried our best to find ways to keep the men occupied and, when possible, entertained. However, we, like them, spent many hours sitting idle and brewing about our situation. More than one fight broke out; these fights represented more than a problem between individuals as the men began to break up into groups. This was aggravated by the fact that the Americans did not enter into the everyday disciplinary problems of the POWs unless things got totally out of hand. Intercamp problems and discipline were the responsibility of the German leadership. Unfortunately, Oberst Reiter began to get depressed and withdrawn. The leadership void was filled by Major Fliederman and his inner circle of strong party supporters. Soon party meetings were being held regularly at night after lights out. To not attend at least some of them was to invite trouble. I found myself doubting everything. I knew that for Germany, and we German POWs, to survive we must stick together and remain proud. However, I also came more and more to realize that perhaps our situation, and all of the killing and being killed that was going on was in part a product of the arrogance of Nazi philosophy. I was still clear on who the enemy was, but I started to have doubts about who my friends might be.

With spring came the return of POWs to the farms. Things started out great but a problem soon developed. One day at work call, after breakfast, many of the men did not show up. Guards soon scattered out and herded everyone into a hasty formation. While the Americans looked on with rather nervous faces and ready weapons Oberst Reiter turned to the assembled POWs and asked what the problem was. Hauptmann Rote stepped forward.

"Sir!" he shouted, louder than he needed to. "It was our understanding that this was a voluntary progam."

"Yes, Herr Hauptmann, that is true."

"Then, sir, I have been asked by the men to say that any loyal

147

German soldier among us will not participate in this American conspiracy."

"Are you saying you are the spokesman for the camp now, Herr Hauptmann?" The captain began to look a lot less confident under the glare from the old colonel.

"Ah, no, sir, just for the men who met last night to ask us officers who have proven ourselves to be the most loyal to dem Vaterland as to what they should do."

"And you 'loyal' officers, without consulting me, decided to tell them to lie around here in camp and act liked common criminals in a prison?"

Hauptmann Rote looked around for Fliederman hoping for a way out from under the glare of Oberst Reiter. Fliederman stepped forward.

"Sir, Hauptmann Rote and I are not attempting to speak for you or the entire camp. We are however, speaking for the loyal Germans who have come to us for advice. We, and they, feel that this aiding and abetting the enemy has gone far enough."

"Very well; however, let me make something perfectly clear: I am the senior officer in this camp and I will decide what will happen or not happen when we as POWs have any choice. I have decided that this program is not a conspiracy by the enemy, but a chance for our men to remain physically and mentally healthy while in this unfortunate situation. Any man who decides to work on the farms can do so without any retribution from me or for that manner, most definitely, not from you. Is that perfectly understood?"

The trucks soon left. They were not full, but many of the former absent workers were now on board.

I thought that the matter was solved and that soon, as the workers started to receive their extra pay, those hesitant men would rejoin the men going out each day. This was not to be the case. Soon, many of the men were suddenly sick and unable to go to work. I brought this to Oberst Reiter's attention, but he chose to ignore it. One of the soldiers who had been enjoying the freedom of getting out of the compound was Beckmann. He had used the opportunity to expand his English and had become a valuable asset to the program. He was assigned to farmer Brewster's farm because it had the

148

biggest crew. Even though he didn't have the rank, he served as the lead man of that crew. One day he did not show up for the work formation. That evening when I returned I went to see him. I entered his hut and asked where I could find him. The two soldiers I made the inquiry to looked at each other in a nervous manner.

At last one answered me, "Sir, he is not feeling well and is asleep; I don't think he wants any visitors."

I snapped back at him, "I didn't ask for your opinion, Soldatin. I asked you where I could find him."

The two soldiers snapped to attention and one pointed to the rear of the hut. There in the dim light I saw a figure in a cot with his back to me. I walked back to the cot and said, "Beckmann, are you asleep?" There was no answer, but I saw him stiffen slightly and knew he was awake. "Juergen, I know you are awake." I said in a soft voice. "You might as well answer me."

After a moment of silence, he said, "Sorry I missed work call today, sir. I just feel real bad is all."

"Have you been to sick call?"

"No, sir, but I will be all right, if I just take it easy a few days."

"Ah, a few days it is to be then?"

"Yes, sir, I am sure I will be better then. I, uh, may go out again then."

"You 'may' go out again? That is about enough Juergen. Tell me just what the hell is up with you."

"Nothing, Herr Hauptmann. I am just not feeling well is all."

"Then if nothing is wrong why won't you look at me?"

He still failed to move so I raised my voice to a command level and ordered, "Jaeger, get on your feet and talk to me as a proper soldier."

Beckmann quickly rolled over and jumped to his feet. He did not remain at attention but a second before he fainted. I caught his fall and laid him back down on his bunk. It was then that I noticed that his face was a mess. Since he wore only underpants I could see bruise marks all over his body.

He soon regained consciousness and I was able to ask, "How the hell did this happen?"

149

"I just fell down is all," he mumbled back.

"FELL DOWN? Like hell you did! I suppose you fell down the flight of stairs we don't even have in this camp. Now tell me who did this to you."

"It was just a disagreement over a card game, sir."

"A disagreement with the whole damn platoon it appears."

"Sir, you know I can't say more. I will be all right; please just let me be. It really would be best for both of us if you did not get involved, sir."

I tried to make him comfortable and left without saying anymore. I knew that there had to be more to him being beaten than he was saying.

I decided to go and check up on a couple of other "sick" soldiers whom I knew were very happy to be out on the farms. I found one writing a letter to his wife. He claimed to have decided that working on the farms was unpatriotic. I found two others, both with signs of a beating; however, not as bad as Beckmann. I went to Reiter, but he told me to just forget it and let him look in to it.

Two days went by and nothing was said to me by the Oberst. Each day, though, there were fewer workers reporting to work call. On the third morning Sergeant Washington, on the way out to the farms, asked Jackson to pull over into some trees. He got out and asked me to follow him. We went under a tree. He sat down and gestured for me to do likewise. When I settled down onto a convenient rock under the tree, he reached in his pocket and pulled out a pint of whiskey. He took a swig and then handed to me. I had not tasted hard liquor since those evenings with the doctor on the boat ride over. I carefully took a swallow and rather enjoyed the hot path it left down my throat. Sergeant Washington, took another drink from the flask, threw it back to me, and laid back looking up into the tree with his hands behind his head.

"Now, cap'n, are you goin' tah tell me what the hell is goin' on or not?"

"I don't know what you are getting at, Sergeant."

"Ah shit Cap'n, I may be dumb, but I ain't stupid. Fo' the last few days we is seein' less workers and you is gettin' mo' and mo' quiet. Now what the hell is up?"

150

"I really don't know Sergeant. I have spoken to my colonel and he said he would look into it."

"I is really goin' to miss the freedom of drivin' 'round the country like this rather than sittin' in a guard tower and watchin' you sittin' in a cage like a zoo animal. I kind of figure you is goin' to miss it too, and that is 'xactly what are goin' ah happen if'n we lose just a few mo' workers."

I took a long drink from the bottle before saying anything. "Damn it, Sergeant, I really am not sure what is going on, but I do think I know who is responsible."

Washington quickly sat up and looked me in the eye. "Then why don't you tell me so maybe I can help your sorry white ass?" This brought a smile to my face, though it did not last long.

"Sergeant, remember how you once told me about the different people in America? Well, in the German army we have some differences also. We have a rather well-defined and respected chain of command. However, there are certain individuals who have special links to the highest levels of leadership and they must be given some special attention by the other members, even those in the leadership chain above them. This has not always been so, but it is now a fact in our army."

"I ain't too damn sure what you is sayin', but I figures that it has somethin' to do with that fella Hitler and his band of Nazis. Am I right, cap'n?"

"Don't you think we ought to get back on the road, Sergeant Washington?"

"OK! Have her your way, cap'n, but just remember that I understand we all live under a few unwritten rules. Gawd knows us black folks do, so if'n you feel there is any way I can help let me know." With that he started back to the jeep.

I stopped him and said, "Thanks, Sergeant. I will say this, I will look into it some more tonight and maybe let you know more tomorrow." Nothing else was said between us about the matter that day.

That evening I lay in my bunk and thought about what Sergeant Washington had said. He may not have been educated, but he obviously was a smart man. I knew that I could not ignore the situation. Sergeant

151

Washington was right. I didn't want to sit out the war in a cage. I really enjoyed the freedom of riding around overseeing the farm program. I decided to do some more investigating. I waited until the camp was dark and quiet. I carefully took a tour around through the huts, avoiding the light, and keeping out of sight of the perimeter guards. All seemed to be normal. In most of the huts I could hear the noise of card games in progress or men talking and singing. However, as I came upon one hut I heard angry voices.

"You Arschloch, don't you give a damn about your country?"

"Sir, please, I have told you I am loyal to der Fuehrer, it is just that I am from a very poor family and this extra money may help them to at last buy our own farm."

"It is obvious that it is useless to talk to a selfish Schwein like you. The rest of you had better take heed and see what happens to people like Soldat Weis. They seem to value their own insignificant lives more than what they know is best for the good of the Reich."

The sound of a scuffle enseud followed by the pained cries of a man being beaten. I hurried to the door and burst in to the hut. There in the middle stood Fliederman and Rote watching as some of their followers beat Soldat Weis, as others held him. As I came in Fliederman saw me.

"Ah, look here my friends; we have a visitor. The oberst's kiss ass and personal handmaiden of the Scharze Sergeant Washington."

"Just what the hell is going on, Herr Major?"

"I could say that it is none of your business, Ami Hund, but I guess it is your business. You are the Arschloch who has caused weak men like Weis to become traders to der Fuehrer."

"And, just when did our Fuehrer start condoning the beating of German soldiers who are following the orders of their commander?"

"If you mean Herr Reiter, he is not fit to be a commander. He lost that right when he decided to sit in his hut and drink the American whiskey the camp commander gives him, rather than stand up to these Schwein by refusing to do their dirty work."

"Who the hell are you to decide what is right and wrong?"

"I am the protector of the party in this camp, and therefore the personal representative of der Fuehrer." Is that not right men?"

152

Fliederman's followers snapped to attention and raised their arms in salute as they hollered "Heil Hitler!" I stepped between Fliederman and the now prone, bloody body of their victim.

"You had better just get the hell out of here, Fliederman, and hope to hell I don't report you."

"Report me? Report me to who you Scheisskopf, your black friend? I think it is time for you to be shown what happens to cowards in this camp."

With that he gestured to his mob and I found myself being knocked to the ground and kicked. As I tried to struggle to my feet I saw Rote swing a club. I was able to deflect it but was sure I heard a bone in my arm snap. As I fell, I felt other blows strike me. I didn't lie there long before I saw a flash of light accompanied by a terrific blow to my head. Just before total darkness flowed over me I heard new voices, this time in English, accompanied with whistles and the sound of many more men entering the room.

I awoke with a terrific throbbing pain in my head and arm. As the world quit rotating and came into focus I saw Sergeant Washington's big black face looking down at me.

"Welcome back, cap'n, I weren't too sure that I was goin' ah see those baby blues of yo's again."

"Damn! Are you sure I am not in hell? It would only be there where I might see such an ugly face. What the hell happened? Where am I?"

"You is in the infirmary, Cap'n. Seems you had a bit of a disagreement wit some of'n yo' friends."

"Was that you I heard breaking up the party before I decided to take a nap?"

"Shore was, Cap'n. Didn't seem that you was a havin' much fun anyway."

"You can say that again, Sarg, but how did you get there?"

"Well, I could tell you had bigger trouble than you let on, and we have been watching that gang of Fliederman's. I figured you was goin' to lead us to the root of the "sick" problem. We was watching you the whole way through camp. I suggest you don't try to become a burglar, Cap'n. You is not what I's call sneaky. Anyway we saw you go inta dat hut, so we listened in a

153

bit. I aint shor what all dat Kraut talk was, but it shor didn't sound friendly. Sorry it took us a bit to realize dat you was a gettin' yo' ass stomped. Well, no worry now. We all done took care of Fliederman, Rote, and da rest of his pack of dogs."

They did take care of the hard-core Nazi party element in the camp. Within the week, Fliederman, Rote, and the key members of his close followers were shipped back east. I was to learn from Sergeant Washington that they were sent to Oklahoma. I assumed it to be to the same camp my tent mates in Texas had been sent to after their attempted escape. Life was soon back to normal and I, after a couple of weeks' recovery, was back out making the rounds with Sergeant Washington. The only real change was that, with the negative pressure off, many more of the camp POWs wanted to work outside the camp. Sergeant Washington and I were soon going further and further as the program spread out of the valley to other small pockets of farms. Some men, those with special skills, were even going to shops such as shoe repair and watch repair establishments in the town. Viewing an American town was a new experience for me.

I had seen several towns from the train, but I had not had the opportunity to actually tour one. Farmington was not much of a town. It was my first experience with American towns so at the time I thought it looked like all towns in America. I was shocked that it was so plain and frankly, so ugly. The Americans seemed to all want a piece of ground. Therefore, the houses and buildings were all spread out. However, they didn't seem to care about maintaining it. Few of the large yards around the houses were well kept, and there were many empty lots. When the wind blew, the dust swirled out of them so bad one couldn't see to drive down the street. Most of the buildings were wood, many in dire need of paint. On the edge of town were large blocks of adobe and ramshackle wood huts. Every one of the yards around these places seemed to be full of Mexican children. I remember Sergeant Washington saying, "These greasers shor ain't got much, do they?" Two things were obvious, the Americans were a segregated people and they for the most part were poor. Believing this, I was shocked when I actually got to go into some of the downtown stores with Sergeant Washington. The stores themselves were mostly in a style I found rather

154

strange. They were one-story buildings, mostly of wood, but they all had a false front to make them appear as two-story. The Americans, for all of their attempt at being a "simple folk", were a pretentious lot. Along the main street this row of square, false-fronted buildings gave the town a temporary look. Their shelves were overflowing with goods, and the customers seemed little bothered by the prices as they left with their arms full. I was further surprised to hear some ladies complaining to a store manager about how hard it was getting by with the newly announced rationing due to the war. Outside the stores the streets were filled with cars. I did not see one wagon. For a person whose country was at war with America, the obvious wealth and the glut of goods was frightening and discouraging. Many people stopped and stared at us as we drove and walked through town. I am not sure if they were looking at me as a POW or at Sergeant Washington and Private Jackson because they were Negroes. I didn't see any other Negroes in the town.

The workers we dropped off at shops in town were very well received. In fact, in the evening when we came back by with trucks to pick them up they seemed quite pleased with the work. Few could speak any English, but it didn't seem to matter. Western Americans, which I can't say about most Europeans, are, for the most part, very patient with people who can't speak their language, though I must say my German soldiers were very quick to pick up the language. In fact, quite soon most of the POWs were able to converse with their "sponsors" (that was the term used for the farmers and businessmen who got cheap POW labor).

Soon more POWs came to our camp. They had been captured in Italy. We had heard from the guards that the war had spread to Italy, but we really did not want to believe it. We were discouraged to find it true, but also encouraged by the fact that the new POWs were still convinced that Germany would win. The war, according to them, was only going bad at the moment because of the cowardliness and treacherous nature of the Italians. The growing camp population led to an even more expanded work program, and the need to spread over a larger geographical area.

A very large change in my, and many other POWs, life was in part spurred on by this increase in population. As the program spread out over the area, the workday of many POWs became shorter due to the longer commuting time. A representative group of farmers came to the camp commander and asked him to let the prisoners stay overnight at their farms. This of course was not something the camp commander could authorize himself, nor something he even wanted. Oberst Reiter was asked to come in to sit in on the meeting. He brought me along to translate if need be. Most of the farmers recognized me and came over to greet me. Since they ignored my commander, not knowing him, I could see Reiter getting a bit sullen and his jaw tightening. I quickly tried to ease the building friction by introducing him to the farmers. I am afraid the damage was already done. Unfortunately, during the meeting when one of the farmers wanted to make a point, such as how well they treated the prisoners, they would turn to me for confirmation as if I were the leader of the POWs. After the farmers had made their point, the camp commander sat in silence, obviously disturbed by the request. I can imagine he was just seeing his career going astray when some prisoners who were let totally out of his control escaped. He turned to Oberst Reiter and asked his opinion. Reiter was still brooding over the insult of being left out of the conversation and was not about to do anything to accommodate those, in his mind, rude men.

He came to his feet and said in a very formal manner, in English (he wasn't about to go through me), "As the Kommander of the German soldiers in this camp, I would not advise that it would be in the best interest of the Americans nor the Germans to go any further with this program. It is clear to me that some individuals (his eyes quickly flicked over to me and then back to the American colonel) under my command have started to forget what their duty as soldiers is. If you allow this program to expand I am afraid both you and I, colonel, will see our command powers being eroded."

The camp commander nodded then turned to the leader of the farm group. "I find myself in the strange position of agreeing more with Colonel Reiter," he told them, "than with my own fellow citizens. However, you must realize that my major concern is for your and the country's security. I cannot let men I am ordered to keep in internment until they are returned to their homeland under the agreements of war free to wander the countryside at will."

156

Several of the farmers started to object, but farmer Becker, their leader, held up his hand, smiled, and said, "Gentlemen, the colonel has made his decision; we just need to talk to the people who can help us." He turned to the camp commander, shook his hand, and said, "Thank you, colonel, for listening to us. I am sure you will hear more about this manner." He quickly left with the other farmers in tow. After they left, Oberst Reiter asked me to leave as he stayed for a chat with the camp commander. I went back to my tent knowing that I was once again on Reiter's bad list.

Surprisingly, I was not ordered to report to my laison duty later that day, nor the at nextformation. I had gone over to the usual spot where Sergeant Washington picked me up to go on our rounds, but he didn't show up. On the second morning I returned to the pickup point. I waited for over an hour but Washington again did not show. I was just about to leave when Private Jackson came by and informed me that I would not be going out for awhile, if again at all. It seems that Sergeant Washington had been called in by the camp commander and given a lecture about his allowing me to become too friendly with the farmers. I now knew what Reiter and the American commander had discussed when I had been sent from the room.

A week went by and I remained in camp. Since I had nothing to do I just lounged around. I did write several letters home hoping, but not really believing, that they would reach my family. One morning as I was taking a long stroll around the compound I noticed a group of cars arriving at the camp headquarters. One was a big, new, shiny black car. I could tell when the visitors gathered together outside the HQ building for a small conference before going in, that one of the men from the big car was the focal point. He was obviously a very important man. Shortly after they entered the building a runner could be seen scurrying to Reiter's tent. Shortly thereafter, a Soldat came running out into the yard and calling my name. I hurried to the Oberst's tent. As I got there I was greeted by Major Gottlieb, the second highest-ranking officer in the camp. Gottlieb was a very quiet fellow who had come in with the last group of POW's. He had yet to take any role in the camp, either because he didn't want to or because Reiter had made sure that he didn't. In any case he had appeared to me as a nice man who was happy to be out from under the weight of a command. On this morning he

157

was quite agitated. I could tell that there was a problem. As I arrived, he looked at me and said, "Ah, Herr Hauptmann, I am happy to see that you are in camp. We have a problem. The Oberst has been ordered to a meeting and he is in no shape to go, what shall we do?"

"Pardon me, sir," I answered, "but what do you mean by he is in no shape to go?"

"I believe he is a bit, ah, shall we say under the weather."

"I see, sir, (I started to understand), but why have you asked for me rather than putting out a call to the senior officers?"

"We don't have time, Herr Hauptmann. The meeting is in ten minutes. Besides, you are the officer who has been to the most meetings with the camp commander. Oberst Reiter has told me that he trusts you."

"Very well," I said trying to cover up my surprise, "but should we not talk to the Oberst first before going to the meeting?"

"Yes, we shall, Herr Hauptmann, but I warn you he his not in a good mood or in the shape to have a very intelligible conversation."

With that he ducked into the tent. I followed. I had to take a quick breath as the rancid smell of old whiskey and an unwashed body hit me. There on the edge of his bunk sat Reiter. He was trying to put on a boot, but was unsuccessful. It was some time before he noticed us.

"Ah, gentlemen," he slurred. "I am glad you came. Maybe you can help me with this damn boot. My feet must have swollen in this damn American heat. I have got to be at, ah, ah, ah, well some damn place."

We could see that he could not get his right foot into his boot because it was his left boot. Besides that, he was far too drunk even to stand up. I quickly glanced over to Major Gottlieb and found his face in a grimace. I looked back to Reiter and said, "Sir, I have just come from the front gate and am here to tell you that the meeting has been called off."

"Just like those damn Amis," he said as he laid back down. He laid there a minute and seemed to try to focus on my face. At last he said, "Er soldiers." He seemed to lose focus, shut his eyes, and I believe was snoring before we got out of the tent.

Once outside, we stood a moment and tried to breathe in some fresh air. "Good thinking, Herr Hauptmann; now I think we had better go to the meeting, Major Gottlieb commented. You are to tell no one that the

158

Oberst is anything but ill. Do you understand?" I assured him of that as we strolled over to the headquarters gate. I was impressed by the fact that we strolled rather casually to the gate. It was obvious that the Major did not want the Americans to get the idea that he, or any German officer, would come running to their beck and call. I noticed he was wearing his gloves and was attired very neatly considering our circumstances.

As we entered the commander's office we could see that there were about seven or eight American civilians in the room. All were standing except for one very well-dressed man who occupied a chair right in front of the colonel's desk. Neither he nor the colonel stood when we entered. We also were not offered a chair. The camp commander was not about to show this visitor, whoever he was, that we were anywhere as important as he. Major Gottlieb reacted in a very cool and relaxed manner. He slowly removed his gloves, motioned for me to stand next to him, but not too close to the desk, in the proper translator position, adopted a very casual stance and then had me translate his greeting.

The camp commander then introduced his visitor. He was a senator; I can't remember his name. He was a rather big fellow with a very reddish complexion. He seemed to make it a point not to recognize Gottlieb. He just glanced up to him from his chair as the introduction was made and switched his attention back to the camp commander.

"To get back to my point, Colonel, I think it is important to realize that the program of having the POWs work on the farms is more than just a little rehabilitation program for your prisoners. Our farmers are being asked to up their production in these hard times and they are short of help. Now, it seems rather clear that you have plenty of labor potential here, and I don't see why you are resisting the continuance of a good program."

"Senator," the colonel answered, "I can understand your concern, but my directive is clear. The use of POWs for work programs other than those right here in camp is to be voluntary according to the Geneva Convention Agreements, and it will not take place if it is detrimental to the security of the country."

"VOLUNTARY! Well, I'll be damned. I thought these Krauts were our enemies, not wards of Mr. Roosevelt's welfare program?

"Enemies they may be, Senator, but they must be treated under the guidelines set down by international agreement."

The senator turned to the farmers and said, "Do you hear that, fellas? The army is more concerned about the welfare of these 'fellow soldiers' than it is the welfare of the hard-working citizens of this country." He turned back to the colonel and glared a minute. He then said, "Colonel, I guess you have got us here. I understand you must operate under the rules set down by your higher headquarters. However, I am sure you understand that your superiors are not going to be too pleased when a certain United States senator drops in to tell them that the community no longer wants this camp located here and perhaps they should relocate it very soon. In fact, I suppose they just might come down here and find it easier to appease the locals by shit canning the officer who caused the locals to feel that way. Now I and these fellows here are going to go down to town and have a beer. If you change your mind about not wanting to continue this program you might want to get word to me by this evening."

He stood up and headed for the door. Before reaching it he turned back and said, "Oh yes, one more little thing. While you are making up your mind you should consider expanding the program. I have been hearing more farmers throughout the area are interested in getting some of these fellows to work on their places." With that, he and his entourage left.

The colonel just sat there and stared at the door. "May I say something, Colonel?" Gottlieb asked.

The colonel motioned for him to sit and replied, "That must have impressed you on how efficient democracy works?"

"No matter what system people like to work under, Colonel, they find a way to use, or should I say abuse, their power. What options do you think you have?"

"Now that somewhat depends on you and Colonel Reiter. I will not violate your rights as prisoners of war. If you do not want your men to live out on the farms then certainly I will not force them to."

"As far as them staying out of this wonderfully appointed living area, I don't suppose the men would object at all. As for Oberst Reiter, I will have the Hauptmann here report back his answer as soon as we speak with him. I know it is not my concern, but are you not worried about my men escaping if they are left overnight out of the compound?"

"Frankly, yes I am. However, if they are foolish enough to try to escape in this damn desert they will no doubt perish and I will be transferred to the front lines with no chance of making full colonel. If I don't let them go they will no doubt become bored to the point that they riot and I will be sent to the front lines with no chance of making full colonel. So go visit with your colonel and I will comply with the dear senator if you so wish."

Gottlieb and I returned to Oberst Reiter's tent. There we proceeded to get the inebriated old man to agree to letting the soldiers return to the farms and to stay overnight if required. Within the hour I returned this information to the camp commander and he in turn sent out a messenger to the senator. Thus, a new phase of my time as a POW commenced.

CHAPTER FOUR

PRISONER OR TOURIST?

As things so often do, it turned out that the decision to allow POWs to stay off site was made just in time. First of all, shortly after we Germans started back to work on the farms and in the villages, a new load of POWs arrived at the camp. Secondly, the area our workers went out to expanded.

The arrival of new POWs was a bittersweet thing. One's first reaction was the joy of having the prospect of receiving new word about the homeland. Perhaps there would be a guy from one's hometown, or at least area, among the group. This was often the case for the soldiers from larger cities, but for us who came from small towns we had to be satisfied with general news of our country. The news we did get often was confusing. On one hand the new POWs talked rather positively about the war effort. Great gains were being made in Russia and the word was that the English were nearly ready to quit. As for their concept of America, they were convinced that the American people were ready to take to the streets to stop the war against the brave and noble German people. When we asked them how they came by that impression, since we certainly had not seen any such activity, they became irate. How could we be negative? Had we given up being soldiers? They knew the truth because they had read it in German newspapers and had, had the privilege to have listened to news broadcasts transmitted to the front. We wanted very much to believe them, but we had seen so much wealth in America, and so much optimism among the farmers in their feelings toward the war, we just were not sure whose propaganda machines were the most truthful. One did not know whether to feel ashamed of one's pessimism or angry at being betrayed and lied to by the German leadership. We each had to wrestle with that question on our own. To express such doubts was to risk being branded a coward and a traitor. To further compound the confusion about the state of the war, it was clear to me that the very presence of new POWs who had been captured in northern Italy was not an indication that the war was going well. The truth of the matter was that whether Germany won or lost became less and less of a concern to me,

162

and I think to the majority of POWs. The real concern was when would the war be over? Whether we went home to a victorious Germany or to a defeated one was secondary to the very idea of just going home. With the new prisoners came the word that the Allied bombing had increased. No one was really sure how extensive the damage was, but the thought of our loved ones being subjected to the terror of bombardments was excruciating. The POWs from the large cities were the most concerned as they knew their homes would be the main targets.

As the work program expanded, so did my travels. Farmers in other agricultural areas began to request, or demand, that they be allowed to use this new cheap source of labor. Being from the West you know that the arable lands are spread far and wide. It became the policy that small "temporary" camps be set up in the major town in each of these areas. These camps were generally on a Festplatz, or as you call them fairgrounds. I was soon to find that even the towns in the American Southwest were a long way apart. Thus, I became a tourist. Since Sergeant Washington and Private Jackson were also strangers to that part of the country so they also took on the persona of tourists.

What a strange team we made, two big-city black men and a German POW (or I should say two German POWs since it became the norm for Beckmann to come along). We not only accompanied the groups of workers being transported to new work areas, but also were sent out to make advance arrangements. When troops were in place we would make the rounds to see that all were being treated properly and to assist them with such things as taking them for minor medical or dental treatment. That was the main rationale behind sending Beckmann and me both together. We could then stand by to translate as two or more soldiers received treatment. Sometimes we would not get back to the main camp for a week or more. Along the way we managed to have quite a few adventures.

Several of these I think you will find interesting as they reflect my growing curiosity about the people who were my captors. For example, one day we were out and about on our rounds on a very hot and dry day. I happened to mention that it was too bad we were not in Germany so we could stop at a Gasthaus for a refreshing beer. As I hoped it would, the

163

challenge that only Germany had good beer was accepted. Sergeant Washington ordered Private Jackson to stop at the next crossroads settlement and we would find a good American beer. With luck we soon came upon a small cluster of buildings, one of which was a bar. We stopped and Sergeant Washington went in to purchase the beer. We heard some shouting and laughing and soon the sergeant came storming out without any beer, jumped into the jeep, and growled at Jackson to get the hell out of there. As we started down the road, Jackson asked, "What happen', Sarg? Where is da beer?"

Washington whispered between his teeth, "What the hell do you think? Damn, we should have known better."

"Bastards," muttered Jackson, and we drove on.

I was quite confused and at first decided it was best that I just keep quiet. But my thirst had been increased by the very thought of a beer. At last I ventured, "Do you mean that that establishment didn't even have beer? I told you it was too bad that we weren't in Germany." Then I really went overboard and jokingly said, "If you fellows were my prisoners instead of the other way around we would all be having a beer right now."

Washington suddenly yelled at Jackson, "STOP DIS DAMN JEEP!" Jackson slammed on the brakes and we skidded to the side of the road. Washington sat there a minute, and then turned toward me with a most menacing look. "Yo' dumb-ass Kraut. Yo' ain't got the slightest damn idea what Jackson and I feel right now. If'n I thought yo' did I would blow yo' damn head off right here and now." He turned forward, looked over at Jackson, who was sitting there shaking his head, then slowly turned back to me. "OK, Cap'n, I guess you really don't understand; so I's gonna tell ya. I went into that bar just like any other soldier in this here army would and asked for a six pack, but you know what, I ain't just any ol' soldier, I is black. Well, that fat-assed bartender just looked at me and said, 'well there, little Nigger boy, I would throw yo ass out but then again maybe yo cain't read.' So naturally I asked him, 'What y'all mean, cain't read?' He just pointed to the wall, and shor' 'nuff there was a sign there that read: NO DOGS, MEXICANS, INDIANS, OR COLOREDS ALLOWED. I tried to hold my temper even tho' dem fellas in der started ah laughin'. I axed him if'n he didn't rec'nize the uniform of a U-nited States Army sergeant and dat set

164

dem redneck bastards to really laughin'. I'da punched dah son of a bitch in dah nose if'n der weren't so many others wit him. Well shit, we might as well get on down dah road."

We traveled a bit further when I said, "Damn! I sure was looking forward to that beer."

Washington shouted at Jackson, "TURN THIS SON OF A BITCH AROUND."   Jackson whipped that jeep around so fast it came up on two wheels. I thought for sure I had pushed Sergeant Washington over the edge and he was going to go back and use his carbine to clear that bar out so that he could punch the fat bartender in the nose. I could see he was real mad. When we got near to the bar he directed Private Jackson to stop. He then turned to me and said, "Now, Cap'n, since you are so damn set on having a beer, yo' take yo' white Nazi ass in der and buy some. We will be right here to pick yo' up when what is left of yo' Hun carcass gets thrown out onto the street."

I looked him in the eye for a moment to see if he was serious. I decided to call his bluff. I stood up slowly, smiled, and said, "OK, I guess someone needs to get the beer, have you got the money?" Jackson started to giggle as Washington fished in his pocket and handed me a couple of dollars.

The interior of the bar was not very well lit so it took me a minute to let my eyes adjust. I had noted that the conversations that I had heard as I walked through the door had all stopped. As I began to focus better, I could see about seven or eight men sitting around tables. All were quiet as they stared at me. I damn near decided to head out the door quickly, but then my thirst got the better of me and I sauntered over to the bar. All eyes in the joint followed me. I had never seen the interior of an American bar and was impressed at the long polished wooden bar. A fat sweaty man, obviously Sergeant Washington's fat-assed bartender, stood opposite me and said, "Well, stranger, what will you have?"

I tried to remember what Washington had called a container of beer bottles, but couldn't remember what he called it, so I ventured, "I would like a couple of boxes of beer, please." The whole crowd started to laugh.

"Gee, stranger, would you mind taking it in a bottle?" the bartender managed to say through his laughter.

165

"Oh, sorry, I meant a couple of boxes of bottles." This really caused some laughter.

"Why, of course, but would you like big boxes," he paused to get his laughing under control, "or little bitty boxes?" he said as he demonstrated size with his hands. The crowd was really into it by then.

"Excuse me, please, but how big of boxes does your beer come in? You see, I am not from here."

"You sure had me fooled, fella. I thought you was a local yokel for sure. Now how 'bout a couple of six packs?"

"Ah, yes, that is what I meant to say. Give me two six packs, please."

The bartender stepped back into a back room and brought out two paper containers with six bottles of beer in each.

"I ain't got no cold six packs. Will these two do you?"

"Oh yes, that is good. I don't want them cold, as long as they are Keller, I mean cellar cold, that is fine." I heard murmurs behind me and more laughter.

"I am not too damn sure what cellar cold is but these sure ain't even cool."

"Well, they will do very nicely, thank you."

"That will be a buck twenty."

That really confused me and I just stood there. I finally said, "How much will the beer be?"

"I just told you, a buck twenty."

"Ah, I have only got two dollars. Is that enough?"

The bartender looked at the crowd and said through his tears of laughter, "What do you think, fellas? Will two dollars be enough to pay for a buck twenty's worth of beer?" This was obviously a great joke because everyone really laughed. He took my two dollars and pushed the two six packs across the bar to me as he asked, "Stranger, you obviously are a soldier; do you mind telling us where you are from?"

"Well, no, I don't mind. I am originally from Potsdam."

"Potsdam you say. I ain't sure that I have heard of it. Is it in New York or somewhere back there? You talk kind of funny like those New Yorkers."

166

At last I caught on that these people had no idea that I was a German, and certainly not the fact that I was a prisoner of war. So I answered, "Yes, New York area; you have a good understanding of dialects."

"Damn straight, one doesn't run a bar as long as I have without having talked to people from all over. But, that certainly is a different uniform, what does the P and the W there on the legs mean."

"Oh that. That is strange, isn't it? Well, it means prisoner of war. You see, I am acting like a German for some war practice we are doing."

"Ha! That is good, and let me tell you, you sure do play the part real well. Why if it weren't for my spotting that there New York accent I'da thought you was sure enough one of them Nazis."

I thanked him and retreated quickly out the door and around the corner to the jeep. I jumped in and said "Let us get the hell out of here quick!"

We pulled up into the next grove of trees to drink our beer. As I handed out the bottles Jackson said, "You must be one hell of a comedian by the sound of that laughter we heard."

Washington took one swallow of beer and almost spit it out. "Damn! This stuff is almost hot. Why didn't you get cold beer?"

"Well, they didn't have any; besides, cold beer doesn't have any taste, and it's not good for you anyway."

"Jesus! I guess I should of known better than send a dumb-ass Kraut."

Warm or not, those two seemed to enjoy the beer almost as much as I did. It was a rather bitter, weak, very fizzy pilsner but it was beer. My first in a long time. One strange thing was that Washington and Jackson didn't find any humor in the fact that a POW could buy beer when they could not. They became real quiet and sullen. I guess one can rightfully say all of us met the enemy that day.

I had several opportunities to meet different Americans during those weeks of travel around the American Southwest. One day we drove into a large American Indian settlement. It was really one big apartment-like complex made of rock and adobe. It did in ways resemble the construction I had seen in northern Africa. As a young lad I had read all of Karl May's books. He was the German author who had introduced the German readers to the Red Indians of North America. Having his stereotype of the noble, brave, warriors living in tents of skins in my mind I was a bit shocked to meet real Indians. I really didn't get to meet them. It is more correct for me to tell you that I saw real Indians, since the people in the village only stared at us as we drove through. To tell you the truth, I don't know if they had ever seen black men, or if their stoic demeanor was solely due to the fact that we were strangers. After I saw them in their own village I realized that many of the people I had seen around the small towns we drove through were actually Indians. Up to then I had just figured they were Mexicans of some kind. They certainly were not red skinned, tall, and muscular savages that Karl May's writings had led me to picture in my mind.

My introduction to Mexican Americans, other than the occasional farmworker I saw on the same farms my fellow POWs worked on, was a rather different experience. On one trip around the outlying farm country, Washington decided to stop in a brothel. He was in one of his better moods and decided that I should also enjoy the "fruits of the countryside." I was given the pleasure of the company of a pretty (a relative term, one must remember I had been long out of the company of females), relatively young Mexican girl named Yolanda. I have never been one to wallow in the hay with paid maidens, but I can tell you that I neither protested the opportunity for the experience, nor detested it. I will not go into the details of the night, other than to tell you some about the conversations we two had while we were sitting in the parlor of the brothel resting from our trips upstairs for more earthy activities.

Yolanda, to my surprise, spoke rather good English. In fact, she was certainly much easier for me to understand than Jackson and Washington. She claimed she was only working at the brothel to earn money to go to California and work in a winery where her brother now worked. She had learned secretarial skills in school and felt that if she could get to California she could work in the office at the winery. She knew I was German, but it didn't seem to bother her. She said she really didn't care what side of the gringo war I was fighting on. The most interesting part of our conversations concerned her view of my guards. She wanted to know more about the

168

Americans I was traveling with.

"Senior German, how can you stand the smell of those niggers?"

"What do you mean, I don't think they smell any worse that anyone else who travels around in a jeep in this hot sun."

"Well, they sure do stink to me, they don't smell like sour milk as do the gringos, but I sure hate laying with them. Don't they ever take baths?"

"That I couldn't tell you, but I think they are nice enough men. Have you met a lot of colored men? I only know them and a few of the other guards at our camp."

"'Colored men'! Look at me. Do I look white to you? Gringos call anyone that isn't washed out like an old dish rag 'colored'. However, if you mean do I know lots of black people, then no, not really. I only have met those guys you are with, and then where I went to school there was a family of niggers."

"Why do you call them niggers? They don't seem to like that name."

"Well, that is because that is what they are. Besides they call we Mexicanos by names we certainly don't like."

"Other than the fact that they smell different to you, what else is wrong with them? They seem about the same as the rest of the Americans I have met."

"Well, I don't really like any of these Norte Americanos, but at least the gringos have some right to be here. On the other hand the Africans were brought here as slaves. Now they think they are better than we are. I am the descendant of Spaniards who were here long before America was even the United States."

Such was the sentiment of Yolanda and, I gather, the majority of the Mexican population. I began to understand that America was a country, not a people, as is Deutschland or as you call it Germany. Deutschland is a country of and for Germans. I began to understand why the Americans could never understand the love of we Deutscher had for das Vaterland, and our desire to bring all German-speaking people into one country.

Another, very fun adventure for me during this time was Juergen Beckmann's and my holiday in America. I call it our holiday because we did

169

it by ourselves. No, we did not escape. Frankly, during that time we had little desire to do so. Our holiday came about because of Washington's and Jackson's, and the other two guards we were traveling with, addiction to the comforts of the brothel where Yolanda worked. On that trip, as most of the trips during that period, we were in two vehicles, a jeep and a small truck. We were taking replacement clothes, mail, and first-aid packages around to POWs on the various farms. Sergeant Washington decided on that trip to stay at the brothel rather than make the scheduled rounds. While a bit drunk, Washington handed me the keys to the padlock on the steering wheel of the truck and said, "Erich, y'all knowed where da farms are, why don't yo' and 'da cheese head'", his name for Juergen which had something to do with his having been born in Wisconsin, "take da three quarter ton and go tuck yo' fellow Krauts in bed or whatever da hell ya'll do."

We didn't have any money to make it worth sticking around the brothel, so off we went. Our intentions were actually to go around to the farms, but then we just decided to drive a bit. We had a few coins for some food and a book of ration stamps for petrol so we just kept on driving. Late in the afternoon we came upon a sign that said Grand Canyon. Both of us remembered something about it from our geography lessons as young school boys so it became our destination. Except for a stop for petrol, a loaf of bread, and some cheese we drove all afternoon and evening. We couldn't understand why it was so far, then we remembered the signs were in American miles, not kilometers. Despite the fact that it was late summer it started to get rather cold in that open truck. The Americans had taken the canvas roof off for more comfortable driving in the sun. We hoped to find a small town, but they are very few and far apart in that country. At last we saw some lights and it turned out to be a small farm, or ranch, as the owners called it. We stopped in front of the house and were debating whether we should chance knocking on their door. For all we knew we might by then have been turned in by Sergeant Washington as escapees. Before we made a decision, the door flew open and a man with a rifle walked out onto the porch. I had a flashback to the story Hauptmann Heimer had told me about how he had been captured in Texas. Do all American farmers have guns that they so readily brandish?

170

"Who's out there?" the man yelled.

"Just some soldiers, mister. We seem to be lost."

"Well, you obviously ain't from here, by the weird way you talk. Where ya aheadin'?"

I didn't understand his question, so I repeated, "We are lost. Could we stay over in your barn until morning?"

"Sure, help yourself; but don't be messin' with my stuff iffn you don't want hot lead in your ass."

We found a pile of straw in the barn and settled for the night.

I awoke to the squeak of the barn door. I dared not open my eyes, because I knew what I would see: a big, burly guard with a rifle pointed right at my head. At last I ventured a look. There he stood, except he was only about one meter tall and had brown unruly hair, big eyes, and freckles. In a small, obviously frightened voice he said, "Papa says that iffn you want any breakfast come on in the house." His announcement completed, he bolted for the door. Juergen and I at first were going to run to the truck and drive out of there as fast as we could go. We instead decided that if by chance the farmer hadn't recognized us as POWs by then he might figure it out quick if we decided to run for it. I recalled my bluff at the American bar where they thought I was from New York, so we went on in.

The house was rather spacious and cozy, in a rural sort of way. It wasn't that different from a Bauernhaus in Deutschland. I remember being very impressed with the large wood cooking stove in the kitchen. Jurgen later told me his parent's house also had such a huge stove, but that was because it was once part of a large hunting lodge that was often full of guests. We ate right in the kitchen, so I didn't see the rest of the house. I remember the breakfast though, it was of beans from a pot on the stove that looked like it was always there, the strange unleavened bread called tortillas, some very good Speck, what you call bacon, and coffee. The beans were very spicy and Juergen and I at first had a problem with them to the delight of the farm family. The family mostly ate in silence. The wife, a small, very thin, seemingly overworked lady, messed around the kitchen and never did sit down. When the breakfast was over the farmer began to talk a little.

"Where you fellas from?"

"Wisconsin," Juergen blurted out before I could use my New York story.

"Been there, nice state, 'cept it's so damn cold. I was in Janesville area. You from around there?"

"No, my father's farm was near Sheboygan." Juergen later told me he was just hoping Sheboygan, where he was born, was not near a town called Janesville.

"Ah, that explains your accents. Lots of you German folks from up there in that country. It's kind of weird you having to be in the army and might have to go over there and fight your own people, huh?"

"Yes, sir," I said, "except that those folks are Nazis and we are German American. We just want to get rid of that Hitler fellow."

"Yeah, I can understand that he must make you guys real ashamed to be of German stock. I ain't been around the army much, but I sure notice you guys are wearin' some strange uniforms. What's the P and the W mean on yer pant legs?"

"Oh these" I replied. "Well, ah, did you ever hear of the Panzer Wehrmacht?"

"Can't say as I have."

"Well, it is a real bad German army unit. My partner and I here are in a special unit, its kind of secret so don't go telling everyone about it. Well, we fellows from German heritage families are being trained to infiltrate into the Panzer Wehrmacht and disrupt them. These uniforms with this 'P' on one leg and 'W' on the other are that unit's work uniforms."

"Oh, that is interesting, but what's the POW stand for on the back"

"That is for Panzer Oder Wehrmacht," Juergen said with a straight face. "That is the full name of the unit. We don't always wear them, but we are on a special trip and we are wearing them to see if other troops are able to recognize us as the bad guys."

Luckily, that seemed to satisfy the farmer and we were soon on our way. We told him we had to get going and find the rest of our unit. We were some ways down the road when I looked over to Juergen and said, "Panzer Oder Wehrmacht?" and we both laughed until we cried.

By midmorning we came to the Grand Canyon. What an unbelievable sight. Neither Juergen nor I had any idea that it was so immense. As Juergen commented, "You could put all of Luxembourg in here and not even see it." We didn't have a long time to spend there, but one little action will always be in my mind when I think of the Grand Canyon. Just as we were getting ready to leave a small Indian boy of about six or seven years old just appeared out of nowhere. He stood and stared at us for a moment then walked over to the rim of the canyon, leaned out, and urinated out into the void. Upon finishing he turned to look at us, gave a small smile, and ran back into the bushes. Juergen and I started laughing, then he looked at me rather funny. I was not sure if he was joking or not so I finally said, "Why not?" and walked over to the rim and joyfully watched my yellow stream disappear down into the depths of the canyon. I was almost too engrossed in the act to notice Juergen beside me doing the same. I can truly say that I left my mark on the great Grand Canyon.

We drove like hell to get back to the brothel by morning. Upon arriving there we found a very disgruntled Sergeant Washington. He was so damn mad he didn't say anything. That is until he noticed that the truck was still loaded. It was obvious that we had not been to any farms. For a few minutes, as he threw his hat on the ground and turned as red as a black man can, I thought he was going to shoot us. Finally he was able to say, "Just where da hell has yo' assholes been?" We explained to him that we had gotten lost. "Like hell yo' has been lost!"
he yelled. "Now what is I gonna tell the colonel?"

"You could tell him we went to see the Grand Canyon while you was in the brothel."

"GRAND CANYON? DATS CLEAR DA HELL OVER IN ARIZONA? Oh shit! I am shore I is gonna tell him we was so busy messin' wit whores dat we didn't notice da Kraut fellas done sneaked off to go on a sightseein' tour all aroun' da whole gawddamn West."

"Well maybe you could say that the truck broke down."

So with Juergen and me under guard in the back of the truck, off we went to finish our rounds and get back to tell the colonel that we had 'broke down'.

Before summer was over, shortly after the sad word came that

173

the Allied troops had landed in Normandy, France, my world changed directions again. First of all the unit guarding us changed. One day when it came time to make a round of the farms, Sergeant Washington informed me that there wouldn't be any rounds for a few days until the new guards were in place. He then told me that his unit was being reassigned. I asked him where he was going.

"Now Erich, yo' knowed I cain't tell yo' dat. But, I will say give me yo momma's address and I jus' might go see her."

My first reaction was a strange one. I actually thought, "How nice that he would want to visit my Mutti." Then it struck me. This strange black man, who had in ways become my friend, was about to go to Europe and engage in warfare against my countrymen. Perhaps he would even be shooting at my own brother (who was actually in Russia at the time, but I had no way of knowing that since I never did get a letter. Later I was to learn that my family didn't write because they thought I had been lost in Africa).

"I guess I should wish you good luck, Sergeant, but then again I hope you never get to pull a trigger. Maybe when this foolishness is over we can get together and drink a decent Bier. I will even find you a cold one."

"I mus' say, cap'n, I never espected to learn to like one oh yo' Kraut fellas, but I, dispite yo' weird taste in beer, is gonna kinda miss ya."

We shook hands and I never heard from or saw him again. I have often wondered if he made it to Europe and if he lived through the war.

Shortly after the new guards got there (they were Caucasians, mostly from the West Coast), I was moved. I was called in one day and informed that I was being sent up to Utah to help set up a new camp. Juergen was going to stay in New Mexico as the main interpreter for that camp. In some ways, I was quite excited to get the opportunity to see even more of America. However, New Mexico, for some strange reason, felt like home. As for Juergen, I was very sad to be leaving him. Despite the fact that he was only an enlisted man, we had formed quite a bond of friendship.

CHAPTER FIVE

AMONG THE MORMONS

Up to the time I was moved to Utah I had thought I had only experienced wilderness in America. The route of the convoy that transported us from New Mexico to Utah traversed some of the wildest land in the world. It rivaled the bleakness of northern Africa. It was also a strangely beautiful land. While in Africa I had never learned to appreciate the beauty of the desert. Up to then I had equated beauty with green. However, the reds, yellows, and ocher of the southern Utah wilderness were a new and awesome sight for me, and will forever define the true beauty of a natural landscape. As we traveled along, foreboding thoughts kept invading my mind. "Where are they taking me? Is there going to be any civilized habitations in this vast nothingness? Will I ever see a real city again? How can I ever describe this land to my family? Will I ever see them again?"

Our destination turned out to be a very small agricultural community called Salina. Salina was a rather plain and sorry excuse for a town, but was situated in a splendid setting. To appreciate the grandeur of the setting one must be there. The town sits in a valley between the western spine of the Wasatch mountain range and the eroded high plateau of central Utah. It lies at about 1,500 meters and the peaks only a few kilometers to the west tower to over 3,700 meters. Since I arrived there in the early summer I was able to witness flowers in bloom with a backdrop of towering peaks blanketed in brilliant white snow. The camp itself was very small and the living quarters bleak.

Immediately after arriving, before the camp was even completely constructed, I was sent out with an advance party to set up farm programs and town jobs for the POWs. Utah's agriculture is even more scattered than New Mexico's, if that is possible, so we covered vast areas. My first area of concentration was centered around the small town of Hurricane, or as the locals called it "Hurrikin", quite a ways south and west of Salina. It is in a dry plain below the beautiful Zion National Park. It was there that I met a totally different group of Americans. The trip from Salina to Hurricane was

175

an adventure in itself. I can not imagine how the first white people in the area ever got around. The area is sprinkled with rock structures that are of the most fascinating hues of red and white. Most of the land is totally unfit for agriculture and one covers many miles without seeing a single village, or for that matter even a human-built structure of any kind. I really wondered how much the Americans must have hated us to send us into such a foreboding land.

I found the people of the region to be very German in many of their ways, and then again as far away from the cultural mores I held as a group could be. This I can only attribute to their religion, since their religious beliefs are so strongly held that it totally controls their lives. Nearly the entire population of the area belonged to a church called the Church of Jesus Christ of Latter Day Saints, or the shortened name LDS. The locals mostly referred to themselves as Members, or as Mormons. Among this population was a strong contingent of very traditional Mormons who were not officially members of the LDS, but adhered to their own version of the Mormon traditions and teachings. Their main divergence was their adherence to the practice of polygamy. Polygamy was once a tenet of the LDS, but had long since been abandoned. It was supposedly an illegal practice, but was openly practiced in that area. I tried to question some of the families I met (I will tell you about them later) about this double standard concerning polygamy, but none would discuss it. Needless to say my experience among the sects of the population that practiced polygamy was very interesting.

I found myself not only associating with these polygamists, but actually living for short periods among them. They were rather reserved in their manner and not so aggressive in trying to convert us as the mainstream LDS people seem to be constantly doing, but were friendly in their way. In dealing with them one did not deal with the individual farmers, but rather with the leader of each sect. Each man was referred to as The Prophet by his followers. Each prophet was in total control of the lives of the people he had collected as his followers. There seemed to be several of these prophets in southern Utah.

I particularly remember one settlement south of Hurricane. The prophet of that clan had fifteen wives and they all lived in one big house. I

176

think he had more wives than any of the other male members of his flock, but they all seemed to have at least three. We Germans were welcomed onto their farms because there was a shortage of young men to do the heavier farmwork. It seems that many of the young men had run away to Salt Lake City or had fled to join the army, a practice forbidden by the prophet. It seems that a problem in these settlements was that when the older men took more than one wife it left the young men without girls to court and to marry. Unlike the farms of New Mexico, illegal alien Mexican workers were not used. When I asked about this I was informed that "those heathens were not fit to be allowed contact with the kind, tender, and virtuous women of the membership." In contrast, they were very comfortable around we Germans. In fact I had the distinct feeling that they shared many of the same views as those more staunch members of the Nazi party.

Disaster almost befell me one night as I was sleeping in one of the barns in the small settlement. I was awakened by someone crawling under my sleeping blanket. I did not react quickly because I was too afraid of what might be happening. Finally a small voice said, "Are you awake, Mr. German?"

"What do you want?"

"I have come to lie with you."

"What do you mean, lie with me?"

"Please, sir, this is difficult enough; can we just get it over?"

"I am afraid, young man, that I really have no idea what you want, but I do know that I will be in big trouble if your parents or one of my guards find you here under my blankets."

"No one will catch us. Besides, I am not a boy."

I jumped to my feet as if I had found myself in the bed with a rattlesnake. I finally managed to whisper, "Himmeldonnerwetter! Spinnst Dm?"

"I am sorry; I don't understand German. You do speak English don't you? That is why I have come to you."

"Yes, yes, I speak English. Now please tell me why you are here."

"I have come to lie with you."

"I can see that you want to lie with me, but don't you have your own bed?"

177

"Of course, silly man, I have my own bed, but I can not have you come there. My husband and the Prophet would kill us if he found us there."

"Kill me! Indeed they will, if they find you here. Now, if you must lie elsewhere than your own bed please do it in another barn."

She started to cry and whimpered, "But you are my only chance. You must lie with me."

"Why is it so important that I lie with you? It is not too cold for you to lie alone."

"Oh dear, I see you do not understand me. Well . . . what I want . . . what I must have is for you to lie with me as man and woman."

"Liebe Gott!" I blurted out as I realized what she wanted. "No, no, young lady, I cannot have you in my bed and I certainly cannot . . . how do you say it, lie with you as man and woman."

"But you must or I will never get to the kingdom of the Lord."

"I don't know about your Lord, or how one gets there, but I know for sure I will find myself in hell very soon if someone finds you here. Now please go, I beg you."

She started to cry again and then suddenly stood up, placed her hands on her hips, and said in a stern voice, "I will not let you prevent me from what must be done. I say to you, either you agree right now to lie with me or I shall yell and scream until someone comes and I will tell them that you dragged me from my bed to do foul things to me here in the barn."

I stood there in silence as my mind raced nearly to the speed my heart was beating. What should I do? If I were caught having sex with this young woman, she could not have been over nineteen or twenty, I would no doubt be shot, or at the least spend the rest of the war in solitary confinement in the terrible camp in the place called Oklahoma. If I called her bluff and she began to yell, I would suffer the same fate. Just as she raised her cupped hands to her face as if to holler, I dropped to my knees and said, "All right, I will do what you want. Just tell me what to do and I will try; though under these circumstances I am not sure if I can."

"Please, do not be mad at me," she said as she dropped down in front of me. "I only do this because I am desperate, and Sister Ora has told me it is the will of God that has sent you to me at this time."

"I find your faith to be a strange one. Do you really think I have been sent by God to . . . lie with you?"

"Frankly, I am not sure, but I know that it is possible, and I can understand your confusion, few Gentiles understand the ways of the true teachings, but I sense that you are a gentle and understanding man. Now please, let us do what must be done." She began to remove the long white nightgown that seemed to be her only garment.

I quickly reached out and stopped her. "Wait, I must have some time. At least tell me a few things."

"All right, but I cannot be here long. I may be missed by Sister Jane. She shares the room with me when it is not her turn to be in the nursery. What is it you need to know?"

"For a start what is your name?"

"It would perhaps be better if you did not know, but if it is necessary, I am Hanna."

"Thank you, Hanna. Now tell me please why is it so important that you lie with me. Isn't Mr. Smyth your husband?"

"Yes, I am his sixth wife. I have been his wife for over two years."

"That does not answer my question; in fact, it makes it more important that you answer me. Why must you lie with me?"

"Don't you see I have been married for over two years and I am still without a child. Mr. Smyth is becoming very upset with me and is thinking of asking the Prophet for permission to marry my youngest sister. She is only fifteen and would like to marry someone else. Besides, if I do not have a child I will spend the rest of my days doing the heavy labor around the house while my sister-wives tend their children. Please do not think me ungrateful to my husband or to my sister-wives and their children. I love them all and am thankful to the Prophet and to God for allowing me to live in the holiness of the church. But I do want to have a child of God with my own body. Besides if I do not, I may not be called out."

"First of all, I understand that the old man may be having trouble getting you pregnant. But he surely does not blame you for that?"

"He is very upset with me. He says that I am not with child because I am not pure of heart and am too selfish to bring one of God's babies down to earth to have his earthly experience so that it can live in eternity in heaven."

"Doesn't he realize he is an old man, and may not be able to have children anymore? My God, he must be near seventy years old."

"Thou should not take the name of God in vain. Yes, he is sixty-eight years old, but he points to the other wives and proclaims to the whole family, 'Why can selfish Hanna not be like my other wives and love me and God enough to bring forth a baby?' I sometimes hear even the children say sister-mother Hanna is a selfish person."

"Hanna, I understand that your husband blames you for your barren condition, but you said that you may not be called out. What do you mean 'called out'? Would it not be better if you were called out of this strange settlement and allowed to live a more normal life?"

"What you may think is a normal life we members know is a life of ignorance to the true word of God. Don't your German women fear that their husbands will not call them out?"

"Out of where?"

"Oh, you poor man! You are indeed one of God's creations who has not been given the light. Please do not despair. It is not too late. I will bring you to the Prophet and he will help you to learn the truth of the Book of Mormon and the teaching of the true church. For now, I will tell you only that when my husband gets to heaven, if he feels that I have been a true and worthy wife he will call me out of my grave or if I am in the other place, to join him in eternity. However, now I feel he is too upset with me to do so. I would not be here if I felt my eternal future were not at stake. But, please, when you talk to the Prophet he must not know of this meeting and what we are going to do. Now is that not enough talking? Are you a man or a question box?"

"I can only say to you, poor sweet Hanna, that you have me very confused and if I am even able to carry out your demands it may be at the risk of my salvation. So with God as my witness that I enter into this without blasphemous thoughts, tell me what I am to do."

"Tell you what you are to do? Oh dear, perhaps I have very much misjudged you. Has no one ever told you what a man must do to give a woman a child? Well, never mind I am sure that God will guide you." With that she stripped the nightgown over her head and lay down on the straw mat I was using as a bed.

I could not tell you if she was a beautiful girl or not; it was too dark in the barn. I had a moment more of hesitation, then I reluctantly removed the undershirt and underpants that I had been sleeping in before this strange woman came pouncing out of the dark into my bed. I positioned myself over her then rolled over on my back and groaned, "Dear girl, I believe the English have a saying that the mind is willing but the flesh is weak. In this case, both the mind and flesh are unwilling and weak."

"'Tis nothing to be ashamed or alarmed about, Mr. German. My husband, though he has sired sixteen children, often has trouble with his manhood. Let me help you."

I will only say here, even after the four beers we have enjoyed tonight, that she indeed did know how to help me gain the proper attitude, physically and mentally, to lie with her. Almost as soon as I finished performing what she required of me, Hanna reached for her nightgown, pulled it quickly over her head, and began to leave. I grabbed her arm and pulled her back down to me.

"Please," I whispered, "stay a moment and at least let me think I am a man rather than a stud horse that has mounted one of the mares."

She at first seemed frightened by my grip on her arm, then she relaxed. "Yes, I am sorry; this has been a bit of a strange thing. I can only say that I have had no other experience other than with the Prophet when I was young and with my husband. You did fine and I am sure you will someday return to your homeland or, God willing, you will see the light and stay here in the promised land and have many of God's children of your own."

"Well, thank you, Hanna. Does that mean that you enjoyed our time together?"

"Oh, as God is my witness, please do not think that I enjoyed the act of coupling. God's children are not to be animals and succumb to their carnal urges. Coupling is for procreation not pleasure. I will tell you, in strict confidence, that I did not find lying with you to be something I did not enjoy, and now I have the warmth in my heart that God indeed must have brought you here."

"That is a comfort to me. But one time does not ensure a baby by any means."

"That I am very aware of, but Sister Ora has been helping me with my counting and I am sure that I am at the height of my monthly cycle and I will indeed bear a child if God is willing."

Before she departed I convinced her that she should not talk to the Prophet about my questions concerning his church. She realized that if she said anything he may ask her how she knew so much about me. She disappeared into the night as quietly as she had come.

I did not see Hanna the next morning and was happy when we moved on to the next valley to check on the POWs welfare in that area. I am not sure if I ever saw Hanna again, since I was never really sure of what she looked like other than she was slender and rather well developed. I did, however, return to that village on several other occasions. Once, right before the snow blew and all of the German POWs were recalled to the main camp, I was on her husband's farm and noticed a young, pretty woman looking at me. When I looked at her she smiled and then quickly averted her face and walked back into the house. She did seem to be starting to show with child.

In the late fall of 1944 the fact that we were indeed living as prisoners under the guard of the enemy was not much on our minds. I had fallen into a routine of nearly daily trips out to farms and villages to check and assist my fellow POWs with any medical or other problems they might have. I look back now on that time and I realize that I had almost forgotten that I was a prisoner in an alien land. My usual guard team of Lieutenant Joe Brooks (a quiet young man from Seattle) and his driver Private Scott McElroy had become just people I worked with. I am not sure if either of them even loaded their weapons. We would drive through the wide open Utah countryside joking and laughing as if they nor I had any remembrance that I was their prisoner, and that they were charged to shoot me if I decided to make a run for it. As for escaping, I don't think it even crossed my mind.

The winter of 1944 was particularly depressing for us. With no one working, except those in the few local shops, there was little to do but sit and listen to the wind blow through our poorly insulated huts. Though access to news was restricted, I often saw local papers and illustrated magazines when on interpreter duties outside the camp. The news of the Allies' success on European soil was of great concern. I realized that much of what I read was propaganda, but still pictures don't lie, and pictures of American and English soldiers in France were proof that my country was suffering setbacks. Even more disturbing was the news of massive bombing campaigns on German cities. Would there be anything left of my homeland? I continued to write home, with no response.

A new group of soldiers appeared at camp. These men had been captured in France. At our first view of them, as they stood as bewildered in the center of camp as I had been so many months before in Texas, we knew that things had changed. These were not professional soldiers, as we had been. By their very demeanor and stance we could tell that they were civilians in uniform. Many of them were very young and some must have been near fifty years old. Soldiers like that bespeak of a country that has depleted its military resources and is fighting a war of attrition. At our first opportunity we pumped these new POWs for information. Not all was negative. As I had expected the invasion of Europe by the Allies was not going as smoothly as the American newspapers indicated. The new POWs related stories of many casualties being inflicted on the enemy. On the negative side they did not deny the stories we had heard of a German fallback, nor did they blame their subsequent capture to a lack of military leadership or skill. They spoke of a lack of petrol and ammunition and of being totally overwhelmed by the enemy's seemingly unlimited supply of men and equipment. My earlier fears at seeing the size and wealth of America seemed to be well founded. I must say that at this point I no longer felt that Germany would find a way to win this war.

A real moral blow came from the descriptions of the Allied bombing on the cities of das Vaterland. No longer was it the word of the propagandist. We now had to deal with actual eyewitness accounts of mass destruction. Would there be a homeland to go back to? Even blacker visions came to me. Was the reason my family did not write back because they were dead? Potsdam was a small city, but since it was traditionally a military garrison city it may easily have been a target.

Though few of my Kameraden left camp during that winter, I was occasionally still sent with a work crew to get supplies in Ogden, or to a base called Dugway, far out in the bleak landscape southwest of Salt Lake City. Dugway was a storage site of some type; however, I have no idea what was stored there. I only knew that it was highly secret and I never was taken further than a group of storage buildings on the outskirts of a large desert

183

valley that seemed to have storage bunkers spread for many miles. I don't think that Lieutenant Brooks or Private McElroy had any more idea what was there than I did. One time we were going from Dugway to Ogden and Brooks decided to take the convoy, we had two trucks with us, on a bit of a side trip. We drove across a very large salt flat. There was no way people at home would ever believe that I drove for miles and miles across pure salt. At one point we stopped and walked out onto the salt. All of us, Amis and Deutscher, were seen to kick loose a piece and taste it. Yes, it was really salt.

I remember the Lieutenant looking at me with a smile and saying, "Eric, you have been such a good guy I have decided just to let you go home. Honest, if you just walk away right now I won't say one word nor will I shoot you." I slowly turned around and surveyed the hills that were all several miles away. They all looked almost as bleak as the flat, foreboding, void of any vegetation salt flats. I also became aware of the icy wind that was blowing. Lieutenant Brooks may have thought his joke quite funny, but to me it was a spear to my heart. I just shook my head and shuffled back to the jeep.

Besides the "business" trips I occasionally went on, I had a chance to partake in some strange social events that winter. Once or twice a week people from the local area would come to our camp to hold "discussion groups". The discussion was always about the Mormon religion. I went to these occasionally just as a way of breaking the monotony of sitting and waiting out the winter. I did find the discussions rather interesting. How could any people buy this strange story with so little evidence? When one questioned the story being told, the speaker seemed to be truly offended that you could not see that it was true just because their prophet had written it. One day two of the discussion group leaders were actually German. They were both from Oberschlesien and had migrated to America shortly after World War I. To my surprise they had converted to their religion before they left Germany, and I had never even heard of the religion before being taken to Utah. After the discussion one of the men asked the guards if it was possible for me to come to his home for a visit. The guard carried the request higher and it was granted. Thus I found myself a guest at a German-American home. I will say that the trust was not totally there since I could

184

only go if Lieutenant Brooks joined me.

Margarete and Hans, my hosts, lived in a small white house near the center of town. Hans was a worker for the highway department. They had lived in the United States since 1934. We held all of our conversations in English, in deference to the Lieutenant. Their English was surprisingly poor for people who spoke it every day. I had come to their house not sure what to expect, other than I expected I was going to get a full dose of missionary indoctrination. Actually, little was said that first visit about much of anything. We mostly engaged in small talk about family, food, and to some degree individual histories. It was during the second visit that we began to delve into more substantive issues.

We were usually gathered around a large table that was located right in the kitchen. It seems that Americans are more comfortable at a table than anywhere else. One evening we were joined by another couple. They had migrated from Sachsen at about the same time as Margarete and Hans had come over from Oberschlesien. The man, Paul, was a very outspoken, but not a very articulate person. The evening was proving to be entertaining until Paul seem to suddenly become rather agitated.

"Erich," he asked in a serious tone as he leaned toward me, "let's get to der heart of what I need to know. How da hell could you Germans have tolerated der rise of Adolf Hitler?"

Lieutenant Brooks got a very worried look on his face and said, "Maybe we should go?"

"No, perhaps this conversation should take place," I responded as I waved him to sit back down. "I am curious why Paul has asked that."

"Good heavens, man, dat should be obvious. Da man is a tyrannical madman."

"Are you sure of that, or is that what the American newspapers portray him as?"

"Are you saying dat he is not? Why I see newsreels at da movie house of him and he rants and raves as if he is near to having a stroke."

"Yes," I said with a smile "he is a bit dramatic, but then you should see the way the Deutsche news portrays Churchill or, for that matter, Roosevelt. But first let me get to your original question as to why he came

185

to power. Were you not in Deutschland during the twenties and thirties?"

"Ya, I come in '34."

"Then you know that life was very hard, especially for the farmers."

"Ya, it was hard here too when we come, but we not turn to a man like Hitler."

"Deutschland needed a strong man to stand up to its neighbors, to do what was needed to turn the economy around. To bring back pride to our people. Are you not proud of being Deutsch?"

For a moment the table was silent, I knew that I may have crossed over a hidden social barrier. At last Hans broke the silence.

"Erich, my friend, please understand dat ve may be of German birt', but ve are no longer Germans. Ve are Americans. I know you find dat hart to understand. However, doe ve still love Germany ve now feel ve belong here and are proud of da tradition of freedom dat being an American brings."

"I certainly don't mean to insult you, Hans. It is just very difficult for me to understand how you can no longer feel that das Vaterland should have the right to consolidate all of the German-speaking people under one Reich."

"Can't you see," Paul interjected, "dat Hitler has turned da German dream of 'one people' into a ploy to conquer all of Europe and destroy any peoples dat do not bow to his vill?

"He has only responded to the tyranny of his neighbors."

"Vat tyranny did der Niederlander bring on Deutschland?"

"The Hollander invited the Wehrmacht to come into the Niederland."

"Ha, I see dat you believe the crap Herr Goebbles spits out."

Lieutenant Brooks quickly stood up and said, "It is late, I think we should go back to camp. Thank you for the fine evening."

That night I could not sleep. The conversation of the evening kept echoing in my head. How could Germans no longer be Germans? Yes, I too had questions about the direction Hitler had taken Germany, but had there been any other course for the German people to take? Were these Germans, or Americans that were from Germany, or Americans . . . or whatever? Were

186

they my enemy, or were we both just victims of a twist of world history? One thing I was sure of: As I tried to defend the actions of Hitler in my own mind, I could not. That was very disturbing to me. It called to question the very reason I sat there in that forlorn land a prisoner. To be a good patriot must I defend the actions and decisions made by Adolf Hitler, or was it enough that I had fought bravely for my people?

I did not go back to visit Margarete and Hans, even though I received invitations through Joe to do so. I spent the rest of that long cold winter huddled up in camp, except for a few trips up to the supply depot at Ogden. On those Ogden trips I was able to pick up a newspaper and sometimes a magazine, something that was not allowed in camp. The war news was, of course, of major interest. I, and I believe most of the POWs, no longer doubted all that we read or heard about the war. Our skepticism had been blunted by hearing the stories of the new POWs who had arrived. Naturally I still knew that what I read in the newspapers was perhaps mostly propaganda, but the pictures in the papers and in the occasional magazine we got hold of were graphic proof that the war was going poorly for Germany. When I smuggled back a paper that talked about a big Wehrmacht offensive near Bastone, everyone was very excited. Some of the guards asked us if we were celebrating some German holiday. We just told them we were getting ready for Christmas. As a group we celebrated, but I must admit that probably more than one of the other men was like me. I, though all smiles during the day around my Kameraden as we discussed the offensive, was not so jubilant inside. I would lay awake and think about how this offensive would lengthen the war and thus my captivity. Then a strong wave of guilt would come over me. How could I be so selfish? Is it possible that a part of me actually wanted Deutschland to be defeated, just so I could go home early? How could a good soldier and a patriot even give a passing thought to the very idea that das Dritte Reich could be defeated? Was I becoming as weak as the so-called Germans I had met in the community? Those poor people who had difficulty speaking their native tongue, but yet could not speak their adopted language with any proficiency. I became very depressed. I am not sure if my hidden nighttime tears were from pity of my position, or from shame at my loss of faith in the cause that had brought all of us here.

Spring comes rather swiftly to the desert valleys of Utah. By April the farmers wanted workers back in the fields, but many of the men seemed hesitant to go. The long winter, and its accompanying flow of bad news, had taken their toll. Many of the men were in a seriously depressed state. Others seemed anxious to get back to doing something productive. Some were even heard to occasionally comment that they were not sure that they wanted to go back to Deutschland when the war was over. No one was heard to speak about an eventual victory.

Indeed, a German victory was not to be. One morning we woke to the cheering of the guards. From the motor pool outside the compound came the blaring of auto horns. At last the word was spread. The war was over! I wandered out onto the parade ground. Slowly the barracks emptied and I was joined by the entire POW population. There was no cheering within the compound. For sometime we all just stood silently and watched the antics of the American troops outside the fence. After what seemed a half day, but was probably a half hour, many of us began to walk slowly around and shake a Kamrad's hand or give each other small hugs. Some men fell to their knees and even sobbed. I don't know if their grief was for Deutschland defeat, or a release of tension. I do know that almost every man had tears in his eyes or running down his cheeks. I have no idea how long we stood out in the cool spring wind. I don't think we even had a formation that day. No Americans that I know of came into the compound. We could hear their celebrations far into the night.

It was not until we were back into our huts that evening that much was said. Then we spent some time discussing what might happen to us now. We all retired to our bunks and lay there immersed in our own thoughts. I doubt if anyone slept that night.

The next day Major Rehms and I were called to the commander's office and told that for now there would be little change in the routine. It was several days before things actually did normalize. One noticeable change did take place. Our soldiers working outside of the camp had always been treated nicely, however the relationship between the American employers and the POWs changed. All of a sudden the Americans were even nicer to their German workers. They seemed to treat them no differently than they would anyone they might employ. In fact, in nearly all cases the Americans started asking many of the workers if they would like to stay in America. The workers were naturally flattered and most a bit confused. If only they could have any idea what lay ahead of them back in Germany. Would they have jobs awaiting them, or for that matter would they even have homes left? The pictures we were seeing in the illustrated magazines foretold of massive damage to the towns and cities. Of course, most of the men were anxious to get back to their families and loved ones, but not all had that to draw them home.

By the first of June, it was all a moot point anyway. We were informed that the camp was being closed and we were all to be shipped to other camps. The American way of operating is quite different from the German way. Had that been a German camp it would have been nothing but a dust bowl days after the decision was made to shut down the camp. However, an American decision seems only to be a reason to start planning a way to carry it out. Though we were anxious to go, since we felt that it surely meant that we would soon be home, it was not a stressful time. We were all in high spirits and even invited the guards to join some of our games and music get-togethers. The concept that we were still soldiers almost disappeared. Then came the shooting.

It happened on the eighth of July 1945. It was late afternoon and I was sitting in my barracks writing a letter to my mother, an activity I did fairly often even though I never got a return letter. Most of the POWs were out in the yard watching a makeshift game of Fussball. Suddenly I heard a machine gun begin to rattle. I quickly rolled to the floor. At least my old wartime instincts were still with me. The firing came in quick bursts and lasted perhaps only a few seconds. It was accompanied by lots of shouting and screams of pain. When I was sure that it had ceased I crawled to the door and looked out onto the compound. The compound was littered with bodies, some lying still and others writhing in pain. I realized that there were many wounded so I jumped up and ran into the compound, dodging and ducking. I expected that at any moment I would hear the machine gun begin to fire and was prepared to hit the dirt. I really don't think I considered the fact that I could have felt the slam of a bullet into my body before I heard the report from the shot. Luckily, nothing happened and I soon was kneeling down next to a soldier I only knew as Soldat Meyer. He was a youngster from Bremen and was quite dead. I jumped up and ran to the next soldier, who turned out to be Walter Vogel, an artillery officer from my barracks. Walter had a bad leg wound so I quickly began to try to stop the flow of blood. Soon many other POWs were flowing into the yard to assist the wounded. It was only after the first major commotion that I became aware that no Americans were in the compound. I glanced to the fence and saw several guards around it on the outside. Many others were running toward the area. Then I noted a group dragging away another guard screaming and struggling. The guards seemed to be totally unorganized and in a panic. I left Walter in the care of a couple of other prisoners and ran to the main gate. I was nearly to it when I realized that I had about twenty or thirty rifles pointed right at me. I quickly stopped and threw my hands in the air. I stood there for a few seconds and then walked slowly, with my hands still in the air, to the gate. I yelled at the guards standing there with their weapons still pointed at me to get some medical help. They just stood there pointing their rifles at me and saying nothing. At last the camp commander, a major, came up and yelled, "What the hell is going on?"

One guard answered, "I don't know, sir, but there must have been a mass breakout attempt."

"Shit!" the major responded, "Let's get these damn Krauts back in their barracks."

I finally got his attention and yelled, "Major, we need to get these men some medical attention."

"In due time. First, you had better tell your men to get back to their barracks."

"But major, we have many wounded and I am afraid several dead."

"That's too damn bad, but they should have thought about that before they tried to break out. Were you their leader in this, Captain?"

"I know nothing of a breakout attempt; I was in my barracks when the shooting started. Now please help the wounded."

Just then the American first sergeant of the camp came running up.

"Sir, we have him locked up."

190

"Locked up?" the major responded. "Who? The leader of this breakout?"

"I don't know of any breakout, sir. We have Private Thayer in custody. He just went berserk and started to shoot the gun in tower three."

"We will work this out later. For now, let's get these prisoners back to their barracks." He then looked over to me and added, "And get the wounded to the clinic."

I spun around and ran back through the compound instructing one man to stay with each of the wounded and the rest to get back to their barracks. I stayed with Walter. Soon American guards were pouring into the compound.

It was nearly an hour before Rehms, the ranking German officer in the camp, and I (because I was the main interpreter) were called to the main gate and taken to the camp headquarters. The same major who was at the gate, I am sorry that I can't remember his name, acknowledged our presence and finally said, "It seems that one of our men had received some very bad news today and went a bit crazy. I am afraid he did some fair damage to your men."

"Just what do you mean by 'some damage'?" Rehms had me inquire. "I know several men were killed and many more injured. Why haven't I been allowed see them?"

"In due course, Major. But first it is your responsibility to see that your men don't do anything foolish."

"MY MEN? It seems that it is YOUR MEN who are out of control!"

"Don't yell at me, Major. Let's damn well keep in mind who are the POWs here. Yes, it seems that one of my guards is responsible, but that is my worry, not yours. For now just go back and make damn sure your men don't do anything that would cause a repeat of this mess. Is that clear?"

Rehms just stood and glared for a moment, then very calmly and quietly spoke in English, "That is perfectly clear. You Americans don't believe in fair treatment of enemy prisoners. I go back now to my soldiers, but I don't forget this." He did a smart about-face and marched from the room with me right behind him.

That evening and night were long ones. Among my barracks mates,

191

only Oberleutnant Schneider was among the wounded or dead (we were not sure who all of them were until the next day). I am sure that in every barracks long discussions were being held as to what to do. Wild speculation was bantered back and forth as to the reason the American guard had opened fire. Many were sure that it was because he was a black-hearted Jude, but most agreed that he was no doubt a Communist. Several of the officers in my building were in favor of a mass breakout. "Why sit here doing nothing just to be slaughtered?" they argued. I felt that such a move would be foolish since the guards were at full alert. Besides that, I must say I had mixed emotions. One part of me was furious. Didn't these damn Ami care that the war was over? Was victory over us not enough? How could civilized men allow a crazy soldier to kill just for the sport? Had we not cooperated with the Ami to have a peaceful camp until our return to Germany? We had not even had one escape attempt while at the Salina camp.

Despite my regenerated hatred of the enemy I somehow understood what could have (and later confirmed did) happen. The young soldier had gotten a letter about a loved one, perhaps a brother, being killed in Europe. I clearly remembered my moment of craziness when the Brits had bombed the hospital and I had tried to shoot the English prisoners. In times of pain and stress it is natural for a soldier to want to eliminate the cause of the pain, the enemy. One thing was really clear to me. Despite my close relationship with Americans such as Sergeant Washington and Lieutenant Brooks, they were the enemy and I was their prisoner.

The next morning when formation was called, many of the POWs were afraid to show up out on in the center of the compound. For the Americans' part, the tower and perimeter guards were at double strength. Those of us who were there had to stand and wait as several orders for morning formation were given. A few more men trickled out of the barracks, but it was obvious that many men were not in formation. In the last weeks it had not been an every morning practice to get a 100 percent count, but this morning the Americans demanded it. I figured that I would eventually see a guard contingent come into the compound and roust the missing POWs out of their barracks. Such was not the case. Evidently the Americans were either trying not to provoke an incident, or were afraid to come in. The loudspeaker finally blasted the voice of the camp commander. "Major Rehms, if you don't get all of your men out to this formation all of you will be standing there all day." Rehms stood quite still and stared forward as if he had heard nothing. A growing murmur was heard from we soldiers standing behind him. He did a smart about-face and glared at his troops. Silence was quickly restored. The Major did another about face, and snapped to the parade-rest position and stood as if made of stone. The warmth of pride swelled in my chest. Captive we were, and our country had capitulated, but defeated we were not. As we stood there I noticed that more men slowly came out of their barracks and assumed their place in the formation. Rehms obviously noticed this too, though is seems he would have had to have eyes in the back of his head to do so. At last he again came to attention and did an about-face. As he did so the company commanders called, "Achtung." I have never seen troops come to attention any sharper than at that moment. The company commanders called for the morning attendance count, turned sharply about to face the Major, and stood in ridged silence. Rehms took his time before calling for the report. After receiving it he spun back to the front and again assumed parade rest. The company commanders, one by one, barked the order bringing their troops to the same position. We all stood tall, proud, and with defiant faces. At long last a formation of Americans marched through the gates and took their position before the POW formation. At a barked order the armed enlisted men dispersed to positions around the formation and brought their arms to the ready. The American commander stepped forward and called for the morning report. It had been the custom of late, when we did have a formal formation, for Major Rehms to give his report himself in English. However, this morning he called for his staff to come forward. The two other majors in camp and myself, as the interpreter, marched forward and took our positions; the majors to his immediate rear, and I on his left side.

Major Rehms remained silent a moment then, without looking at me, said in a calm quiet voice, "Report that the soldiers of the Third Reich, being detained under the international rules of war in this camp, are all present, except for those troops gunned down while engaged in a fussball match. Then add that, since I have not even been informed about the

193

number of wounded and dead from that barbaric incident, I can not give a proper report."

I barked out the ordered report in a voice that I hoped would carry to the ears of all of the troops assembled, German and American. The American commander winced and almost stepped back away from my loudly proclaimed report. He was seen to get his composure back before he said in a low cold voice: "Very well, have your men report to morning mess." He quickly made a left-face and marched toward the gate, failing even to return the salute Major Rehms had rendered.

Later in the morning Major Rehms and I were called to the camp commander's office and informed about the casualties. Eight men were dead, and eighteen wounded, two of whom were in very serious condition. I must say that I do feel the American major was very conciliatory and remorseful as he informed Major Rehms of this. We also were given permission to visit the wounded, instructed to plan a funeral ceremony for the following day, assign a ten-man burial party, and to assemble a grave-digging party which would be transported that afternoon to the nearest military cemetery where the dead would be interred.

The next day, I accompanied Major Rehms and the burial party to a small cemetery at Fort Douglas in the hills above Salt Lake City. To our surprise we first were transported to a large cathedral in the center of the small city where the caskets were lined up in the courtyard to the rear of the cathedral (which we were to learn was the Mormon Tabernacle). There a solemn ceremony was held. We were a bit taken aback at the gall of these people to bring soldiers from another culture, and no doubt other religious faiths, to be blessed at their holy site. I tried to tell myself that this was done not as an insult, but as the ultimate expression of remorse by the local community that this slaughter took place in their homeland. After this brief ceremony we again loaded our dead and were transported to the cemetery where they were buried with dignity and military honor. I must say that the American burial squad carried out their duty with respect and dignity. I will always remember the list of dead as they were read slowly by Major Rehms:

Walter Vogel

Georg Liske

Gottfried Gaag

Ernst Fuchs

Adolph Paul

Otto Bross

Hans Meyer

Fritz Stockmann

To our surprise, after the burial we were asked if we would like to pay our respects to other German soldiers buried at that cemetery. Not only were there quite a few new graves for prisoners from other camps in Utah, but there was a large area contingent of World War I Soldat. I had no idea there had even been German POWs in America during World War I and certainly not in the far West. What must have been the conditions for those unfortunate souls?

During the next week one of the seriously wounded soldiers, Friedrich Ritter, died and was taken to the same burial ground. Friederich was well known in the camp. He was one of the older soldiers, at forty-eight years old, and was always laughing, even when times were tough. I understand that these men are still buried in Utah and their graves are carefully maintained.[12]

That was my first visit to Salt Lake City. I had seen some of it on a couple of occasions as we had driven by the western outskirts on our way to Ogden where there was a large supply depot from which we drew rations. It also gave me a chance to visit with the POWs held in a camp near there, for they worked at the depot. Up to that point it was the largest American city I had been in. I was impressed by the wide streets and the overall plan. It was only later that I learned that it was an anomaly among American cities as most are very poorly planned and show little sign of unity.

The Salina POW camp never did return to the quiet routine of preincident days. Few crews went out. Though schedules to do so were given, the men most often reported sick or, if they did go, performed their work so poorly that the farmers quit asking for them. Many of the men who worked in shops in town continued to do so, realizing that it was not the fault of the shopkeepers, whom they had come to know, that some of their Kameraden had been shot.

195

CHAPTER SIX

THE MAGIC VALLEY

Word came down that at last everyone was being moved to a large camp in the Midwestern region of the United States. We were all very excited because we knew that this must just be a step in returning us to Germany. My jubilance, however, was short-lived. Early one morning I was called into the commander's office where I was introduced to Second Lieutenant Charles Atwell. He and his driver, Staff Sergeant Douglas Sermons, were from a small POW camp in a small town called Burley somewhere to the north of Utah in the state of Idaho. They were sent down to bring a German officer back to Burley to help handle a problem they had there. I was to be that officer.

My good-byes were cut short and within the hour I was packed and on my way north with my new guards, or, as we Germans had begun saying among ourselves, my Wachhunde (the watch dogs). Very little was said among us as we began our journey. It gave me a little time to reflect on my situation. First, I got a little depressed. The manner by which I was spirited out of the camp was certainly indicative of my position in life. Being in the military should have well prepared me to move on at a moment's notice. Such had happened to me before, but never by myself. Being in a specialty unit I had gone through training and every move with the same men. As I rode out of camp I felt as if I were nothing but chattel. My second thought was about my packing. Had I forgotten anything? I quickly inventoried all my belongings and made a mental note that they were indeed packed; this caused me to break out laughing. The lieutenant and the sergeant both quickly looked back at me with expressions on their faces that were a mixture of curiosity and concern.

"What's so damn funny, Captain?" the lieutenant asked.

"I just realized how much I just packed onto your trailer."

"OK, but I seem to remember only a small box and a ditty bag. Did I miss something?"

"Ha! No, it is just that when I was captured I had the clothes on my back, a compass, and an empty water flask. Now I have been a POW for over two years and I travel like a tourist."

"Glad you're having a great time."

"Please don't misunderstand me. I just was laughing at my worry over whether I forgot anything. It seems that no matter what a man has in life, such is his treasure. Have you ever been stripped of all you own, Lieutenant?"

"Can't say as I have, except when I got to Officer Training Camp."

"Ah yes, I do remember the feeling of being stripped naked on my first day at officer training. Was your training a long process?"

"No, I am a rattsie officer."

"Rattsie?"

"That is R-O-T-C. It stands for Reserve Officer Training Corps. It was part of my course work at college. I am not a professional soldier. I just had to put off my teaching for awhile so I could ferry important people like yourself around on their holidays."

"Sorry to inconvenience you. So, you are a teacher? I am also, or at least was before the war."

"Say, how about that, Sarg; you have the privilege of two teachers in your presence. Maybe we can teach you a thing or two."

"God help me," grumbled the sergeant. Then he added as he looked up at his mirror and caught my eyes, "That is the damn army for you. I quit school to see the world and I end up driving through the gawddamn Utah desert with two teachers. What the hell did I do to deserve this?" He ended his tirade with a hearty laugh, which I was able to join in on, feeling much better.

Our first stop was at the Ogden supply depot. They had left a crew of POWs and guards there the night before to load their three trucks with camp supplies. Just as we were getting ready to leave a large flight of bombers took off from the air base that was just to the east and circled overhead until all of the formation was together and headed west over the Great Salt Lake.

"Wow," the lieutenant shouted, "no wonder you Krauts gave up." He looked at me and obviously saw that pain in my face as I thought about my family and wondered about their fate. "Oh sorry, I guess that was a bit

197

insensitive. Was your family bombed?"

I shrugged and looked him in the eye as I said, "That is all right; war is war, and to answer your question, I have no idea what has happened to my family, but I am very worried since they have not written me. I don't even know if they know that I am alive."

"What a bitch. Well, Captain, let's hope that you get to go home soon and you find them all safe. This war shit is sure stupid."

From the tone in his voice I could tell he meant it. He was embarrassed that he had caused me pain. He had obviously never experienced war, for he seemed not to have any hate or understanding that what enemies do is kill one another.

What a strange feeling it was to be riding in the back of a jeep, not really under any noticeable guard or restraint, as a prisoner, but yet being treated as an equal. Could one simple document of surrender, or whatever had been signed, do that? I remained cautious, the memory of the massacre still clear in my mind.

The road north began to climb out of the large Salt Lake Valley. I looked back to see a dynamic panorama over the green irrigated valley flowing down to the incredibly large Salt Lake that disappeared into the summer haze. One could not feel anything but a national pride if one were to view such a dramatic and scenic country with the knowledge that it was yours. As for me, it left a wonder in my heart why the Americans seemed to take it for granted. Soon the road was winding around through the gray green foliage called sagebrush. I had tasted the leaves of this bush and found it certainly had no taste relationship to the spice Salbei which I had heard the Americans call sage. The hills were very reminiscent of the hills just south of the agricultural areas in north Africa. Soon we dropped down into a large flat plain dotted with a few groves of desert trees, but for the most part very barren. The sergeant looked into his mirror again to catch my eyes.

"You know, Captain, I figure that if you Germans and that fella Hitler really wanted land to spread out into, we Americans should have been nice and given you this here beautiful chunk of real estate."

The lieutenant chipped in, "Damn, that is a good idea too late for

198

its time. It would have saved a lot of hassle. What do you think, Captain?"

I could see that they were either playing with me or testing me so I casually said, "It wouldn't have worked. We Germans would have turned it in to a garden and you guys would have been pissed."

Luckily my retort was taken for what it was, and a good laugh was shared. I don't think old Sergeant Smith, back in Texas, would have responded the same. After a couple of hours we snaked our way back up into some mountains and climbed over another pass. At the top of this pass we even came through some leftover winter snow. The convoy stopped and the POWs in the trucks enjoyed a snowball fight as if they were ten year olds. Lieutenant Atwill asked me why I didn't join in. When I answered that it was because I was an officer. He didn't seem to understand. It seems that American officers had a much less formal relationship with the men under them. I often wondered how the American army could have had the discipline to fight a war. I assure you that the respect and perhaps fear of one's superiors that comes with distance is a great motivator.

Shortly after remounting the trucks we were descending to a large valley. I could see a large river, the Snake River it was called, slashing through it. Large patches of the land reflected the verdant summer green of agricultural fields. The sergeant yelled out, "Captain, welcome to your new home, the Magic Valley of the Great State of Idaho. The land of potatoes, potatoes, and more potatoes."

During the entire trip I was surprised that no mention was made of the reason I was being taken to the Burley camp. At last I ventured to ask. Atwill and Sermons just looked at each other and remained silent. At last the lieutenant said, "Sorry to act so secret, but my specific orders were not to discuss the troubles with you. I will say this, though, since you seem to be a rather nice fellow. I think the trouble lies with the Kraut, excuse me, German commander in the camp. I would just ask that you talk to the men a bit first." After a pause he added, "Say, do me a favor and don't mention that I said anything to you, OK?" If I was worried before about the reason for my move, I was really worried after that bit of information. What possibly could be happening?

199

At last we reached the camp at Burley. To call it a camp was a stretch of one's imagination. Actually it was a group of tents in the middle of a Festplatz, or what you Amis call a fairground. There could not have been more than fifty POWs there. Upon reaching the camp I was taken directly to a tent that was set aside from the others. Atwill informed me that it was the officers' quarters and that a bunk was set up for me. He said I should catch a night's sleep and he would see me in the morning. He said that he was dropping off one truck of supplies at Burley then was taking the other two over to the bigger camp, Camp Rupert across the river. He would be back later tonight, but would not see me until morning.

As I entered the tent, a large red-faced man who was sitting on one of the cots looked up at me and laughed. His laugh attracted the attention of two other men who sat up from the cots they were stretched out on. "Ah so!" chortled the big man. "The new camp savior has arrived. Let us all greet the man the Amis have brought in to straighten us out." He stood up and clicked his heels together as he performed a short bow. "Can I show you to your quarters, sir, or would you rather take mine?" he said with a grand gesture of his arm toward his cot. One of the other officers jumped up with a smile, obviously enjoying the performance. The remaining officer just sat there with a disgusted look on his face.

I walked by the big man and placed my bags next to the one empty cot. I spread out the two blankets that were folded and stacked on it, then turned to the waiting faces. As I held out my hand, I smiled and said, "My name is Erich, and as for all the savior part of your fine greeting, I haven't the slightest idea what you are talking about."

"If you truly are ignorant of your reason for being here, perhaps you should keep it that way," he said as he ignored my hand.

"Sounds good to me, sir, but would it hurt for me to know your names?"

"Hauptmann Willy Bruenner, officer in charge of this shit hole of a camp, my adjutant Oberleutnant Rafer (he pointed to the standing young officer), and Leutnant Volk."

Rafer just smiled, and Volk got up, came forward, and shook my hand as he addressed me, "Welcome to our humble abode, Hauptmann."

200

"Well, how civil of you, Volk," the overweight Bruenner said. "Rafer do you detect a bit of butt sniffing going on?"

This brought a hearty laugh from Oberleutnant Rafer. Volk's face got very cold as he looked at me, shrugged his shoulders, and went back to his cot and laid down. I took the clue and also went to my chosen cot and began to unpack and prepare my area.

"Sorry to seem unfriendly Kameraden," I said with what I hoped was a casual tone, "but I have had a long journey through the beautiful American countryside. Perhaps we can continue this charming conversation in the morning?"

As I at last settled on my cot Bruenner rolled over on his and said, "One last thing Hauptmann, just keep in mind who is in charge here." After a rather fitful night, I finally fell off to sleep wondering what the hell I was in for this time.

I awoke in the morning to the sound of men moving around outside. My tent companions seemed not to notice, so I dressed hurriedly and went out to see what the commotion was. Men were assembling around trucks parked in the center of the grounds. Soon they loaded up, and the trucks, one by one, not in convoy, pulled out of the camp. As the last was leaving Sergeant Sermons walked up to me.

"Good morning, Captain. I hope you slept well."

"Good morning, Sergeant, and yes I did thank you. Could you tell me what is going on?"

"Oh this is just a normal workday; the men are headed out to their various work sites."

"Isn't there a morning formation?"

"Not since the end of the European conflict."

"Well, what about breakfast?"

"Oh, of course! I bet you are hungry. It should be served in about an hour, over in that area under the racetrack bleachers."

"Thank you, Sergeant, but actually I was referring to breakfast for the workers who just left."

"Oh, yes! Well, they eat at their respective workplaces. In fact, the farmworkers eat all of their meals there. Before I forget, our captain would

201

like to talk to you right after breakfast. Just come over to the main gate and ask for me."

I wandered over to the bleacher area and found several men in the process of getting the small kitchen area, which was in a room under the stand of seats that faced out onto a race oval, up and running for the morning. I hoped that I could scout up a cup of coffee. As I walked into the area I could hear the men laughing and enjoying the beautiful morning. Their conversation and laughter quickly ceased when they saw me and recognized me as an officer. This was not an unusual response within the German army, but here I could detect more than a silent respect for rank. In fact the mood was one bordering on sullen disrespect. I sat at a small table right near the kitchen. Before I could ask, a cup of coffee appeared. I sipped my coffee as I lit up a Lucky Strike, trying not to seem like I was eavesdropping on the kitchen workers.

A young private came out and started to wash down tables. He very carefully avoided even looking at me. At last I got his attention and he came over to me and snapped to attention.

After giving him "at ease," I asked him, "How many men do you feed here in the morning, Soldat?"

"It varies, sir!" He remained at parade rest as he barked out the answer.

"Please relax, Soldat; I am not here to interrogate you. I am new and trying to figure out what the routine is. Now, about how many do you expect most mornings?"

He relaxed slightly as he said, "This morning there will be only five or six, sir."

"Is that all that is left in camp?"

"No, sir, there are probably about fifteen of us here."

"What is with the others? Where do they eat?"

"Since we stopped formation, sir, not everyone gets up, except for the ones who work in the camp office."

"How about the officers?"

A cloud of caution again spread over his face. "Well, sir, Leutnant Volk always comes in before he goes over to the office."

"How about Hauptmann Bruenner and Oberleutnant Rafer?"

"Sir, they normally come in later and we serve them. Would you like breakfast right now, sir?"

"No, thank you, Soldat, I will just have coffee and will eat when the men get here."

After the private left me I could see the kitchen sergeant call him over and question him as they each glanced over at me.

Soon a group of men wandered in from the tent area and received their breakfast of toast, boiled eggs, bacon, and coffee. They sat at a table as far from me as possible and only whispered to each other as they ate. Occasionally, one or two of them would glance at me. I also noticed some hand gestures vaguely in my direction and assumed they were talking about me. The young private brought me my breakfast. As I was eating I saw Leutnant Volk come over to the area. He hesitated, then walked over and picked up a cup of coffee and a couple of pieces of toast. He looked at me, again hesitated, then walked off toward the main gate. I assumed that he was headed to the office for his morning duties.

After breakfast (neither Bruenner nor Rafer showed up) I wandered over to the gate and asked for Sergeant Sermons. He soon was seen walking over from a long building. He led me back to the same building explaining to me that it was the former exhibit building for the county fair that used to be held on those grounds every year. As we walked in I saw the area had been divided into office spaces and sleeping quarters by makeshift panels. Leutnant Volk and several enlisted POWs were working at desks in the front area. I was led back to a small area, where Lieutenant Atwell was sitting with his feet up on a desk having a cup of coffee. He put his feet down and gestured to a chair for me to sit.

"Good morning, Erich." (The familiarity of first name put me a bit at alert. Was I about to be used in some dispute between prisoners and the Americans?) "Would you like a cup of Joe? Hey Wolfgang," he yelled, "bring your captain a cup of coffee . . . and don't forget the cream."
He smiled at me and said, "Excuse me for not asking how you like it, I just know that you Germans don't seem to drink it black. Sleep well?"

"Thank you, Lieutenant. Yes, I do drink it with cream, though I am not sure why. Your American coffee is more like colored water." This brought the expected laugh which helped to ease my tension.

"Did you have a chance to meet the other officers in the camp?" As Atwill said this, his brow wrinkled a bit as if he was suddenly more than casually interested in my answer.

"Rather briefly, I am afraid." I tried to disarm the question with a smile and a bit of a joke. "I was a bit bushed after our long exciting sight-seeing tour yesterday." I paused a short while, then asked, "Just when is it, Lieutenant, that I am going to be told why I have been brought to this camp?"

"I suppose that will be this morning when we go over to visit the captain."

"Go over?"

"Yes, Captain Sneed is the commander of the camps in the area. He is physically located at Camp Rupert, which is across the river."

"Are there more camps in the area, or is that a military secret that I as a POW have no right to know?"

This brought a smile to his face. "I suppose it would have been an improper question last year, but the end of hostilities has changed things a bit. There is one other German POW camp in the area down in Twin Falls, but it is also just a small one in a fairgrounds such as this one."

"Since things have changed, perhaps you can also tell me when we Germans can go home. I like your country and your hospitality has been superb, but I am a bit homesick."

"Now that is a military secret, Erich. One I don't even know, unfortunately. However, I must admit, I am not too anxious for it to happen."

"Please don't think me impertinent, but do you find being a guard over soldiers of a defeated army interesting or exciting?"

"Ha! No, I assure you that this is not the exciting job I had hoped to have when I pinned on these bars, but I am not sure I am really up to the excitement that will come next."

"Excitement?"

"You Germans seem to think that the only war was the one you started in Europe. Well your Jap friends are still to be reckoned with. I am sure that as soon as this camp is closed I will be headed to some jungle playground to help root out those slimy bastards."

I did not reply to that tirade. Though I did find it odd that this man could be so cordial to one enemy and so bitter toward another. I supposed that it was much like my feelings toward the English and the Americans. I still was on my guard around Americans, but by that time had learned that most did not really hate us Germans; only Hitler and the Nazi party. As for the English I still regarded them as a ruthless people.

Soon we were off to Rupert, which proved to be just a short drive north across the Snake River. Captain Sneed turned out to be a rather old man; I assume in his late forties. He did not strike me as an officer who had a lot of ambition or drive. He got right to the point about the reason for my being transferred to Idaho. It seems that nearly a quarter of the men being held at Burley had filed requests not to be sent back to Germany when such a time should come. The captain told me that this was not proving to be unusual. In every camp some POWs wanted to stay in America. Some had fallen in love with the shopkeeper's or farmer's daughter they worked for, and others just felt that there was no future for them back in Germany. However, at no other camp had such a large percentage of men requested not to return home. In addition to that, it had been noticed that, even with the announcement of the end of the war in Europe, the men held at Burley were not as jubilant as those at other camps. Naturally, no Germans were content to be prisoners, but at least most seemed to go about their daily lives in such a manner that did not make one believe that they were being oppressed or personally punished for a crime. I seemed to have gotten a reputation as a German officer who held no grudges, and had the men's welfare in mind first and foremost (I supposed it was left over from my run-in with the Nazis in New Mexico). Captain Sneed only asked of me that I look around and see if I could determine the cause of the discontent in Burley and report to him if I felt that it was something he could correct. On the drive back to Burley my head was spinning; what was I to do, how could I help my Kameraden without helping the enemy? I did not like being asked by the enemy to spy on my Kameraden; after all, the Americans were definitely still the enemy as long as they chose to hold us as prisoners. On the other hand, if large numbers of POWs were refusing to return to das Vaterland, and to their loved ones, something indeed must be wrong and should be investigated. I decided to play it by ear. Before going back to my tent I asked Lieutenant Atwill if I could tour the workplaces in the capacity I had in New Mexico and Utah, as a liaison between the POWs and the Americans. He seemed to have already decided that such would be my duty at Burley.

That evening I was surprised to be joined at the dinner table by all three of the other officers. At first I was treated almost as a guest, especially by Bruenner and Rafer. Volk remained a bit sullen and kept his thoughts to himself. It also became very obvious that Bruenner was the boss of camp in more than rank. Whereas a Soldat brought out the meal for the rest of us, the kitchen sergeant personally served Bruenner. In fact, the Feldwebel hovered around the Hauptmann like a honeybee to a flower. After lots of small talk, Bruenner finally got down to what I am sure he went there to say.

"Well, Herr Hauptmann, did you have a wonderful chat with Captain Sneed?"

"Brief, but interesting. How did your day go?"

"I would say that depends on what you two talked about. Is it a state secret or am I, as the OIC of this camp, going to be informed about it?"

"No big secret. We just talked about what my role here is to be." I felt it best that I not reveal much, at least for a while, until I figured out just what was going on.

"Excuse me, Hauptmann, but I am not a man who likes to play games. I take my leadership role in this camp very seriously. Now just what the hell is it you and the Amis have decided is your role?"

I sipped my coffee and methodically lit a cigarette before I looked into the deepening red face of Bruenner and answered. "I am to resume the role I have had in every camp I have been in. I, because of my language skill, serve as a liaison to our troops to make sure their needs are being taken care of. As for our relationship, Hauptmann Bruenner, I will report my findings to you if corrective action is necessary. However, I detect in your tone that you don't approve of my presence here. Well, frankly neither do I, but it may surprise you to know that we are prisoners of war and I don't, nor you for that matter, really have a choice of where I am."

206

"Very eloquent, your mother must be proud of her educated son. But it is best that you keep in mind that these Amis are indeed our enemy and anyone cooperating with them should know that it is their duty as a soldier of das Vaterland not to assist them with their treacherous programs, or they will suffer the consequences." With that he stood up and marched off to our tent, with his faithful Oberleuntant Rafer at his heels.

After he disappeared, Volk spoke for the first time. "I am afraid that he means what he says. I would walk a cautious line if I were you, Sir."

"Thank you for the advice, Leutnant. Can you tell me what the hell is going on in this camp?"

"Why of course, Herr Hauptmann. We are trying to survive the best we can here and in the future. One must ask himself, is the comfort of the present worth risking the fate of the future? Good night, Sir."

My next week was spent touring with Sergeant Sermons. We went from farm to farm and checked the working conditions and health of the POWs. We also visited several shops in town where POWs performed a variety of skills, such as clock repair and shoe repair. I had expected to find very unhappy troops, due to the nature of the warnings I had received. Such was not the case. Admittedly they were somewhat reluctant to speak with me, viewing me as some sort of threat, but I still could see from the way they worked and interacted with their American hosts that they were basically happy. The fact of the matter is that they were more what we would call Gastarbeiter, guest workers, than prisoners. This became clear to me in my first tour into town. As Sergeant Sermons drove us into Burley we passed a German I recognized from camp. He waved at us as we passed. Sermons did not seem to see him and just drove on. I finally said, "Sergeant, did you not see that POW walking alone down the street?" He told me he had and even knew his name. I inquired why he did not stop, and he informed me that the POWs were free to walk around or go on tasks if their employers desired so. There obviously was full trust that the men would not try to run away.

Around the camp in the evenings, I saw another general attitude. There was a notable lack of fooling about, which I believe you Amis call horse play, and it was rare to see any sports being played. When more than four young German men get together and no one starts to kick around a

Fussball, something is drastically wrong.

During the week no inquiries were made by the Americans about my impressions. Even Bruenner never came right out and asked me what the hell I was doing, but he it was clear to me that he definitely wanted to. Not only did he ask probing questions each evening, but also I became aware that his lackey, Rafer, was suddenly very chummy and was trying hard to get on my good side. Leutnant Volk remained aloof and stayed out of contact as much as possible.

I vividly remember two visits we made that were very important pieces in the puzzle of what was going on at Camp Burley. The first was to a farm owned by a young couple named George. The Georges' farm was west of Burley right near a large dam on the Snake River. This dam, the Milner Dam, formed a reservoir that provided the water for a large system of irrigation canals that watered the many farms on the high desert plateau surrounding the river. The Georges' had three POWs assigned to them. The only one I recall by name was an older Schwaebischer Bauer named Kurt Tahlmeister. Soldat Tahlmeister seemed to enjoy his work and professed no problems, but I did sense that he was very uncomfortable talking with me. After the men went back to the fields to irrigate, Mr. and Mrs. George invited Sergeant Sermons and me into their house for a glass of iced tea, a drink common in that area that I learned to like very much. Mrs. George didn't seem to be the type who would hold her tongue long if something was on her mind. Her husband was a bit the opposite, being a very quiet man. No sooner had we sat down at their kitchen table and were served our tall glasses of iced tea than Mrs. George looked Sergeant Sermons right in the eye and asked, "Now just what are you going to do for Kurt?" The sergeant's brow wrinkled and he looked to Mr. George. The young farmer grimaced and studied his glass as if enthralled with the way the drops of water appeared on its surface and trickled down to the table. At last he spoke.

"I know that Kurt is a German soldier, Sergeant, but I don't think he is one of those nasty Nazi fellows. I just don't know why he can't stay here if he wants to."

"You know that is not up to me, don't you?" Sermons answered. "For one thing he hasn't even made a request."

"Well, of course not if he did he would be punished.

"Who told you that?"

Mrs. George interrupted, "Why that seems to be common knowledge. In fact, all of the POWs who have worked here told us that."

"Well, ma'am, as I told you before, the decision of whether any soldiers can refuse to go home when the time comes has not been made yet. We are aware that several of the Germans have expressed interest in staying here, but no formal policy has been issued on the subject. Captain Sneed is concerned about the morale of the prisoners at Camp Burley. In fact, the captain here was sent here to investigate just that."

Mr. and Mrs. George quickly turned to me with inquiring looks on their faces. I had not wanted anyone to know what I was up to, but now it was out. I held up my hand and said in a quiet tone. "Please, I am not really sure why I am here, but I do know that if the word gets out that I am investigating anything I will surely find out nothing, even if I knew what I was looking for. So, I beg of you to say nothing to anyone about me, but I will tell you that I am confused by why men would not want to return to their families at the soonest possible time. For now would you let me just get to know the men and see what is on their minds."

Mrs. George looked back to the sergeant and said, "I hope you know what you are doing trusting this German officer. From what I have heard from the men, in their army the officers think they are some kind of kings."

I spent the rest of the afternoon at the George farm on the pretense of trying to learn about American agricultural practices (I did find them fascinating). I spent the time shadowing the men in the fields as they diverted water from the canal into furrows that irrigated the rows of beans and sugar beets. I stuck very close to Soldat Tahlmeister. At first he seemed to have to concentrate so hard on his work that he could not talk to me. However, as I asked him to show me how to set the water, and about the farm itself, he loosened up. At last I felt it safe to ask him about himself.

"You seem to have a love for the land, Soldat. Have you a farm at home?"

He stood up and looked to the distance with a sad look on his face.

209

At last he answered, "Yes, sir, I have lived off of the land all my life."

"Is your farm as large as this?"

"HA!" he exploded. "Now do you suppose if I owned this much land I would be here? No, sir, I would have been able to buy my way out of the army as other rich land barons did. Actually, I work my father's land with my brother. We have only twenty Hectar."

"Are you married?"

"Yes, sir, to a fine woman."

"Children?"

"None; that is, none alive," he answered slowly. "We lost two and never were blessed with another. That is why I was the one chosen to go off to the war. My brother has two sons and a daughter and so he was able to stay on the land."

"Yes, it has been tough to be separated so long, but maybe the time is near that we can go home, won't that be a fine day?"

The soldier suddenly looked and acted far older than his age. I think I detected a tear in his eye. I said nothing, hoping my silence would give him confidence to tell me what was on his mind. At last he spoke, in a quiet voice. "I have been thinking, sir, perhaps I won't go home."

"I don't understand. Don't you think the Ami will let us go home? I am sure they will actually be glad to get rid of us. Keeping prisoners must be expensive, if for no other reason."

Kurt seemed on the verge of opening up to me further, then he shook his head slowly and began again to give total concentration to his work. I finally came right out and said, "Soldat Tahlmeister, I really don't know what the hell is going on with you, or for that matter many other soldiers in this camp, but I do know I can not help you if you do not talk to me." With that, I walked away and went back to the farmhouse. There I found Sergeant Sermons sitting on a fence watching Mr. George feed his cattle, which were enclosed in a large paddock.

"Find anything interesting, Captain?" Sermons inquired.

"Quite," I answered.

"Do you mind telling me, or is it a high German command secret?"

"Not at all, Sergeant. I found that they grow a phenomenal crop of bears and sugar beets here in these fields. Someday you Americans will feed the world."

"I am sure Captain Sneed will be thrilled to hear that," Sermons answered with a smile.

"All right, Sergeant, the truth is I don't know what is going on, but something is definitely bothering Tahlmeister and he doesn't seem to want to talk about it. Do you think the Georges know more about it than they have spoken to us about?"

"Well, let's find out." He called out to Mr. George, "Hey, Richard, could you come over a minute?"

The farmer sauntered across the paddock. He climbed up on the fence and perched beside us. He sat there for some time before he spoke. "Fine looking animals, are they not?" the young farmer said as he gazed out onto his herd with a satisfied look on his face. "Do you farm in Germany, Captain?"

"No, I am a schoolteacher; at least I was, but I am not unfamiliar with farming."

Mr. George again sat in silence for some time. I could see that he was working something over in his mind. At last he spoke. "Can't see as how anyone could live off the land; it must be awful to live in a city. You see, life here on the farm is more personal. Take this here bunch of mangy beef in my corral. I know each one of them, not by name, but I know the peculiarities of each critter. You see, each of God's creations is a special individual— even those damn chickens Erma insists on keeping."

"I can not speak for your animals, Mr. George, but I damn sure am worried about some of the men from the camp. Can you tell me why Kurt Tahlmeister does not want to go back to Germany?"

After contemplating for awhile, he said in a very quiet, but firm, voice, "It may hurt your German pride a bit, Captain, but perhaps he just likes America more. Can't any man, even a German, even if he was, or is, a soldier, live where the hell he chooses?"

"I am not sure if I know the answer to that, Mr. George, but we will never know unless some good reason is given. You might pass that on to Soldat, ah, Private Tahlmeister."

211

I got down from the fence and walked toward the house and the jeep.

The sergeant trotted after me and murmured, "Talkative fellow, ain't he?"

As we got to the jeep, Mrs. George came out of the house with a bucket of scraps for the hogs. I stopped and thanked her for her hospitality and turned toward the jeep, thought better of it and turned back to ask her, "Dear lady please do not think of me as an enemy, which I guess, even if the war is over, I still am. I truly would like to help soldiers like Private Tahlmeister to do so I must know what he wants and why he wants it. Can you tell me why he does not want to return to his wife and fatherland?"

She smiled and said, "We are all the children of God, Captain, and I do hope that this war brings an end to hatred. As for Kurt, I only know that he feels that he can not go back to Germany."

The puzzle became no clearer the next day when we visited shops in Burley where various POWs were detailed. One particular man, a Gefreiter Hofmann, was almost a double of Soldat Tahlmeister. He seemed to have a lot to return to at his home in Frankfurt am Mein—a family, a skilled position in a shoe repair business owned by his father, and many friends whom he openly wondered if they had survived the war, but yet he asked me how he could petition to stay in America. When I directly asked him to tell me why, he visibly began to get angry, and then got himself in control and looked me in the eye as he coldly said, "Do you not have enough information in your officer book, Captain? Now, please sir, I have many shoes to repair today. May I go back to work?"

After I had several such conversations with POWs in the camp, and a further discussion with Captain Sneed, I felt that I should take some more direct action. I decided to turn up the pressure on Leutnant Volk. I asked Lieutenant Atwill to have Volk stay in the office late one afternoon. When Volk reported back to Atwill's office he was surprised to find me as the only one there. I got right to the point.

"Leutnant, I think it is time that we talked; have a seat. As you no doubt have guessed, I have been brought here for a reason. I have been asked to try to find out why the morale in this camp is so low. Furthermore, I am

212

trying to determine why so many of our soldiers do not want to go back to Germany."

My self-exposure did not seem to phase Volk, who just sat there in silence. It was clear to me that he considered me a traitor who was in some way working for the Americans. I had to make him see that I had the welfare of the POWs in mind.

"If you give a damn about your fellow soldiers and our fatherland then you had best talk to me. Damn it, man, I am not an American sympathizer. Can't you see that if many of our soldiers choose to stay here, which I am not even sure is possible, we as a people have totally lost. The war itself has been lost, but we must all work together not to let these people rob the dignity of our soldiers. Think of their loved ones back in the fatherland. Must they lose even those soldiers who were not sacrificed on the battlefield?"

"It is the welfare of these men that you don't seem to understand," Volk finally responded. "If they do not stay here they, and their families, will be disgraced."

"Disgraced? I don't seem to understand how that can be. Getting captured is not a disgrace. These men did not run from battle. In fact, just the opposite is true. They stayed to fight, but circumstances beyond their control caused them to find themselves prisoners of war."

"Yes, yes, I understand all of that, but all of us, whether because of, as you say, circumstances beyond our control, or out of free choice have done things that now will be used against us."

"I know of no actions that anyone in this camp has taken that would lead to some sort of punitive action."

"Don't act so naïve, Herr Hauptmann. You know perfectly well about the report book kept in every camp."

"Report book?"

"Report book, incident log, commanders log, I don't know what the actual thing is called, but I know it is kept in each camp, and it has sure and the hell been kept very well here." Volk became visibly shaken as he began almost to shout. "In fact, I am sure that this little conversation will be fully recorded. But I am telling you, Herr Hauptmann, I don't give a damn

213

anymore." Volk jumped to his feet.

"Please, Fritz, please sit down," I said quickly. It was the first time I had used his first name and it seemed to shock him. He hesitated a moment and then sat down with his elbows on his knees and his face in his hands. "I am now in my fourth camp in America and I know nothing of any logbooks being kept. Now, I must give you an order. You must tell me about this book and who keeps it."

Volk slowly looked up at me. His brow was wrinkled and he had a very strange look on his face. "Sir, are you trying to tell me that it is not customary for a company logbook to be kept that reports any crimes that have been done by soldiers against die Wehrmacht or das Vaterland?"

"I know of no order to keep a logbook, but of course it would be the duty of any officer to report a crime if he was aware of it. Is that what you are afraid of, Fritz? Have you committed a crime?"

Volk sat and looked at me in silence. At last his chin began to quiver, and he bit his lower lip. He finally answered in almost a whisper. "I don't know who to believe anymore, but I guess it does not matter. It is all written anyway. Yes, I suppose I have."

"You have what, Leutnant?"

"Committed a crime, maybe lots of crimes. Who knows what is in my file?"

"You know that it is your duty to report any such thing to me, but you know as a man that you do not have to freely admit to me what crimes. However, for me to judge if such crimes have actually taken place it would behoove you to tell me."

"Sure, why not?" He jumped to his feet and came to attention. "Sir, it is clear that I have aided and abetted the enemy by working here in the camp office. Furthermore, I have accepted special privilege from the enemy."

"Accepted special privilege, how so?"

"Sir, isn't it very clear; I come and go in the camp as I please. I even walk out the main gate each day and come here to work where I help the enemy keep records of the other traitors in the camp who work for the Americans on the farms and in the shops."

"And you feel that these actions are crimes?"

214

"No, sir, I do not feel they are. I am just trying to keep busy and trying to help those other soldiers who do not want to sit and watch their lives go by here in this foreign desert do something. But, it does not matter what I think; it is what he thinks. Is that not what will be presented to the higher command when we return to das Vaterland?"

I gave the order of "at ease" and asked him to sit again. "To start out Fritz, what you tell me I in no way feel are crimes. You are just doing your duty as a soldier. Secondly, you speak of a report to be made to a higher command. What command, I ask you? Unless the American commander and the American press is out and out lying to us and the American citizenry, Der Fuehrer is dead and the high command has completely capitulated. Do you not see, there is no higher command? I think we will return to a Vaterland full of turmoil and destruction. Perhaps I am the one who has sold out to the enemy for saying this, but I have only sadness and trepidation in my heart when I dare to think of what we will find when we return. I do know, though, that no one in Deutschland will have time to be concerned about the so-called crimes of each and every prisoner who has worked here in America. You also said that 'he' thinks it is a crime. Who is 'he'? Are you speaking of Captain Sneed?"

"No, of course not, sir. Herr Hauptmann Bruenner keeps the log I speak of. He has kept a complete record on all of us. In fact, I know that he now has several entries on you. Are you serious when you say that these things will not be used against us when we return to Deutschland?"

At last I had an inkling of what was going on. The dear asshole Breunner was holding each soldier in some kind of a power hold by threatening to expose their crimes against Germany and the German people. I answered Volk in a very serious tone. I was the one who was now having a hard time controlling my emotions. "I can not promise you anything, leutnant; I do not know what is in store for us when, and even if, we return to Deutschland, but I do know that if what you told me is true then a very serious crime has been, and is being, carried out, and it is not by you or me. It is being acted against us by Bruenner. Will you please help me expose the Arschlock for what he is?"

"Sir, even if it causes me to go in front of a firing squad I would gladly do anything that would get to Bruenner and that queer scheisskerl, Rafer."

"One last thing, Fritz; does he actually have a list of crimes that I have committed?"

"He joyfully read it to us the other day when you were late coming back from the farms." Volk could not help himself from saying this with a big smile. "It seems as if you are a major sympathizer to the Americans, and are almost singlehandedly helping them to turn our soldiers against the fatherland. He told us that you will be no doubt punished severely when you return to Deutschland."

It did not take me long to hatch my plot against Bruenner. On the next Sunday while all of the men were in the compound I had Lieutenant Atwill call Hauptmann Bruenner to the office. As soon as he left I went over to his area and started to search through his things. Rafer saw what I was doing and quickly ran over to me screaming.

"Get out of that area! You have no right there! I will report this to the Hauptmann." He started to run toward me, but was interrupted by Volk. Rafer seemed very surprised that the quiet Leutnant Volk would take a side. At first he sneered at Volk and said, "Out of my way you bastard, or you will be reported along with this other traitor."

"Reported to whom, your lover Bruenner?" Volk retorted with a mocking smile.

This stopped Rafer in his tracks. He seemed very confused before he said, "Can't you see if I don't stop you from this I will be written up also. I don't want to stay here. I want to return to see my mother." He was obviously on the verge of crying.

"Oh for God's sake man, shut up and stay out of our way," Volk said in an almost comforting tone.

Rafer went back to his bunk and sat with his face in his hands. I continued my search until I found a set of notebooks. A quick perusal assured me that I had the right ones. It seemed that each man had a section devoted to his "crimes". I found my name in the newest of the books. For only being in the camp a short time I had an interesting record. I was no doubt a major conspirator with the Americans against the people of

Germany.

I looked back through the other books and soon found mention of Oberleutnant Rafer. "It is now very clear to me that Oberleutnant Rafer is a homosexual," Bruenner had written. After this declaration in his notes, Breunner had gone on to expose the deviant, criminal behavior of this "disgusting piece of humanity." I looked over to Rafer and signaled Volk to step outside, which he did.

"You know what is written here about you, don't you?"

"Yes, sir," Rafer whispered.

"Why then, could you please tell me, are you supporting and defending this piece of shit."

"It started shortly after we got here. Breunner caught me . . . well, in a compromising position with one of the guards. He showed me that first report on his books and said that he would report me when we got back to Deutschland unless I, as he put it, cooperated with him. You know that would mean prison or death, don't you. What was I to do?"

"What did this 'cooperating' entail?"

"I helped gather information on each of the soldiers' criminal activities. I also was to make sure that each soldier knew that Bruenner was aware of them and would report them."

"What was the reaction of the soldiers when you told them that their superior was keeping a record on them?"

"Some, like Volk, just seemed to ignore it, though I am sure that they were worried. Others, such as Soldat Tahlmeister, would get very angry and then say that he could go to hell because they would find a way not to go back to Deutschland. Many would beg me to have Bruenner forgive them and take their names out of the books. Most of these men would offer to pay Bruenner to do so."

"Pay him what?"

"Some, like the men in the camp kitchen, would offer extra food or service, some would offer money."

"Would Bruenner accept these bribes?"

"Yes, of course, if they were enough. Sometimes I would go back several times to the offender to get the right price."

217

"How would they know that Bruenner had removed the information from his books once the bribe was made?"

"Naturally, they wouldn't know that. In fact, Hauptmann Bruenner never eliminated any information. He told me that he would be sure that all of the traitors would be eventually prosecuted."

"Why did you keep cooperating with him knowing that? Did you not realize that he was also continuing to keep this record on you?"

"I had no choice. You see, he held my life in his hands no matter what. He knows what I am and knows how to exploit my weaknesses. Now I suppose everyone will know and I will not live to see my mother."

"That remains to be seen. If there is any hope for you, you must tell me everything. So, is there anything else, Oberleutnant?"

Rafer began to sob, and turned away from me. Finally he answered, "Yes, of course; he made me perform several acts with him."

"Acts?"

"Please, don't make me be more specific." He turned toward me and could see that I was intent on pressing him further. "Oh all right, what difference does it make now; he had me perform oral sex and submit to his sodomy when all of the other prisoners were out on duty."

"How long has that gone on?"

"For over a year."

I had, of course, always known that there were some homosexuals in the German army, but this was the first time I had actually been in a position of leadership where something had to be done about it. You must understand that in the German army it was absolutely not tolerated. Men found to be homosexuals were hauled away by order of the high command and never seen again. I have always assumed that they were shot.

I told Rafer to keep quiet, and ordered him to stay confined to the tent, except for food and toilet breaks. I went out into the yard and found Volk and discussed with him what he thought should be done with Bruenner. We decided not to tell the Americans right away. Volk felt that they would just haul him away and the rest of the soldiers would think he was getting rewarded for his dastardly activities. We decided to have a camp meeting that night. I did go out to the camp operations office and asked the lieutenant to ignore any disturbances that evening.

Hauptmann Bruenner came back from Burley just in time for the evening meal. After the meal he retired to our tent. The rest of us officers, Rafer included, stayed out at the officers' table. Minutes after Breunner went into the tent he came storming out, started to come over to our area (one could tell from the look on his face that he was in a state of fury), then almost ran to the front gate. There we could see him wildly gesturing but could not hear what he was saying. After a while one of the guards strolled over to the operations building, was inside for about five minutes (which seemed like twenty), and then strolled back to talk to Bruenner. Bruenner let out a string of curses that we could hear, and then began to holler, "Herr Lieutenant, I know you are in there. Damn it, important documents have been stolen from me and you must, as camp commander, come out and help me. These criminals will, and must, be prosecuted. If you don't come out I will see that your commander will prosecute you." No response was heard from the operations building or from the guards on the other side of the gate from Bruenner. What his tirade did succeed in doing was to alert the whole camp that something was going on and everyone who had returned to the compound, or were resident workers, stormed out of their tents to see what was happening.

Bruenner at last could see that he would not get help from the Americans. He managed to get control of himself and very confidently strolled back to our table, came to a halt with clenched fists on his hips, and glared at us. His eyes noticeably fell on the notebooks on the table before me. I had kept them hidden during our meal. Finally a vicious smile spread on his face and he spat out, "I suppose you feel that by stealing my books you will be saved from your just rewards. Such cowardly action will just be another nail in your coffin. I will be open for discussion on the matter if you care to come to my tent, Hauptmann. Rafer, come with me." He spun back toward the tent, took several steps, and then looked back to see Rafer, his head down and eyes on the ground, but still sitting at the table. "Just as well, you gutless little shit," he sneered. "Just know that as soon as I tell everyone about you, you will be a dead man, woman, animal, or whatever you are." With that, he returned to our tent.

All of us sat and waited for the return of all of the out-of-camp

219

workers. None of the men returned to their tents. They knew that something very big was happening. As workers returned they too saw the growing crowd and joined it. When the last of the workers came in I asked Volk to go to our tent and invite Bruenner to join us. Volk came back with the word that the Hauptmann had told him to go to hell. I decided to start the camp meeting without him. I stood up on the table and motioned the men to gather around. When all were assembled I held up the notebooks.

"Men, I hold here an interesting set of notes taken by the, up to this time, leader of this camp." A murmur spread though the men. "Don't worry, I am not about to reveal the specifics of these notes. However, as probably most of you know, they were not compiled to bring praise upon you when we return home." A few in the crowd actually laughed at that statement. "I have no idea whether any of the accusations in these documents are true. I suspect very few are; however, true or untrue, it does not matter. I will see that these notebooks will be destroyed." The men began to cheer. Suddenly on the table next to me Bruenner appeared. At first the crowd hushed, then the men began to hurl insults at Bruenner. He stood there, hands on hips, feet wide apart and glared at the men in his most defiant way. I held up my hand and called for silence. At last the crowd quieted down.

"It is proper that we should hear what the good Hauptmann has to say," I yelled. "Quiet, everyone, and let him speak."

Bruenner at first just stood there and glared. At last he spoke, "I stand here in shame." Many in the crowd made expressions of surprise at this sudden confession, but their surprise was not to last long as Bruenner continued. "I once fought with men of character, men who believed in the German cause, men who would die before giving one crumb of help to the Vaterland's enemies. Now I stand in a midst of the rottenest infestation of cowards that could possibly exist. I am ashamed that I must go back to my homeland and report that the men under me were such a despicable lot. Right now this turncoat standing next to me, and the worms who support him, think they have saved your hides by their cowardly act of thievery. Do you think that I need the actual camp notes of the acts of treason that have gone on to get each and every perpetrator prosecuted? Who do you think our superiors will believe: this refined, English-speaking coward, or a faithful

220

officer like myself?" Another murmur spread through the men. I could see many shaking their heads in agreement with what he said. He continued, "I know that I do not stand alone in this camp and many of you who know you are innocent will stand with me against these agents of our enemy." He started to come toward me. Before I could react, Volk jumped up onto the table between us and caused Bruenner to hesitate.

I held up my hand again for silence. The arguments that had started to break out in the crowd finally settled down. I addressed the men again. "I find some of what the hauptmann says to be true. You were proud faithful soldiers. But what I disagree on is what you are now. You are still faithful Germans. I am not sure if any of us feel proud of the fact that we are now prisoners being held in a foreign land, but we really have no reason for shame. We have shown the enemy that we are not the murdering dogs that some of them once thought we were. We can leave here proud of the fact that those we have met and worked with know that the German people are a hard-working, honorable people. The Hauptmann also speaks of our superiors. I ask you just who are these people? Have you not heard that the war is over? Do you not believe that our superiors capitulated to total, unconditional defeat? Neither I, nor you, nor Hauptmann Bruenner know what has happened in Deutschland. None of us is even sure if there is a Deutschland." This declaration caused some to become agitated. "We do know several things, however. We know that when a country is defeated the leaders are no longer the leaders. The victorious army designates new leaders. Do you suppose that these leaders give a damn about the individual acts of each former prisoner of war, especially when the only one who claimed them to be treasonous did so to gain personal favors. How many of you bowed to his extortion?" The assembly's mood quickly changed and began to become increasingly hostile. I continued, "I also know that, though the Deutschland we left may not exist, the same German people still exist, and these people will welcome you back into their arms in joy and gratitude for what you have done. Who will join me in destroying these books?" A loud cheer arose from the men and nearly all of them began to yell their support. They surged forward and soon a fire was started. They cheered wildly as I began to rip up the first book and toss pages into the fire. A new roar would raise with each new batch of hatred descending to the flames.

As the flames devoured the last of his despised books, Bruenner waved his arms and nearly jumped up and down to get the men's attention. At last they let him speak.

"That was an interesting display, gentlemen, but it was for naught. It is I who will have the last laugh as many of you are exposed for the criminals and perverts that you . . ." His speech was cut short by a terrible cry as Rafer suddenly sprang up behind him with a knife from the kitchen, which he plunged into the startled captain's back. A commotion broke out as men ran to and fro, some trying to get out of the melee and others trying to get at Bruenner. Shots were fired and guards suddenly appeared to break up the assembled POWs. We were all ordered to our tents.

I spent a long night going over what had happened. Had I done the right thing? Was I responsible for the attack on Bruenner? Was he alive or dead? What had happened to Rafer?

Early the next morning I was called to the operations building where I found myself in front of a desk at which sat Captain Sneed. He was busy writing out a report. I remained standing before the desk. At last he looked up, and without asking me to sit said, "Quite a party you had last night, Captain. I don't remember in my discussions with you that you were told to take matters into your own hands. Now look at the mess of reports I have to make. One man in the hospital in critical condition. One man in the local jail accused of assault, and I have a camp of workers I must hold in confinement. Soon I will have local employers beating on my door demanding their workers. Yes, all in all Captain, you have done one hell of a job. I won't even ask you what the hell was going on, because it doesn't matter. What does matter is that I will have the damn colonel down my neck, big time. I should send your damn ass to Oklahoma, but for now consider yourself confined to quarters. Dismissed!"

I walked out of his office and out through the front area. Lieutenant Atwill was there. As I passed him, he winked at me and nodded. I also saw Sergeant Sermons in the background and he gave me a thumbs up.

During most of that week all of us stayed in camp. I was called in to operations and questioned by an officer and sergeant from what the

Americans called the JAG (the Judge Advocate General). I did not reveal individual comments made in Bruenner's books but informed them of the general gist of them and how Bruenner had received bribes from the men to have their records supposedly expunged.

The mood in camp began to change. Everyone began to treat me with utmost respect. Even the kitchen sergeant personally served my meals. Several of the men came up and thanked me for stopping Bruenner's tyranny. Private Tahlmeister stopped me one evening on my way to my tent. He had tears in his eyes as he saluted me and said, "Sir, I think you are right. I shall go back to my family." I shook his hand and assured him that perhaps soon we would all be able to go back. I wasn't sure if I believed that myself or not.

By the end of the week the workers were again going out to their assigned workplaces. I was back to making my rounds with Sergeant Sermons, or occasionally Lieutenant Atwill. The coming fall was bringing some of the most beautiful weather I have ever witnessed. The days were warm and dry; the sun never seemed to go away in southern Idaho, and the evenings were cool. The harvest of potatoes and beans started, and I soon could see why the people of Idaho called the state the "Land of Famous Potatoes." The size and quality of the potatoes was truly amazing. I must say, though, that while I was in America, even in Idaho, I missed the flavor of the small-yellow fleshed German Kartoffel. The days moved by without much change. However, one day Lieutenant Atwill took me to some places that I will not forget.

The first of these excursions was to a local sporting event. One evening he asked me after our normal rounds of the farms if I knew anything about football. I, as all German boys, naturally spent my youth on the fussball field. I proudly told him that I had been a pretty fair torhueter (goalkeeper) well into my college days. He at first seemed a bit confused then replied with a laugh, "No, not soccer, the real football—the kind we Americans play. I then remembered that the Americans naturally had their own way of doing everything, and considered it the "real" thing. I had seen the guards playing a game with an elongated ball much like the English rugby ball. I never could really figure out what the object or the rules were, and told him so. "Well we will fix that," he said. That evening he and

223

Sergeant Sermons took me along as a truckload of guards journeyed over to the town of Rupert. There, at a large field next to a school, we met a contingent of guards from the Rupert camp, accompanied by Captain Sneed. The meeting of the two groups was a reason for much laughing, verbal sparring, and wagering on the game that was to take place on the field that evening between the high school rivals, Burley High School and Rupert High School. I gathered that none of the soldiers were actually from one of the towns, but the game offered a good reason for some friendly rivalry between the two camps. I was surprised that no beer was in evidence. Captain Sneed's group had brought a washtub full of iced sodas. I was offered a bottle of a soda called root beer. I almost gagged on it, much to the delight of the Ami guards.

As crowds of local citizens arrived, each camp group joined the respective village's hometown crowd on opposite sides of the field. Each side had their own band and, to the delight of the soldiers, a group of short-skirted young ladies who danced and jumped to the tune of the band or to the organized cheers of the crowd. At last the teams from each school came running onto the field. At first I was impressed with their unique uniforms and the obvious muscular build of the individual athletes. Then it was clear to me that each player had his uniform stuffed with some sort of padding. To add to the medieval look, each player wore a helmet. The game began with the kicking of the ball from one team to the other. I then recognized that the game was a version of rugby. However, the player who had caught the ball was quite selfish and never passed off the ball as he ran downfield, even after encountering players of the opposing team. He was soon knocked down and an official in a striped shirt blew his whistle. As play resumed, it was clear that the game bore only slight resemblance to rugby. Through the course of the game I began to gather the objectives of the game, but never really figured it out. What I did comprehend was that Americans were a people well suited for war. This game was obviously a favored sport in the country, since all of the soldiers I accompanied, no matter where they were from, had played the game and were very fanatic in their love for it. The game itself evolved around the entire team forfeiting their bodies by slamming into the opposing players so that one man could advance the ball toward the goal. It was clear that only the actual ball handlers were the heroes, and all of the rest of the players were quite content to sacrifice themselves to make them that way. Such unselfish group patriotism is the most important ingredient in war. Only a few will be revered when the victory is won, but many must sacrifice to achieve it. I still think Fussball is a superior game, but it is a much more selfish sport, and each player can have his individual moments of glory. That makes for an exciting sporting event, but is not the essence of war.

I have little recollection of the actual game but know that "our" side won and much rivalry resulted. After the cheers were over, and the wagers collected, we piled back into the truck, hidden bottles of whiskey appeared and the trip home was a wild party. I found myself as just one of the boys and was allowed to let the tension of the previous weeks flow out of me. Soon after the night of the game another tour out of the camp helped me to get a glimpse of American life.

A large load of supplies arrived from the big warehouse in Ogden, Utah. With the assistance of a detachment of POWs, with me as their leader, Lieutenant Atwill was to deliver supplies to the other camps. Our first trip was west to Twin Falls. The camp was actually at a county fairgrounds in a small town west of the community of Twin Falls. We drove right through Twin Falls and I was quite impressed at the neat, orderly layout of the town. As all of the Mormon villages I saw, starting with Salt Lake City, the streets were wide and straight, being laid out in a very orderly grid. Twin Falls being situated in such a flat area was a natural for a rigid grid system. The real fascinating thing I saw in the area was a short side trip we made to see one of the river falls that the city was named for. To my surprise, there was no water coming over the falls. I knew that there was plenty of water in the Snake River thirty miles upstream at Burley. I also had seen lots of water below the dam near the George farm, which was between Burley and the big falls. American ingenuity was at work. The little water that was not taken off for irrigation was routed around the falls through an electrical generator. I was told that this happened at both of the large falls on that section of the river. What a sight those tremendous falls must have been when water actually ran over them. The thought crossed my mind that it was too bad the

Germans and the Americans had not become allies. With our joint ingenuity and propensity to work hard, to say nothing about our strong ethnocentric tendencies, we could have brought great things to the world. I wondered if the American people would ever realize that the German people were not the monsters that the American press had built us to be. My faith in Adolf Hitler had long eroded and I was becoming very hesitant to justify his actions, even to myself.

The Americans were being very sanctimonious, especially when they brought up the treatment of Jews and other minorities by us Germans. I, at that time, had no concept as to what had really happened to these peoples during the war. I am not sure I really do even now. Our third stop of the day provides a good counterargument that I am not sure many American of the time would have been able to respond to.

We left Twin Falls and headed back east, then north across a long suspended bridge over the Snake River Canyon. The canyon at that point is very deep and is but a mere crack in the earth's surface, with shear rock walls plummeting nearly strait down to the river. I would not ride in the jeep, and definitely not in a truck, over this chasm, and chose to walk across. I may have been a former parachutist, but no one issued me a parachute to brave being that far above the jagged rock floor below. I felt that a people who could dry up rivers could have built a more substantial bridge than that swinging strand. We continued on to Camp Rupert to deliver their supplies. Much of that stretch of country was not developed and I was able to see what the area may have looked like before white settlers changed it. It is hard to describe the before and after difference that irrigation brought. Our third stop was a camp northwest of Rupert.

As we drove across the railroad tracks north of the town we saw a young American corporal standing beside the road with his duffel bag at his feet. He held up his thumb in the universal sign and we stopped to give him a lift. As he threw his bag in the back of the jeep and climbed aboard, also into the rear since the lieutenant was driving himself (the desire of American officers to drive themselves I found strange), two facets of his being caught my attention. First, he was limping and sported a walking cane. Secondly, he was Oriental. I was not sure what his ethnic origin was, since I had had very

226

little contact with Orientals. His name tag informed me that his name was Nakamoto, but that meant little to me. He spoke in a very distinct American slang, with no hint of his ethnic tongue.

"You wouldn't be getting near the area of Camp Minidoka, by any chance?" he inquired.

"Damn lucky day, Corporal," the lieutenant answered. "We are actually on our way there."

"If that isn't the cat's pajamas, first break I have had since gettin' to this land of Eden. You wouldn't happen to have a smoke, would you? I have been out of weed since yesterday."

As I offered him my pack I could see him studying my uniform. I was not wearing my issued POW garb (by this time many of us had started to wear some store-bought clothes such as the new-to-us western blue jeans, but had topped it with my German officer's field cap, the last vestige of my German uniform).

"Excuse me for asking, but are you some kind of officer, sir?"

"I guess that is a matter of some opinion, Corporal. To some I am a Hauptmann, some a captain, and to others a mere vassal."

"Oh!" he uttered with a confused shrug. Atwill just laughed. Finally the corporal asked, "Seriously, Sir, I ain't never seen a uniform like yours. Just what are you?"

"I am a temporary guest of this fine nation, Corporal, and this upstanding young lieutenant is being kind enough to serve as my tour guide."

"Ah shit!" Atwill managed to utter from his laughter. "Soldier, ignore this pompous ass. He is a prisoner of war, being incarcerated for his foolish opposition to the superiority of the good old U.S. of A.

The corporal quickly sat back in his seat, as if trying to get the maximum distance from me. He looked back at the truck following us as if to assure himself that other, hopefully armed, American soldiers were about.

"Excuse me, Lieutenant, but shouldn't he be under guard, in handcuffs, or somethin'?"

"Don't worry, Corporal, these Germans are a docile bunch, and they certainly wouldn't try to escape. Why, they are too damn dumb to find their way to the latrine, let alone back to Germany." As he said this, he looked over to me with a grin on his face and winked.

"I don't mean to dispute what you say, Sir," the young soldier said very seriously, "but the Krauts I met up with in Italy certainly weren't docile. I am not so sure I would call them dumb, either. I think cunning, mean bastards would be a better description."

Any fun I was having to that point on the trip was suddenly dashed. I sat quietly and stared out the windshield.

"Italy," Atwill asked. "Is that where you were awarded the cane?"

"That's a strange way of putting it, Sir, but yes, I got mine in some little I'tie wide spot in the road. I was lucky. Most of my friends were award-ed, as you put it, wooden boxes." After a few minutes of riding in silence— obviously wrapped in some old, not so pleasant thoughts—he looked for-ward and said in a rather humble voice, "Sorry, Sir, I didn't mean to lecture you, and as for you, Captain," he directed toward me, "I guess I don't really hold any grudges; war is what it is. Were you in Italy?"

"Corporal, I certainly understand; war is a shitty way for bigwigs to conduct schoolyard disputes. As for Italy, no, I never got beyond North Africa."

"That's good; to tell you the truth, I am not sure if I could ride here with an enemy who maybe put this hole in my thigh, to say nothing of what happened to nearly all of the rest of my outfit."

"Yes, I can relate to that; if you were English I might need those handcuffs you asked about. Do your parents live in this area?"

With pain in his face at my question, he answered before he lapsed into silence for the rest of the trip, "Yeah, I guess you can say they also live here as 'guests' of this great nation."

I soon learned why the corporal was so affected by my ignorance. After driving through a stretch of rugged volcanic terrain and patches of wild sage that grew to nearly two meters high we came to a large entrance gate made of volcanic stone. The gate was manned by armed soldiers. The guards checked Lieutenant Atwill's paperwork and allowed us to pass through; our hitchhiker had to dismount and stay at the gate. We quickly came to anoth-er gate, this one made of barbed wire. It led into a large compound

228

surrounded by a three-meter high barbed-wire stockade fence which sprouted tall guard towers at each corner. The guard towers were manned. The interior of the compound was filled with black tar paper-covered wooden barracks aligned in straight rows along dirt streets. Many young children were playing in the streets; women could be seen carrying out household chores; and men, mostly elderly, could be seen sitting on benches talking or watching the children at play; they were all Orientals. Before we got to a large building that was obviously some sort of warehouse, I asked the lieutenant just what sort of a place this was. He quickly told me that this was a relocation camp for Japanese Americans who lived on the West Coast. Before he could say much more we pulled up to the unloading point. There we were met by an unarmed American sergeant and an old Japanese man. The sergeant saluted Atwill and the Japanese man bowed.

"Herow Rootenant," the Japanese man greeted us with a strong accent, "Do you bring us many good things?"

"Howdy, Mr. Nakamoto," returned the lieutenant. "Of course I loaded up only the best canned beans and premium Spam for you."

"Do you bring us good news about the war?"

"Now you know that I can't bring in newspapers, but I hear that the Japs are getting their ass whipped."

"Aw, very good, old Tojo needs to be kicked very hard," the old Japanese man said with a smile.

"Say, Mr. Nakamoto, didn't you say you had a grandson in the 442th Division?"

"Yes, but we have not heard from him since he was in the hospitow in Engran. Do you bring this o' man some good news?"

"Well, maybe so, perhaps you should go to the front gate. Maybe you could have a visitor."

Tears welled up in the old man's eyes and he started to leave. Then he seemed to remember his manners and dignity. He turned back to the lieutenant, and bowed. "Your name wir be on the rips of many generations to come. Please forgive me but I must find my famiry and check out your possiber good news." With that he hustled off and we saw to the unloading of the truck and the signing of the paperwork by the sergeant.

229

Only after the truck was unloaded and we were enjoying a Coca-Cola (an addiction many of us picked up and spent some of our wages on) did I learn more about relocation camps. It seems that President Roosevelt had ordered all of the people of Japanese descent, regardless of their citizenship, relocated away from the coast for purposes of national security. I asked Lieutenant Atwill about what happened to their homes and businesses, but he had no idea what was done with them. I could understand the need for national security and the conceived threat of large populations of Japanese on the coast. After all, even in Germany we knew of the cunnings of the Oriental people. I knew that the Japanese were part of the axis, but I never really thought of them as trusted allies. What I really could not understand was why they were being confined in such conditions as I was witnessing at Camp Minidoka. Yes, they were obviously Japanese, but the lieutenant had assured me that most were American citizens. What a strange people these Americans were. I, as a known and admitted enemy, was being held under far better conditions than members of their own citizenry. I wondered if Germany had been placing the Jews, who I knew had been relocated from das Vaterland, into camps of such squalor.

As we left I saw Corporal Nakamoto surrounded by a large group of camp denizens. He was in the clutches of a crying woman I took to be his mother. It was later that I asked the lieutenant how a boy whose family was being held in confinement could be forced, expected, or even permitted to serve in the military. He first of all informed me that these people were not being confined. They were only being isolated from the general population for their own protection from people who may do them harm simply because they were Japanese. When I asked if Germans were being interned in the same manner, he seemed confused. "Why, of course not," he replied, "unless they were not American citizens." I chose not to pursue this dichotomy. As to Corporal Nakamoto, it seems that many young Japanese chose to volunteer to serve. In fact, their regiment had been instrumental in many battles in Europe. I remember thinking to myself, "I sort of doubt if there had ever been a Jewish regiment in the Wehrmacht."

It was shortly after that that word came for us to pack up and be prepared to move. The rumor was that we were going home. November

230

1946, two years after my capture, we were loaded onto trucks one more time and taken back to Ogden where we boarded a train full of German POWs from all over the west. I did not get to say much to Sergeant Atwill nor Sergeant Sermons in the way of good-byes. That was not because we were enemies, but because that is the way of soldiers; one day you are together and the next day you go your own way.

I found myself once again on a train, this time headed east toward home. The trip left far less of an impression on me than the trip west had. Naturally, I had gotten more used to the wide open landscapes in America, but also I was more concerned about my personal thoughts about home than I was about the country I was passing through. The route was different from my western odyssey; we stayed further north, right through the heartland of America. Though I was not glued to the window I could not help but notice mile after mile of farmland we crossed, and the size and obvious productivity of the large cities we went through in the eastern portion of the journey. No matter what the status of the war upon the entrance of America to the fray, Germany had neither the food nor the material to stem the tide of such wealth.

232

Section IV
ENGLAND

CHAPTER ONE

RETURN TO ENGLAND

If I were to make a recommendation to you based on my experience in sea travel, I must without a doubt suggest that you only travel west to east when crossing the Atlantic. Whereas my first shipboard experience was filled with discomfort and onboard and offboard hazards, the trip back to Europe was a rather nice experience. We were loaded aboard the USS Fremont on the very same day that our train arrived in New York City. On that morning we had been unloaded directly onto buses at a large train station and taken through the streets of the city to the docks. New York was a bit of a shock to me. I had expected a city of great architecture and wealth but saw, for the most part, row after row of very poor rundown housing. The only sign of wealth was the very large number of autos. I wondered how any people so poor as the housing seemed to indicate could afford to own autos. We Germans were also impressed with the segregation of the population. Each new neighborhood seemed to be filled with people of different races or nationalities. One could see this not only from the look of the people themselves, but also from the signs on the many small shops.

Once at the dock we were herded into a large warehouse where we sat on our possessions and awaited further processing. Nothing took place all day. In fact, they did not even feed us a midday meal. That was not too disturbing because it seemed everyone had stashed away some food either at their home camps or from the stores offered for sale aboard the train. In the early afternoon at least one more trainload of POWs arrived. Somewhere around 1600 hours they started to form us in lines. We then were filed by tables manned by clerks for processing. Once we were checked out by the clerks and given a very cursory exam by a team of doctors (or at least people in white coats acting as if they were doctors), we boarded the ship. As I reached the top of the entrance ramp I was recognized as an officer and directed to a cabin just below the deck. The cabin already had our bedding and some clean towels and linen stacked on the bunks. The accommodations were much the same as those in the officers' quarters of the USS Buccaneer.

234

Later that evening a box for each of us was delivered to the cabin. It contained two sandwiches, an apple, and a candy bar. I found myself in the company of some officers who had spent their incarceration at small camps in California. They were all tanned and seemingly none the worse for wear from their time in captivity.

After a night secured to quarters we felt the ship begin to cast off. After only about an hour a guard came by and escorted us to breakfast and then onto deck. We got there just in time to see the famous Statue of Liberty fading into the distance. We were allowed on deck until the enlisted POWs began to crowd the deck for their morning fresh air time, a routine that was to take place the entire trip. Thus started a week of uneventful, very regimented sea travel. The trip could not be called boring because of the high level of excitement and anticipation that boiled deep within each of us. What was missing was talk about what we expected to find when we returned to our homes, an event we all expected to happen very soon. We all exchanged war stories and stories about our experiences in the camps, but no one seemed to want to let the others know about their personal fears concerning what the future might hold for them, or the fate of our loved ones.

As to my arrival in England I think I will leave that part of my story for you to learn from someone else. I have a surprise for you. Can you come down to the Gasthaus at the Strand beach next week?

235

CHAPTER TWO

AN OLD FRIEND

After a week of anticipation, as soon as I got off duty on Saturday afternoon I anxiously headed down to the campground on the Rhine River where Erich had a summer place. There I found Erich and his wife entertaining an old friend. I was introduced to his friend, a small man, though stoutly built, of a very mild and rather gentle manner. I was quite thrilled and surprised to find this man to be none other than Erich's former first sergeant, Oberfeldwebel Otto Schmidt. Otto was certainly different than I had pictured him from Erich's story up to that point. I had imagined him to be a man of large stature and a rather boisterous manner. To my further surprise I learned that Otto was now living in the United States. After a night of many beers and listening to the talk of old friends (mostly in German so that I was lost most of the time), I was able, during the next morning, to spend a few hours with Otto alone as Erich and his wife had another commitment. The story in this chapter is his.

I guess Erich has related to you our times in Africa; though I am sure he painted himself as a hero. As you and I know it is the noncoms in an army that make it run, but I must say for an officer he was all right. Well anyway, I guess you know how I ended up in the United Kingdom.

My first POW camp in that foggy damp country was in a small camp in Edinburgh, Scotland. It was known simply as Camp 193. I don't remember a lot about it because I was in a tremendous state of pain. They did give me lots of morphine, but naturally when doped up on it I didn't really know what was happening either. I am really not sure how long I laid around in that state. My shoulder was numb, but the area around it was a mass of shooting pain. I must have been there about a week, or perhaps two, when a German army doctor came around checking us out. When he reached me he stripped off my bandages. As soon as he did so he stepped back and made a gagging sound. He yelled for the orderly on duty. "How long has this man been lying here?" he demanded. "Why hasn't anyone changed this dressing? Couldn't you at least smell it? My God! Get him up

236

to the hospital immediately!"

Thus I found myself once again in a clean bed in an honest-to-goodness hospital ward located in Edinburgh Castle. Luck was with me. The doctor who found me was also a POW, but more important he was a well-known orthopedic surgeon from Berlin. After three operations over a period of the next year he was able to save my shoulder and, as you can see, give me back some use of the arm. During my time at the castle I remained a patient and was not assigned any duties. The interesting thing was that I was again in a mixed ward. There were German, British, and American soldiers side by side in the beds. All were being treated by the German doctor. There was little animosity shown by either side. If some bitterness did emerge that individual was quickly moved to what I assumed were segregated wards.

Most of the patients were British or Americans. They, especially the Americans, treated me very well. I think I sort of became a mascot to them. They all made it a point to try to teach me English. The Americans were especially anxious to teach me their slang because it irritated the Limeys. I would get mad at times due to the condescending way they treated me, but I kept it to myself. I liked the run of the place and decided if I was going to be a prisoner of war, I might as well be a comfortable one. I knew that my actions were not what was expected of a good German soldier; I had been at war for nearly three years and fought hard, but I never really figured out why we were fighting in the first place. Anyway, I had carved out a good position for myself at the hospital and was getting excellent care for a wound I had thought would surely kill me. I was nearly able to stay at the hospital until the end the war. In early 1945 the doctor was sent back to the continent to help the many refugees and I was transferred to a larger camp near Southampton where I stayed only a short time.

After that I found myself in Camp 15 near Dursley small town southwest of Cardiff, in South Wales. The camps did not have names, only numbers. This was, I assume, so that we could not set up an escape through letters we were allowed to write to our families. The mail was delivered by the Red Cross.

Luck was again with me when the sergeant of the guard who escort-

237

ed my group to Camp 15 was also being transferred there. He got me assigned as a baker in the kitchens. I had done some baking at Southampton when they found out that I had been a baker before the war. The sergeant told the commander about my Streuselkuchen and I was soon the commandant's personal baker. I did not have to show up at the bakery every morning at 0200 hours like the rest of the bakers unless I had to make some Kuchen or Torten for a special occasion. It was during that time when I started to sneak out of the camp some afternoons and nights. I got to know the countryside fairly well, and even had a couple of pubs where I would drop in and pretend to be a Polish soldier. I soon learned that these men I had fought on the battlefield were not enemies; they were soldiers, just like me. I felt a strange camaraderie with them, even knowing that if we faced each other in battle again we would try just as hard to kill each other.

Excuse me, I have digressed from what I think you want to hear. In addition to my duty in the bakery, I served as an assistant to the camp sergeant major's batman. The sergeant major was a rather nice fellow, but liked to exercise his authority by yelling. In fact, we Germans referred to him by the nickname of Sergeant Major Wauwau. In English, I guess that would be Sergeant Major Bark Bark. One of the benefits of being his batman was that I used to get taken into town when he had business there. It was a bit demeaning in that he liked to show off to the local population that he had a POW servant. It was a bit like, "See, look how tough we British soldiers are. We have reduced the mighty German Army to the level of servitude." The upside is that I got to see the surrounding countryside which was of value to my extracurricular activities outside of the camp. One day Sergeant Major Wauwau took me with him to Cardiff. A boat load of POWs was arriving from the United States at the port. He was there to observe and supervise the detail that was going to pick the POWs assigned to Camp 15 and transport them back to the camp. Since I took every possibility to get out of the camp, even for a few hours, I was thrilled at the opportunity to go along.

We arrived at the docks with the convoy of lorries just as the ship was being secured to the dock and the gangways set into place. The plan was to take off the first one hundred prisoners and load them directly onto our lorries. None of the prisoners seemed to be assigned a number or a specific camp. Each camp was given a quota and that would be the only criteria for sorting and distributing. It was as if we were to pick up a specific number of boxes of freight.

As the first men began to file off the ship we were struck by the volume of their personal baggage. Every man was carrying at least one suitcase, box, or large bag in addition to the standard duffel bag. Some were even carrying musical instruments. They seemed to be all suntanned and some were even sporting sunglasses. I remember Sergeant Major Wauwau exclaiming in his loud voice, "What the bloody hell is goin' on? I thought we were retrieving a load of bloody Huns, not a blinkin' gaggle of tourists." As the men staggered down the gangway it was clear that they still had their sea legs and were having a tough time negotiating on dry land, especially under the weight of their loads. I stepped forward to help one small man who seemed to be having a particularly hard time, but was stopped by Sergeant Major Wauwau. "Let the bloody bastard carry his own crap. If this is not a bunch of shit. Me own family has almost nothing to eat and these bloody bastards are loaded down with more goods than a Chinese merchant."

I had long ago quit trying to find people I had served with among new prisoners. I was one of the few men in the camp who had served in Africa. Therefore, it took me a minute to recognize Erich. At first we just looked at each other then I said, "Nice of you to come and visit, Herr Hauptmann." At first he just stood there with his mouth open. Then he managed to sputter, "Is that really you Otto?" I could only laugh and assure him that my ghost would be much younger and more handsome. I was a bit shocked when he dropped his bags and gave me a hug. Our reunion was soon broken up by the sergeant major as he snickered, "I hate to break up this lovely reunion of you two sweethearts, but if you don't get your bloody Hun arses aboard that lorrie I'll be forced to break your bloody skulls."

That is how Erich and I were reunited. Needless to say I took care of him at the camp and he soon was assigned to a soft duty, like I had.

239

CHAPTER THREE

PRISONER LIFE IN ENGLAND

I just can't explain to you the shock and joy I experienced when I saw Otto standing on that dock. Many is the night when I had lain awake and pictured my last moments with him in Africa. I was plagued with guilt feelings at having left him there to die. Now I was hit with guilt feelings at finding that he was not mortally wounded, as I had surmised, and may have suffered less if I would have taken more time to dress and care for his wounds. However, the guilt feelings did not prevent my joy at finding him standing there with that silly grin on his face. I must say that that was the first time in my military career that I hugged another soldier. I don't remember anything about our transport to the camp other than Otto and I sat next to each other in the back of a lorrie and began the long process of catching each other up on what had transpired in the last years.

My adjustment to the camp was swift. I had changed camps so often that the novelty had long worn off. Otto was able to get me assigned to the kitchens where my English skills were put to work in the storeroom as the officer in charge of POW workers. After the relative freedom I had experienced in America, life in the stockroom was very boring. The only things that kept my sanity were the occasional supply runs I would get to accompany, and the extracurricular activities with Otto.

Normally, twice a week a supply run was made. These trips were to an American stockpile area near the docks and trips into a farmers market to buy fresh vegetables and meats. The canned and dried products from the Americans were for the prisoners and the fresh foods were for the guard staff. I enjoyed my visits with the Americans at the supply depot. They got a big kick out of the slang I and other POWs had picked up in America. The Brits would get mad at us because they could not always understand what we were saying to the Amis. One day I was speaking to a young soldier from Georgia. I said in my best imitation of the infamous Sergeant Jones, "Y'all ain't a goin' ta make us tote this har marterial clar ta that thar truck is ya, Sarg?"

"Shit, if yo' ain't the gol' brickenist Natzi I err done heard."

240

"Cain't hep it, Sarg; I done larnd from yo' southern crackers."

"I'll cracker yo' ass if'n y'all don't get a move on."

Such conversations would always end up in a laugh. We Germans would always look over to the Brits when we laughed and they would respond right on cue and step in with a mad tone and tell us "to quit talking that gibberish and get to work" (they no doubt thought we had been making jokes about them to the Americans). This naturally would piss off the Americans, to have their slang be called "gibberish," and a verbal fight would begin between the two allies. Sometimes, these altercations would go beyond words and a fist or two would be thrown. Such times really made our day.

At the farmers market we had to be careful. The locals were none too happy to have Germans among their midst. Sometimes I would slip away from the truck and go up to a stand that had several people in front of it and buy an apple before the seller realized I was a German. I would take a big bite of the apple and say, "dankeschoen." The seller would do a double take and start yelling curses. I would retreat back to the truck and all of my men would get a good laugh.

Our major break from the day-to-day boredom was provided by a way out of the camp Otto had discovered. Every evening when the night guards who lived in town would arrive they would tend to leave the gate they came into, which was right behind the back of the bakery, open for the day guards to leave. There would be about a fifteen-minute break before the guard exchange took place. During one of these breaks Otto had changed the chain that the lock was secured to with a chain with a link that could be twisted open. This allowed us to leave and reenter the camp at will. A flood-light was located near the gate but a pole in the yard behind the bakery that secured one end of the laundry line for the baker's towels and aprons had been placed strategically by the bakery crew so that it cast a shadow on the gate. When the line was full of laundry it also provided a trail of shadow as well as fluttering in any breeze, which tended to make the guards less vigilant of movement in that area. The guards would also walk the perimeter, but the night crew could not resist stopping in at the bakery for sweet cakes and tea. When they were inside, a blackout shade on the back window was

241

opened a bit to let a small sliver of light show, thus providing a signal to anyone outside the fence that the passage back in was clear. Most of the bakers occasionally took strolls in the surrounding woods just for their physical and mental health. A few like Otto and me, whose English was at least passable enough to be confused with an Eastern European patriot, would even venture into local villages.

Otto and I had several favorite pubs that we would wander into and have an ale or two. We would play the part of Polish patriots and were accepted by the locals. One of our favorite games was to engage the old veterans with talk about the war. It was amazing to me that Germany had not lost the war much sooner. To listen to the locals it was obvious that the English must have whipped us "Bosh" in every engagement. Why, even Dunkirk was looked on as a victory by the English. Otto and I would have a hard time to keep a straight face. Sometimes we were amused, but more often we would be seething inside. This was especially true when the discussion settled on the war in North Africa. The English seemed to have a mystical respect for Feldmarschal Rommel, but were absolutely convinced that General Montgomery was the greatest warrior of modern times. From the stories we heard "Sir Monty" had chased Rommel, the so-called Desert Fox, all over Africa. I don't think I ever heard one of those veterans even mention the Americans. In America, the stories were that the Americans bailed out the British. Once I asked an old pub patron if he didn't think that England would not have been able to win the war if it were not for the Russians. He almost turned purple as he choked and spewed out a mouthful of beer before he roared on about the "bloody red bastards" that were not an army, but rather nothing more than a rabble of peasants. "Why, if it wasn't for Monty taking the Western Front the bloody Huns would have squashed the bloody red blighters." I then brought up the idea that the Americans had saved the day for the Allies. I thought that Otto and I were going to be tossed out into the streets. The crowd became quite hostile toward us foreigners even thinking that the English needed any help. Luckily, a large man who was also a veteran stepped in and said, "Now let's be calm, mates. I had a chance to fight with members of the Free Polish Brigade and they were a damn good lot. 'Tis not the fault of these poor blighters that they might think the bloody colonials was the ones that won the war. Why let's face it, mates, the Yanks did help distract the bloody Huns long enough for Monty to slice through them." Another, much younger farmer type interjected, "Indeed, mates, 'tis a fact that the Yanks were a big help, but as was in the paper the other day, the only problem is that they are overpaid, oversexed, and over here." The crowd all laughed and I quickly bought a round of bitter and Otto and I were once more friends of the pub.

The only time that things really got ugly was when we went to a pub that sat on the edge of one of the market villages. I believe it was Tetbury. Otto and I were enjoying a quiet ale when we noticed that one of the locals was staring at me. He whispered something to his companions and they all began to stare at us. I was just about to tell Otto that we should get out of there when one of the young drinkers came over to the table and asked, "I know all of the men in this village, and you two ain't one of them. Where are you from?" I quickly gave him our story about being Polish soldiers. He then said, "Well I thought I had better ask since me friend over there seems to think he remembers you buying an apple from him at the market last week." I knew that we were in big trouble, but decided there was no harm in continuing the bluff.

I looked around at the man he was pointing to and said, "Excuse me for not recognizing you, but I probably was more worried about the fine apple you sold me."

The apple farmer stood up and said, "See, I told you he was there, but he was with a bloody bunch of Hun prisoners."

I tried to laugh and say, "Oh, now I remember; I was just playing a joke on you by saying dankeschoen to see your reaction. I am sorry if it was not so funny." This seemed satisfy the farmer and he sat back down. The young man glared at us for a moment then returned to his group.

Just as Otto and I were breathing a sigh of relief, a man who was sitting in the back of the pub came forward and spoke to us in Polish. Everyone in the place looked at us in anticipation. Otto, having served in the Polish campaign, luckily knew a few words of Polish and answered. The man smiled and said in rather good German, "That was clever, my friend, but you speak Polish with a strong Plattdeutsch accent." He then turned to the

243

others and said, "You know, fellows, I think we have a pair of bloody Germans here." Before he could say another word, Otto jumped up and shoved him into the nearest table full of drinkers and we both bolted for the door. We were well down the lane when the entire crowd emerged out of the pub in hot pursuit. We headed into the fields in the opposite direction of the camp. We soon were in a thicket and were able to lose our followers. We circled around and ran back to the camp. We finished out the night shift in the bakery and were in the shower room when a general assembly was called. We hid out in the showers. We were later told that a group of locals asked to look at all of the prisoners so that they could pick out the suspected escapees. When they did not see us they asked if that was the entire camp. They were informed that there were men on duty in the kitchens and they were escorted there. During this time we managed to get into the back of the formation in the yard. The locals, escorted by guards, came stomping out of the kitchens and walked right by the formation, but luckily did not look our way since they had already inspected the group. They were heard to say, "Well the blighters we saw last night at the pub probably are still loose in the countryside. You should notify your superiors." With that, they left. It was some time before Otto and I dared to wander out again.

Even when we did sneak out again we mostly stayed right in the area, just enjoying the woods and fields. It was on one such evening that we met Vera. I think it best to have Vera tell you the story. In fact she is going to join me next weekend; could you come on down and join us for dinner?

CHAPTER FOUR

VERA'S STORY

After the surprise of meeting Otto, I was anxious to hear another voice in this ongoing saga. Vera was a small Englishwoman who seemed to have a weight on her shoulders. She was hardly to be seen without a lit cigarette in her hand. She had a bit of a nervous twitch in her hand, which would increase when she reflected on the past. An almost instant bond developed between us. It was as if we had been friends for a long time. Because of this bond she confided in me more than if I had just been a stranger (as I truly was).

It seems strange now, but I was quite a vivacious person back then. It seems so long, long ago. When war was finally declared in '39 I was working in a shop selling shoes, or to be more specific, stacking shoe containers. One had to be with the shop at least a year before you were considered trained enough to actually help the customers with the proper fitting and assist with their selection. I was terribly bored. The social life around the village had nearly come to a total stop. All the men were either already off to training or could only think about when they could and would join. At first, no females were allowed in the military, but soon the powers that were in control of such things realized that many necessary jobs could be done by the fair sex. I was one of the first to answer the call. My life went from one of drudgery to one of excitement and patriotic fulfillment. I found myself working in an underground complex helping to chart incoming German bombers and the status of our opposing brave fighter squadrons. The hours were long, but they went by quickly as each of us, no matter if one was a high-ranking officer directing the forces, or a lowly soldier like myself moving the symbols on the map, were all so involved in the moment that we felt we were right in the sky with our brave men. On the few quiet days and nights there also was little sleep. Life had become too precious to waste on sleep. We danced and partied as if there were to be no tomorrow. My family had very mixed feelings about my service. In part, they were proud of their daughter for serving, especially my mother. However, they also felt that I was a bit too risqué.

245

My father would hint at the term "tart" in reference to my being a part of the free life of the military. Proper girls stayed home and knitted socks for the boys at the front. I didn't know many men who actually got into battle. I don't know a one who was killed; however, I dreamed at night of handsome pilots who would sweep me off my feet, but would later all perish under the guns of the bloody Huns.

When peace was declared my life suddenly changed. The England of defiant parties and the live-for-the-moment attitudes became the England in ruin and sorrow for those lost. There were many more men available to dance and flirt with as the troops came home, but they certainly didn't want to be seen with a woman who was wearing a uniform. My service work also suddenly changed. I no longer was in the center of a humming, exciting war room. I was in a large, drafty, poorly lit room full of desks and cigarette smoke, typing reports. I had reached the rank of lance corporal, but really had no leadership duties. We were women in uniform, but it was a stretch to call us soldiers. We certainly were not treated with the same respect as the men. We were just glorified secretaries. Slowly the ranks of the uniformed females dwindled and were replaced by men or by civilians. Once again life became boring.

In the midst of a particularly gloomy time I decided to take a holiday. I had a few weeks of leave built up so I headed home. The war changed a lot in England, but it sure hadn't made an impact on Nailsworth, my home village. It was the same boring dreary place that I had left. I just did not know what to do with myself. My outlook for the future was as foggy and dreary as the Welsh weather. I spent a lot of time just walking about the countryside and thinking about my future. It was on one of these walks that I met Eric.[13]

That evening it looked like it might rain, but that didn't stop me from going on my usual walk. After all, in England it almost always looks like it is going to rain. I did not have a destination. I just went where my feet took me. I had been home for over a month and knew I should go back, but really didn't want to. That morning I had received another letter from my commander. "Vera won't you please come back," he had pleaded. "We really need your experience to help with the peacetime transition." He never once wrote a threat, as he well could have. You see I was AWOL, absent without leave. I guess legally he could have had me hauled in. However, as I mentioned, the women in the army were not really looked on as soldiers. Several of my platoon had gone AWOL since the end of the war, but nothing was done to them, other than a discharge if they finally refused to come back. I just didn't know what to do. I knew that there was no real future for me in the army, but at least there I was on my own. I knew that the proper thing to do was take my shop job back and begin the age-old quest of finding a steady man to settle down with and have children. I just had too much independence and desire for adventure to relish the thought of spending my life as a proper English wife and mother. I proposed arguments on both sides to myself as I walked along smoking. Oh yes, I was a chain smoker even then! Naturally, I had started to smoke while in uniform. I was a soldier, after all. My walk had taken me into the woods and fields to the east of the village. I suddenly realized that it was about to rain.

At first I started to walk briskly back toward the village. However, as the first drops began to fall I decided to run across the meadow to a shepherd's hut that I knew stood there. I reached the rock-walled hut just as the sky turned threateningly dark and opened up to let down a torrent of rain. There was no door in the doorway, and there were no windows in the hut. Just before I ran into the hut a flash of lightning blinded me and all I could see was a dark interior. The rain was not coming through the door so I leaned against the sill and watched the lightning and the rain. I don't know how long I stood there before I lit a cigarette, but it probably was not too long; as I said, I was a chain smoker. I remember the draft made it difficult to light my cigarette so I turned my back to the open doorway and tried again As I struck the match I saw them. There sitting with their backs to the rear wall were two men. I don't think I yelled, but I certainly must have let out a gasp. I got control and finished lighting up. Naturally, the flare of the match blinded me again, so I could no longer see them. I did hear at least one of them get up. I calmly said, "Excuse me I was just dropping in to light up." I quickly turned and headed out the door. Just then a gust of wind blew the rain right in my face and brought me up short. A calm voice right behind me said, "Don't be foolish. You will drown out there. Come on back in and at least finish your cigarette." I don't know what possessed me to, but I did go back in. The two men backed up to the rear of the hut to give me space and I am sure to give me confidence that they meant no harm.

For some time we just remained silent. Finally, the younger one spoke.

"Sorry if we startled you. We were sitting out the storm when you came running in."

"Why didn't you say something?"

"We didn't want to scare you."

"Well, sorry about that. You really did give me a start."

"Again, I apologize. Are you from a nearby village?"

"Why yes, I am from Nailsworth. I take it you are not from around here."

"No," he laughed, "we are not from anywhere near here. We are, you might say, just visiting here."

"Well, then, if you are not from here you have an excuse for being out without proper rain gear. I am afraid that this is not unusual weather for this spot of God's domain. The big question is why the hell am I out and about without even a bloody slicker, or even an umbrella. It's not like I am a stranger to this soggy place, now is it? Why I . . . Oh, hell! Excuse me, I seem to be rattling on as if I were a schoolgirl. I am sorry. I, uh, well, I uh, damn it! I am sorry; I guess I am just nervous."

"That's quite all right. What are you nervous about?"

"Its not every day that a girl finds herself in a shed with two perfect strangers, but you're right; I shouldn't be. Why, I am sure you are perfectly nice fellows and besides, my brother was right behind me and should be here any moment."

"That we are, miss. Excuse me, would you happen to have a lighter or match? We both are out of them and standing here smelling your cigarette makes me want one."

"I am sorry. How rude of me. Yes, I do. Would you like to try one of mine?" I offered him my pack.

"No, thanks; I have my own." He stepped forward and pulled a pack out of his breast pocket. As he did so, I noticed they were American.

"Oh, thank God," I said. "You are Yanks, aren't you? Ha, I must admit I caught your accent and I am sorry to say that I thought you might be Germans. You can imagine the pickle I would be in if you had been."

He leaned over and lit his cigarette on the match I held for him. I turned around, leaned on the open door casing, and looked back out at the rain. I noticed him stepping up beside me and leaning on the other side. I heard his friend sit back down behind us.

"Does it rain much in the States?"

"I guess in parts of the Northwest and in the East, but New Mexico and Utah are really dry."

"That where you are from?"

"Yes, I came over from there about two months ago."

"Your friend too?"

"No; Otto has been here a lot longer."

"Otto? Now that is strange. You have an accent and you call your friend Otto. Are you trying to frighten me?"

"I would never do that, honest. Tell me, you were standing there and looking so concerned before we suddenly appeared. Are you in trouble or something?"

"No just having to work things out. You see, I am in the army and now that the war is over I just don't know if I should go back."

"I'll be—a soldier, huh? You been in long?"

"It seems like forever, but not really, just for the last five years. Have you been in long?"

"In?" he said this with a worried tone.

"In the military. You are in the military aren't you?"

"Yes, I guess we still are, but who knows what our status is now that the war is over."

"That is a silly answer, but you know that is just what I am trying to sort out. Am I still a soldier, or am I just a female worker in uniform? During the shooting we gals were definitely soldiers. We may not have been up on the front shooting Huns, as we really wanted to be, but we were doing important duty. Now I am not so sure. Where are you stationed? I didn't know there was a Yank camp near here?"

249

"I hope you will understand. We are from Camp 15."

"15?"

"That's right. It probably has another name, but we know it only as Camp 15." He pointed to the west and said, "The camp right over there."

"The POW camp? I didn't know they had Yank guards there?"

"They don't."

We stood there side by side, saying nothing. My heart was racing so fast that I thought I would either faint or have to run as fast as I could. Was he really telling me he was not a Yank, but a bloody damn German? Did he believe my story that my brother was right behind me?

Finally he broke the silence. "I know you must be terrified to find yourself in this small hut with two German, or, how did you say it, Hun, prisoners of war. However, I assure you we mean you no harm and will leave if you ask us to."

I was, as he said, suddenly very terrified. There I was, face to face with the enemy. I had always imagined how brave I would be at such a moment. I must admit that in lulls in the action in the flight control center, when there were sometimes hours of boredom, I had engaged in daydreams where I was at the front or on a spy mission. When confronting the enemy I would blast them away with my pistol. Sometimes I would dream that I was captured and would bravely defy my snarling, vicious German interrogators as I lit a cigarette and casually threw flippant comments at them. However, this was not a dream. This man standing beside me, and his silent partner right behind me, were real men. Not just men, they were the enemy! Being brave? I was not. In this, the first real moment of my meeting the enemy face to face, I stood frozen in place trying casually to smoke my cigarette, but found my hands shaking so much that I could hardly get my cigarette between my lips, and was in fear that I was about to pee my pants.

"Do you want us to leave?" he finally said, almost in a whisper.

"No, I guess that is not necessary. It is still raining very hard; and after all, if you are going to kill me you would do it no matter what I say."

"Kill you? Why in God's name would we do that?"

"I didn't know Nazis believed in God. Besides, unless someone has been making things up for the last six or seven years, I do believe you and I are enemies at war."

"I had the understanding that the war was over. As for being enemies, I have come to the conclusion while being held in confinement for nearly three years that our countries were at war, so they were technically enemies, but does that mean that the two of us must consider each other as enemies for the rest of our lives? Perhaps you and I should talk about more pleasant things as we wait out this storm."

And such we did, not even noticing that the rain had stopped. I can't even recall what we talked about. I only know how strange I felt that I was able to talk about things to this man that I dared not talk about to others. The German soldier's friend joined in on some of the conversation, but it was clear that his English was not nearly as polished. It turned out that the younger soldier had been in England studying before the war and had been an English teacher in Potsdam, his home, before going off to war. We did not discuss the war, other than wondering what would happen to Europe now. Suddenly, I noticed that it was very late and the storm had ceased. I started for the door.

"Wait," he said. "I don't even know your name."

"Vera, and you?"

"Excuse me, the war has even seemed to spoil my manners. I am Erich." He held out his hand and we formally shook hands. "This is my friend and former sergeant, Otto." Otto also shook my hand.

"I am afraid I really must go."

"And not wait for your brother?" Erich said with a grin.

"Oh dear, I forgot him. He must have headed home thinking he had missed me," I managed to stammer, knowing that my ruse was not successful. I at last stepped out into the night. Eric quickly put his hand on my shoulder and stopped me. A wave of fear returned. Was this where the game ended and reality of them being Germans was to begin?

Instead of a garrote or a knife he only accosted me with kind words. "This has been quite a treat for us. Being prisoners we have missed the company of normal people. Would you please meet us here Thursday evening? We usually stroll around on Thursdays."

I really wanted to ask how, or why, they were able to walk around

251

free if they were prisoners, but then thought better of it. "I really don't know what my family's plans are, but perhaps I will try," I said as I began down the path, at first casually, but then in nearly a run. How could I have been so bold, or more correctly, so dumb? I looked back over my shoulder expecting them to be in pursuit. After all, if I told the authorities that I had been held in a shepherd's shack by two German POWs, I was sure they would be in very serious trouble. Though they were not to be seen I kept to a very fast place all the way home.

The next Thursday evening I did go for my regular evening walk. I certainly had no intentions to go back to the shepherd's shack. I did, however, find myself walking in that direction. I tried to delude myself into believing that I was only going to get within sight of the shack and try to see if Eric and Otto showed up. I was sure they would not, and that would definitely be the end of that. It was already growing dark when I reached the edge of the woods at the meadow where the shack was. I stayed in the trees and strained to see any sign of life at the shack. I could not detect any. I started to go across the meadow, but thought better of it and took the path that stayed in the woods. As I walked along I congratulated myself on at least having enough intelligence not to meet with German POWs again, even if they had seemed to be nice. I walked on toward the old stone quarry, again trying to decide what to do about the army. Suddenly I heard someone running down the path toward me. I could make out two men running as fast as they could. I then could hear someone blowing a military whistle further up the path. As the two men came closer they jumped over a stone wall along the side of the path. I was about to yell a warning since I knew the quarry to be on the other side of that wall. I was too late. I heard crashes and groans as the two men obviously tumbled down into the quarry. I started to run to the wall and see if they needed assistance when two more men ran down the path toward me. As they came up to me I could see that they were soldiers. Both were out of wind, but one was quite overweight and was wheezing like an old steam engine. They came to a halt before me and managed to catch their breath long enough to speak to me.

"What are you doing out here, ma'am?"

"I am just taking a stroll. Why, is something the matter?"

"Don't you know that there is a POW camp right up this path about a half mile?"

"Yes, I know that, but I am not planning on going that far."

"Well, ma'am, I suggest you turn right around and head back to the village. We think that there might be a couple of prisoners on the loose around here. You didn't happen to see anyone, did you?"

"No, not a soul," I lied (why I don't know). Are they dangerous?"

"Probably not, sometimes these guys will sneak out just to get some exercise or just to see if they could do it. However, it would still be advisable for you to head home, and in the future do not walk out this way in the dark. Do you want an escort?"

"I don't think that will be necessary, but thank you anyway. I will heed your warning and head right home. Do you think they are trying to get back to Germany?

"No, I doubt it. Since the war is over they are not too anxious to get back. If they were actually escaping rather than just out for a lark they would more than likely be intending to hide out in England rather than go back to Germany."

"Why wouldn't they want to go back to their homeland?"

"Strange thing is, ma'am, that most of these fellows are pretty decent men. They are not all Nazis. In fact, many of them seem to be a bit ashamed of the fact that the Germans fell for Hitler's lies. However, I would not take chances, ma'am."

I bid them good night and headed home. They headed back up the path toward their camp.

As I made the turn toward the village when I reached the meadow, I thought I heard someone behind me. I didn't look back. I just started walking as fast as I could. I could not hear anyone following me, but the further I went the more spooked I became, and the faster I went. By the time I reached the village I was at a full run. I slowed to a walk as I reached my parents' lane so as to catch my breath before I got to the cottage. As I neared the house I heard a voice call, "Vera, Vera, please wait a moment." I stopped and looked back to see Eric running up the lane. He had a decidedly bad limp.

"I am sorry we were a bit late getting to the shack," he said. "We were a bit detained. You might say we took a wrong turn. Did you wait long?"

"Well, no; in fact, I didn't stay at the shack at all. I saw that you weren't there and so I just continued my stroll."

"Didn't you think we would show up?"

"I don't know what I thought. I don't even know why I went there."

"Yes, I understand. It must be strange to meet former enemies under these circumstances, but please remember I only want to be friends."

"I didn't notice you to be limping before. Did you hurt yourself during the week?"

"I am afraid I did take a bad tumble this evening in the dark, but I am all right."

"You had better come into the house so I can see under the lights how badly you are hurt. Just don't let my parents know that you are a German. If they find out they would have a cow and I am sure they would turn you in."

As he came into the house I could see that his shirt was ripped and he had mud all over his clothes. He also had blood running down his forehead. In addition he had a bad bruise on his cheek. I took him right into the kitchen and sat him on a stool. My parents came in to see what was happening and my mother naturally ran for some sanitary wraps and salve. I explained to them that Eric was a friend of mine, and he had had an accident on his motorcycle. Eric stood up and shook their hands and mumbled with his hand on his cheek as if he were in a bit of pain. His ruse worked and they did not notice his accent. My father muttered about how stupid it was to ride those damn noisy machines, and went back to his wireless and newspaper. My mother started to play nurse to Eric. I stopped her and took her aside and whispered, "Mum, let me do it. Why don't you go in with Daddy?" I even winked at her. She naturally thought that I wanted to be alone with this new young man to "kiss" and soothe his wounds. Her desire to get me a local boyfriend was stronger than her mother's instinct and she went into the sitting room with my father and shut the door.

254

Eric was not seriously injured, but seemed quite embarrassed when I let it slip that I had witnessed how he had hurt himself. He told me that Otto was all right; however, his shoulder was hurting him too much to continue and he was going to try to sneak back into the camp. As I was dressing the wound on his forehead I found myself with my face inches away from his. We both just froze and gazed into each other's eyes. His were light brown with flecks of gold. I suddenly felt my face flush and diverted my eyes back up to the wound. I quickly finished cleaning it and putting some salve on it. I put my hand on the side of his chin and gently pushed his face over so I could look at the bruise. I swear I felt a surge of energy go through my fingers and up my arm. (I hope you don't think I am being too sappy. It is just that I wanted you to know how I was feeling.) Well anyway, as he looked away I tenderly touched the bruise.

"Does that really hurt?

"Not really, in fact your touch really feels good."

"Quit being silly," I said trying to be stern when actually I was pleased with his comment. "Do you think you could have broken a cheekbone?"

"I don't think so. Perhaps if you rub or touch it again I can concentrate more and tell you."

I touched his cheek again. This time I watched his face. He winced at little, but not as if I had really hurt him; in fact, I am sure he enjoyed it. I continued my touch and studied his profile. This was the first real look at him since our first encounter had been in the dark. He was quite handsome. His dark brown hair was rather long and combed straight back on his head. His face was nicely tanned and his jaw had a rather square, rugged, manly cut. I found myself again flushing and feeling very warm. I quickly turned around and busied myself at the sink washing the pan out that I had used as a wash basin to clean his face. "Thank you," he said, "we could have used you at the front." The irony of that statement caused me to gasp a bit. "Oh dear, that was a stupid thing to say," he quickly said in a near whisper. "I suppose had we met at the front it would not have been on such a friendly basis. Please forgive me. It is just that I can't imagine that we could be enemies now or even in the past, and I sincerely hope you will let the past

255

be the past."

I turned around and faced him and said, "It certainly is awkward, isn't it. But let's not discuss it now; after all I let you in just to fix your wounds."

"Yes, of course. Well, I uh, I uh, guess I should leave."

"Will you be in much trouble?"

"No, at least not unless they catch me."

"Now how do you suppose they will miss the mess you have made of your face?"

He touched his bruised cheek. "Oh this. Why, I fell in the bath you know."

"Not a bad comeback, but you sure must have a dirty bath with all of that mud on your clothes. By the way, why were you in the bath in your clothes in the first place? Are you bashful?"

We both started to laugh.

"Seriously, I should go; I just wanted to see you again to see if I was only dreaming that I had met such a beautiful, charming lass in the meadow. Just like in a fairy tale."

"If all Germans are as big of rakes as you are, indeed no Fraulein would be safe. But, I can't let you go back to the camp looking like that. The guards would know it was you who was out and about tonight when they see those muddy clothes. Skin out of them and I will get Daddy's robe for you to wear as I tidy them up.

"No, really, I will be all right. I should get back."

"Don't argue; remember who lost the war and who is the prisoner. Do as I say," I ordered with a grin as I left the room to get the robe.

As I walked through the sitting room carrying my father's robe he looked up from his paper and let out a "harump" of disgust and shook his head. Mum smiled at me and winked, obviously pleased with my "progress." Their reaction flustered me a bit and without thinking, I walked right into the kitchen to see Eric standing there in his skivvies. I could not help noticing what a fine figure of a man he was. Not wanting him to catch my embarrassment, nor my appreciation, I walked right up to him and handed him the robe and bent down to pick up his pants and shirt that were lying on the

256

floor. As I did, he said, "Now this is what I call a bit awkward." His comment caused me to look up. As I did I found myself looking directly into the gap in his white boxer shorts.

"Oh my God!" I blurted out as I quickly stood up and carried his clothes out of the kitchen toward the washroom.

As I again went through the sitting room my mother jumped up and took the clothes from me saying, "I will do that, dear, you just go back in there and make your young man a spot of tea."

When I went back into the kitchen Eric was still standing where I had left him, with a silly look on his face. He was obviously very self-conscious about standing around in front of a strange girl in a robe, to say nothing of being caught in his underwear. I tried to make him feel at ease.

"Please don't feel self-conscious; I have seen it before . . . um . . . I mean, I have seen men in their skivies before." If I would have turned off the overhead globe in the room at that moment, there would still have been enough light to read by from the red glow from my cheeks.

We looked at each other for a moment and then both broke out laughing. "Let me brew you a cup, I finally offered."

As the water heated, and then the tea steeped in the pot we sat there and made small talk about our childhoods and other subjects, everything but the war. My mother brought in his clean clothes and hung them behind the kitchen stove to dry. We must have talked more than an hour over our tea before the clothes were dry. I then got a needle and thread and repaired his clothes as we continued our talk. When they were finished I left the room so Eric could get dressed. He lingered on for another cup of tea. During this time we did tell each other some funny stories about our times in the service, but nothing controversial. At last, he bid his adieu and headed home. My father never said anything about him. However, my mother did try to pump some information out of me, but I kept quiet as if I were teasing her. She did ask me about his "strange" uniform. I just assured her that the forces had a large variety of duty uniforms other than the dress uniforms she was used to seeing. She bought that; after all, I was a soldier; I should know. After that evening we continued to meet either at my place or, on occasion, his camp.

257

CHAPTER FIVE

A NEW WAY OF THINKING

That chance meeting with Vera caused me to do some rethinking. I had become comfortable with the fact that my opinion of the English, after my first visit to England as a student many years before, was wrong. I had been infatuated with their manners, ethnocentrism, and humor. However, during the course of the war I began to realize that evaluation of their character was incorrect. What I had thought was straightforward pride of nationality, and dry humor, I had later concluded was really arrogance and self-embellishment. These people of fine manners, even when born to poor circumstances, were the same people whose "refined" culture led them to the atrocities I witnessed in the desert. Now I was faced with another view through the actions and personage of a charming woman. Vera had displayed none of the negative traits I had come to associate with Englishmen. She was a brave, straightforward person who had looked me in the eye and remained calm when most females, or I should amend that by saying most people, would have been consumed with fear. She had also displayed a sharp wit and a charming sense of humor. The compassion she had shown in taking me into her house and cleaning and repairing my clothes was certainly not one of a cold-hearted person. I knew one thing, English soldier or not, I wanted to get to know her better.

Upon returning from my little "night out" after getting pampered by this delightful English girl, I found myself in more than a bit of hot water. At morning formation Otto and I were called to the sergeant major's office. Though I was an officer, POW or not, I would normally not be expected to come to attention for a sergeant major. However, there was something about old Sergeant Major Wauwau that caused a quick straightening and hardening of the spine. Therefore, when I walked into the office with Otto at my heel, I found myself marching smartly to the front of his desk and snapping to attention. Otto followed suit.

"You requested our presence, Sergeant Major?" I snapped out in top military form.

The sergeant major did not respond orally. Instead, he stood up stepped around his desk and slowly walked around us, inspecting us from head to toe. At last he spoke.

"Nice bruise, Captain. I suppose you slipped in the bath. Did you report to sick call with that cut on your forehead?"

"No, I didn't feel it necessary; it is not bad. Yes, the bath explanation will fit."

"Last night it seems that at least two of our 'guests' decided to cavort around the countryside. You wouldn't know anything about that, would you?"

"No, sergeant major, I haven't had any of my kitchen detail say anything to me about it."

The Sergeant Major stopped in front of Otto and looked him right in the eye. "It seems one of the men was a short, stocky fellow with what appeared to be a gimpy arm." He moved on to me, "And one fellow was a taller bloke, perhaps a pair such as you two. Isn't that a strange coincidence? Now you two innocent fellows stand here before me in nice fresh uniforms, something you damn Jerries are not known to do too often, and here on the innocent captain's uniform I find fresh repairs. WHAT KIND OF A BLINKING IDIOT DO YOU TAKE ME FOR?"

"I am not sure what you are talking about, Sergeant Major," I tried to say in a casual voice.

By this time the old sergeant's face had turned the florid red it was famed for when he was "having fun." "LET ME TELL YOU A BLOODY BIT OF INFO, YOU WORTHLESS PIECES OF NAZI SHIT! IF I EVER CATCH YOU OUTSIDE OF THIS GATE I WILL SEND YOUR ARSES BACK TO THE VATERLAND IN A BOX! Do I make myself perfectly clear?" He walked around to his chair and sat down. In a nice calm friendly voice, he said, "Otto, do you think I could get a plate of those spicy little cakes you make only for the colonel?"

"Yes, Sergeant Major; it would be my pleasure," Otto quickly responded, "and perhaps some ginger cookies?"

"How thoughtful of you, my dear fellow. As for you, Captain, being that you are a friend of my little pal here, I don't suppose that a nice cut of lamb might find its way to my wife from the camp's cooler?"

"Strange that you should ask, Sergeant Major. There seems to be a very nice rack of lamb that is not enough to be used for the camp menu and would otherwise go to waste."

Such was the politics of the camp. No different from any military camp in any army.

Though it was much more risky now that the sergeant major, and I assume all of his guard staff, was more aware that some of us occasionally left the camp unauthorized, I still managed to sneak out for visits with Vera. We sometimes met at the shepherd's shack, occasionally at a little pub in a village on the opposite side of the camp from her home village, and even sometimes at her home. Her bedroom was on the second story, but had a nice trellis next to the window that made my clandestine entrance to it not very difficult. I never stayed out with her all night, but sometimes I would have to run hard back to camp to beat the light of dawn. The more exciting rendezvous, especially for her I am sure, were at my camp.

Sometimes Vera would come to the back gate and we, Otto and I, would sneak her into the camp. She was lured into this exciting and perhaps foolish behavior by desire for a good meal. The general British population at the time was having a rough go of it. The normal table fare in most commoners' households was quite sparse. In the camp, on the other hand, being that we drew regular rations from the Americans, we had a rather full menu. With me being the controller of the kitchen supply room and Otto and his chief friend Karl providing their culinary skills, we could set a fine meal. I know the American saying, "The way to a man's heart is through his stomach." I can guarantee that the same holds true for females if they are forced to endure the skimpy diet of the English.

Vera's and my relationship began to take on more than a casual meeting of two former enemies who came together out of curiosity. We became comfortable enough with each other to begin to explore each other's values and dreams. Our values were surprisingly compatible. I say surprising because we both assumed that due to the fact that we had once been enemies, one would think that we would be on opposite sides of most issues. It seems the only issues we were actually at total odds with were the reason

Germany went to war, and the justification for it to do so. On issues as important to the war as our opinion of Germany's and England's allies and enemies—France, Russia, Italy, and America—we shared nearly the same opinions. Even on delicate matters such as our feelings toward the Jews we found ourselves shockingly in near agreement. Concerning the Jews, the information on the death camps was just coming out. Despite my doubts at that time that many of the atrocities being reported actually happened, I, like her, was appalled that hate could have caused such atrocities. Our closest bond, other than some strange chemistry that caused us to cling to each other like magnets, was our goals for the future.

We were both aware of the fact that our relationship was too bizarre to withstand the reality that I was a German POW and she was an English lass, to say nothing of her still being in the English army. For the most part we ignored this salient fact and just tried to enjoy the moment. Our trysting came off without many problems. All of this about came to a disastrous end one evening.

Otto and I were both going to meet with Vera at the Golden Arms, a small pub in a village southwest of the camp. Otto and I arrived early and were sitting in a dark back corner, enjoying a pint of bitters. Suddenly through the door came no other than Sergeant Major Wauwau. He had the homeliest, round-bodied little tart under his arm that one could imagine any man being seen with. From the way they both carried on it was obvious that they both were very drunk. Otto and I hunkered back in the shadows and were enjoying the spectacle. The sergeant major was too engrossed with his 'lovely' lady to notice us. All was well until Vera walked in. At first she didn't see us, but then she caught sight of me and waved as she yelled, "Eric, there you are! Are you two trying to hide from me?" Sergeant Major Wauwau may not have noticed us, but a pretty girl was another matter. When Vera hailed us, his eyes, and the rest of the patronage of the pub, looked to see who the lucky fellow was. We knew the game was up. Right on Vera's heels came the sergeant major, dragging his tart.

"Well, I'll be damned. Look what we got here, luv. I do think it is me friends from the camp."

Otto and I both jumped to our feet and said together in good

261

English soldier fashion, "Good evening, Sergeant Major."

"Could we be buying you a drink, Sergeant Major?" I quickly added.

"That ya may, laddie. I think I have a bit of a thirst. Lads, I want ya to meet my pretty friend, uh . . . uh, damn it, it is on the tip of me tongue . . ."

"Elisabeth," the beauty prompted him.

"Ah, yes, my dear friend Elizabeth. Lizzy, me luv, this is two of the blokes that works for me at the camp. The little bloke is Sergeant Schmidt. The one that makes the finest cakes a man could bite into, and the tall blighter here is, uh . . . uh, Otto's friend."

"'Otto's friend'. What a strange name," the drunk little tart giggled as we all shook hands.

"And aren't you going to introduce me to your friend?" the sergeant major said in a bit of a drunken slur, as he smiled at Vera.

As I introduced her, he gallantly (if a drunk can be gallant) bowed and kissed her hand.

"A bit of flair I picked up from the bloody Frogs," he whispered back to us as if Vera could not hear him.

We all sat down and toasted each other with round after round of ale. The more the sergeant major drank the more he leaned toward Vera and soon was almost in her lap. The round-bodied Elizabeth was getting madder and madder. At last she stood up, and with her nose in the air dramatically said, "Well, I can see that no one here appreciates a true lady." She affected a fine stage right exit, except for the fact that she stumbled down a small step and rolled arse over teakettle, coming to rest on her stomach with her dress up over her ample bottom. The sergeant major, ever the gentleman, jumped up to go to her rescue, but this knight in shining armor was also a bit into his cups and also tripped and fell, ending his less than graceful swan dive with his nose inches from Lizzy's exposed bloomers. The patrons of the pub were rolling in their mirth at the spectacle. The sergeant major tried to cover her bottom, but only ended up grabbing her fleshy cheek. To this indignity she shrieked, came to her knees, and tried to crawl away. Her drunken intended rescuer tried to stop her to explain, but didn't quite let go of his

262

hold on her bloomers and thus pulled them down exposing a blob of white flesh that would have caused Captain Ahab to yell in delight, "Thar she blows!" Elizabeth managed finally to get to her feet and head for the door trying to pull up her drawers. Out the door she staggered with old drunk Wauwau in apologetic pursuit.

Before he came back in, I whispered to Vera, "Please go along with what I say. If the sergeant major wants to, he can get us in a lot of trouble." The sergeant major came back in and sat down.

"Let's have a drink, lads, it seems that the lady had to go home. Now I think it be proper of me to ask what you lads are doin' outside of me camp."

"We were sent here to find you, Sergeant Major. You are wanted back at camp."

"Tis that so? And just what is it I am wanted for, if that would not be too much to ask?"

"Not at all, Sergeant Major, but first a toast." I held my glass high and looked to Vera. "To the beautiful women of England, even if they only have eyes for sergeant majors."

After a hearty gulp and a nod to Vera, the flattered old sergeant said, "To my question lad, what err I wanted for at me camp?"

"Oh yes, it seems that maybe some of the inmates have decided to have a walk outside of the camp."

"Indeed! Now I wonder what two sneaky blighters that may be?"

"Two? I only said 'some' of the unfortunate members of the defeated forces."

"Aye, that you did, but I am a bettin' on the number two, and thinks I may know the bloody bastards. Another toast," he loudly proclaimed as he raised his glass to Vera. "To you, my dear, and may I ask, be it true that you like sergeant majors?" He emptied his glass in one draught and loudly called for another round.

"Not exactly," answered Vera with a smile, "only certain sergeant majors—those with charm."

"If its charm ya like, luv, then ya have found the right sergeant major." He raised his glass in tribute to his fine retort to her flirt, and took another hearty swallow.

"Hadn't you best let us retrieve ya to the camp, Sergeant Major?"

"Can't you see I am busy, Captain? I have plenty of time to nail you two scoundrels' hides to the wall. Now, luv, where were we before we was so rudely interrupted by this son of Hitler's bitch dog."

"I do believe we were getting ready to, let us say, enjoy ourselves in a more private setting. But perhaps you, being so important to the camp, should go straighten out the problems the Captain here speaks of. In fact, I would love to go with you."

The old drunk tossed off his drink and offered his arm to Vera. "Then it is off we are, and you two lads had better come along before I am forced to call the guard."

We all headed out to his waiting Land Rover. With some effort we convinced him that Otto should drive. After he reluctantly agreed to this and, with more persuasion concerning his rank and position, he was talked into riding in the front passenger seat rather than in the back with Vera; the spot I ended up in. As planned, he fell asleep minutes after leaving the pub. We drove up to the gate and were passed through when the private on guard recognized the sergeant major and was humorously convinced that the old boy had taken us out of the camp on a detail and we had stopped by a pub. This did not surprise the guard, but he was a bit hesitant to let Vera pass. I convinced the private, with a wink, that Vera was the sergeant major's girlfriend and if she was not allowed to join him for the evening, the old man would be more than upset with the guard responsible for turning her away. We dumped the passed-out old sot in his quarters. Vera left an item of personal clothing, and she and I retired to my quarters for an evening of togetherness before she slunk out the back gate.

The next morning a smiling, seemingly no worse for wear, sergeant major came jauntily sauntering into the dining area for his morning tea and sweet bread. He called for Otto at his table.

"Otto, you sneaky little blighter, you know I should have you and your captain friend shot. However, being that I had such a lovely time," he winked at Otto, and after looking around to see that no one else was looking, took a flimsy piece of cloth from his pocket, sniffed it, and put it back. "I will let it go this time, but don't let me catch you again. Is that clear?"

CHAPTER SIX

LAST DAYS IN ENGLAND

Not long after our brush with the sergeant major, the word came out that they were closing our camp and we would be returning to Germany. Naturally I was thrilled, but there was one bit of remorse. I would have to say good-bye to Vera. What would I say? How would I say it? I wasn't even sure of my own feelings. How could I possibly relate them to her? I took the easy course of action: I procrastinated. Nearly two weeks went by before I slid out of camp one night to go to her house. I would have probably talked myself into waiting longer, but I knew that in one week I would be gone. Since there had been several requests by my fellow POW's to stay in England, and nearly all were being turned down, I knew that the closer to the depart day it got, the tighter the security would become.

As I approached Vera's cottage, I saw her standing on the stoop smoking a cigarette. When she saw me she dropped the cigarette and crushed it with her foot. She then turned and started to walk into the cottage.

"Please, Vera, we must talk." I knew she would be mad at me for not showing up for so long.

She stopped and turned toward me. "Are you sure you have the right house?"

"I know you are mad because I haven't been out lately, but I can explain. Will you walk with me?"

"All right, for a short time. Let me get my wrap."

When she came back out she was wearing her sweater. As we walked down the lane, she refused to look at me or even to hold my hand. We walked quite a ways before either of us said anything.

"Vera, I am sorry it has been so long. The security at camp has gotten rather tight and I think the sergeant major has been watching Otto and me very closely."

"I am not mad about you not coming. I am just mad, or perhaps frightened, at what you will say to me. I know that is why I haven't seen you

265

for awhile."

I stopped and put my hand on her arm to stop her. "I am not sure I understand what you are trying to tell me." I saw tears in her eyes.

"Please, Eric, let us not draw this out. Tell me; just what do you plan to do?"

"Do? Do what?"

"You know; now that the camp is closing, what are you going to do? Are you going to go home? Will I ever see you again?"

I turned her toward me and put both hands on her shoulders. At first she did not look at me. Then she slowly raised her eyes to meet mine.

"Liebchen, how did you hear of the camp closing?"

"Everyone in the village is talking about it."

"Well, yes, my dear, it is true. The camp will be closed in a week, and all of us will be sent back to Germany."

"Then . . . then it's true . . . You are leaving. Can't you stay?"

"Yes, I am leaving. I must go. There is no choice."

"But that's not true. I have heard that the butcher in Fairlawn's daughter is going to marry a prisoner and he will be staying."

"Yes, I know Heinz, and yes, her father came to the camp and made an appeal and it seems he is staying in England."

"Then I will come to the camp and tell them we are to be married and then you can stay."

"It is not that easy, Liebchen. In Heinz's case he obviously did more than cut meat when on work release. His intended is pregnant. Besides, his request came in even before we knew the time we may leave."

"Can't we try? You do love me, don't you?"

I took her into my arms and, after I gathered my thoughts (it was only at that moment that I myself knew what I must do) I said, "Please understand, Vera, I must go home. I have not heard from my family since before I was captured. I don't even know if they are alive. I don't know if they know I am alive. I have heard that things are very bad in Germany, especially in the East. Don't you understand? Even if there was a way to stay, which I believe there is not, I would have to go."

Her sobs increased, and she held me tighter. "Do at least tell me you love me, and that you will come back soon."

After her sobbing subsided, I put my arms back onto her shoulders, pushed her to arm's length, and looked into her eyes. "Vera, yes I do love you very much, but I can not make any promises at this time. I do know that I could not make a living in this country. I am a teacher, and I am sure that no English school will allow a German to be a teacher in their school for a long time, if ever. I will promise you that I will not forget you, and when I am settled enough to support us I will come back and ask you if you are ready to go to Germany with me." She started to speak, but I put my finger on her lips and whispered, "Please, love, don't say or promise anything now We are in the fast current of events and circumstances far beyond our control. When I come back, then you can decide. So many things can happen. For now, let us enjoy each other as if there were no tomorrows."

So ended our strange relationship. After a blissful night in each other's arms, I bade her good-bye and stumbled back to camp with tears streaming down my cheeks.

268

SECTION V
DAS VATERLAND

CHAPTER ONE

ON GERMAN SOIL

One would think that on that day, of all days, all of us would have been acting like a bunch of schoolboys on the last day of school. After all, we were going home. For some of us, such as myself, it would be the first time we would step on German soil in over five years. However, the general mood of the camp was rather somber. Of course, there were those who were joking and dancing around with smiles on their faces. They were mostly men who had not been in captivity for a long time. The majority of us went about the business of packing and preparing the camp for closure in a very serious manner. I can only speak for myself as to what was going through my mind.

I kept trying to remember what Potsdam had looked like when I had last been there in 1941, but only childhood moments would pop into my head. Scenes of Mutti setting a roast goose on the New Year's table right in front of Vati so he could cut it up and distribute it to the family, with my brothers and me poking each other under the table with excitement. Flashes of days at school with my friends. Marching out of town with the class group who had all joined the forces in one patriotic cluster. These were the mental images that were my personal treasures during these many years of conflict and captivity.

Other thoughts were also on my mind. What would I find when I finally arrived home? Had the town been bombed? Would our house still stand? And the most horrible questions would pop into my mind, as hard as I tried to suppress them. Who would still be alive? My father was not in good health when I last saw him. Mutti, I was sure, would be there right at the stove as always. Not even a war was tough enough to bring my mother down. My brothers were another matter. Helmuth, the oldest, had been on the Russian front the last I had known. My younger brother, Friedrich, was still in school when last seen, but was hoping to join the Luftwaffe as a flyer. The youngest of my brothers, Manfred, was only ten years old when I last saw him. I had faithfully written while a POW, but I had not received one letter back. This was not that unusual. Many of my fellow POWs had not heard from their families. The younger POWs (age was determined by how long one had been in the camps, not chronologically) had related stories to us of the destruction and disruption of normal life in das Vaterland, and of the many families who were now refugees as they were displaced, especially in the East. Therefore, despite the paucity of mail, we all held hope that our families had not received our mail, and therefore not written back.

Besides my fears and trepidation for my family and future, there was Vera. I wanted to go back and see her, but the guard was now strengthened to the point that made that impossible. There was no way I could even write to her. To my dismay, I realized that I did not even know her address. In addition to my inability to contact her, I was frustrated by the realization that I did not know what I would say to her if I were suddenly able to hold her in my arms. Had our relationship just been a passing fancy? Was she just a charming and alluring girl whom I had taken advantage of so that I could feel once more like a man? The dull ache I had in the pit of my stomach when I thought of her belied that possibility. In some moments I would have jumped the fences and run through gunfire to reach her, but in others I reminded myself that she was English, and I German, and no matter what we felt our future could not be together.

At last the day came. We filed onto lorries and were transported to Cardiff to board our last enemy ship, which would transport us to our beloved Vaterland. Strangely enough, I can not even tell you what nationality the ship was that took us to Bremerhaven. I only know that we sailed in the late afternoon and arrived in Bremerhaven late the next day. If some expected some sort of welcoming crowd, or ceremony, they were very disappointed. We filed down the gangway onto a quiet, fog-shrouded dock. The few buildings we could see were either burnt skeletons or were showing serious bombardment damage. There certainly was not a waiting crowd, nor banners, and no band. The dock was nearly deserted except for two Land Rovers with mounted machine guns, one on each side, and a scattering of armed guards forming a corridor to some waiting lorries. We were driven to the Bahnhof and put aboard freight cars with locked doors. We immediately headed south. I don't think one word was said for about an hour, when one POW spoke up, "Willkommen in Deutschland." That actually brought a laugh. My mind wandered back to my train ride from Texas to New Mexico. Was this the luxury train one could expect in the "new" Germany?

We traveled throughout the day, stopping only once. Our midday stop was on a sidetrack in a wooded area. There was an American army mess tent set up where we were fed a bowl of potato soup and a Spam sandwich. Our toilet needs were taken care of in the open woods. We had each been given a small packet of toilet paper. There were not many guards and I am sure that more than one POW slipped away. I do know that one of the soldiers on our car did not get back on. He was not one of the soldiers who had been in America, so had few possessions that he left behind. We did not know whether he escaped or had chosen to go aboard another car with friends. The evening meal was in a bahnhof, I believe in Hamburg-sued. The guard was rather tight in the bahnhof and so I doubt many, if any, men slipped away. We were making slow progress; the rail line seemed to be in disrepair. We passed many wrecked, burned out locomotives and rail cars that had been pushed off the track and were now lying there rusting.

After another night of travel with no breaks to relieve ourselves we arrived at our destination. There were enough gaps and holes in the walls for men to urinate through, with lots of rude comments from their comrades, but one end of the car had to be designated for defecating. Those who could not hold it went to that end despite the protests and complaints of those of us who had to smell their Ami Spamscheisse. We were very ready to get out of those stinking cars. We were unloaded in Heidesheim (yes, the same Heidesheim just up the river from here) and marched, with all our duffel, to a camp near there.

The camp at Uhlerborn was overcrowded and the men had to find shelter under some tarpaulins that had been strung up in the trees. I, as an officer, found an empty cot in a large tent. Our guards were French. There certainly was no love lost between the guards and the prisoners. There was no joking banter as there had been with the British and especially the American guards. The next morning we were all assigned to work sections. Every day each section was taken, under heavy guard, to various Kasernen in the area to repair war damage and clean up the facilities for housing of the occupying troops. A few details were assigned to help clean up the extensive damage in the city of Mainz am Rhein. These details were made up of men whose homes were in the East. I guess they felt that we would not be so likely to escape. I was in charge of one of those details.

CHAPTER TWO

A PRISONER IN ONE'S OWN LAND

After so long as a prisoner, one would think that I would have been adjusted to the role. However, being a prisoner in my own country was another matter. I began to become very bitter, especially under the French. Why were they holding us? We were not criminals. We were prisoners of war, and the war was over. We were told that we would be freed as soon as the new German government was organized to the point were they could process us out of the military. This was a handy way to blame our continued incarceration on our own people. In the meantime, we were a handy work force for the occupying forces. Despite the circumstances, I was not opposed to the work I was doing.

Mainz was a mess. For a city that had had the reputation of not being a war manufacturing city, it had taken a severe pounding by American bombers. The entire city center was a pile of rubble. The city had been bombed on three occasions; the last and most destructive was that of the night of April 1, 1945. On that occasion a large flight of American Bombers dropped phosphorous bombs on the city that resulted in the near total destruction of the city center. Over 2,000 citizens died in the resulting fires of that one night. Our job was to try to clean out the streets so that traffic could move through it to facilitate the cleanup and rebuilding of the few structures that were salvageable. At this task we commenced with all of our strength. Our details worked hand in hand with the surviving citizens, mostly women, children, and old men. There was a sense of pride in that we all felt that what we were doing was rebuilding Germany. Crumbled may our cities be, decimated were our ranks, but we Germans were not wiped from the face of the earth. We would rebuild. It may seem to you that in seeing the destruction and havoc brought on by American bombing I would have become very bitter toward the Americans. Such was not the case. I somehow did not associate the death and destruction around me with the Allies, the Americans, or for that matter the enemy. What I witnessed was simply the result of war. War was, by then, to me a fact of life, not a result of anyone's overt acts. During this time my anxiety for my own family increased with the days of seeing the destruction in Mainz. What would my own home be like?

After about a month or two, men from our camp began to be released, but none from the East. We were told that it was still difficult to transport us back to our homes. The French offered no explanation. We felt that they were keeping us as a cheap labor source to clean up their zone rather than let the Russians use us for the same purpose. Later I was to learn that the Western occupying forces had found out that the Russians were reincarcerating German soldiers who were being released in the West and sending them to camps in Siberia. In fact, many of these men either died in those camps or were finally returned to their homeland many years later, some as late as the mid-1950s.

Life was not easy in a POW camp run by the French. Not only did the French have difficulty providing necessary supplies; they also were, for the most part, carrying grudges and hate toward us Germans. If it were not for the supplies we got from the Americans, many more of our ranks would have died in those camps. I was in wonderful condition when I arrived in Uhlerborn, but was losing weight fast and deteriorating while there. However, despite our sparse living conditions, we were far better off than the average citizens. As meager as my rations were, I found myself hiding some of them and carrying them with me into Mainz to give to some of the poor wretched souls who were trying to survive in the rubble of the once prosperous city. One is taught as a youth that one's good deeds will be repaid. Such was the case for me.

While on a detail that was working in the remains of a Luftwaffe Kaserne that had occupied a hill southeast of the city Centrum (the facility is now occupied by the University of Mainz), I met an interesting man. Herr Doktor Wilhelm was a former professor of English. During the war he had worked as a translator of intelligence information at the Mainz Kaserne. He was a man of about fifty years old, but looked much older when I met him. He was prematurely gray and was nearly a skeleton. He had hidden his identity as a former intelligence worker from the French. This subterfuge had allowed him to avoid imprisonment, but had also left him in a desperate

275

condition. Since he knew no one in the area, and had no house or even remains of a house to shelter in, he was forced to live on the street with what few belongings he could salvage from the rubble. When I first met him I just considered him one of the many struggling masses. Then one morning as I was assisting him in moving a large stone it slipped and hit him a glancing blow on the shin. "Bloody bastard," he let slip in his muttering of pain. I answered in English.

"Maybe you are too old for this work; why don't you retire?"

"Up you ruddy red arse, sonny," he said with a grin.

We continued to work side by side for some time in silence. At last, I could not hold my curiosity any longer.

"A very nice King's English you speak; have you been there?"

"Perhaps, and how does a fine member of Goering's elite happen also to speak such clear English?"

"Thank you. It could help that I just came from a fine resort there where I stayed at the king's expense. Or it could be that I was, and again hope to be an English instructor."

"Indeed! Then I can tell you that I also am a member of that fine profession, and like you I will only find use for it in properly cursing stubborn stones."

From that humble beginning, Doktor Wilhelm and I became friends. I like to think that my meager offerings of food helped him to survive. I also was instrumental in finding him more substantial housing. One day when we were clearing a pile of rubble, I detected an opening to the remains of that building's cellar. Upon crawling into it I found it to be in remarkably stable condition. The furnace had not been entirely collapsed and the coal bin was half full. I showed the cellar to Doktor Wilhelm. Together we camouflaged the entrance and tidied up the interior. Over the next couple of days we were able to salvage an old army cot and several wooden boxes to serve as furniture. I was later to learn that the Doktor lived in that cellar for nearly a year until the University of Mainz was again functioning and he obtained faculty housing. That chance meeting was later to prove a critical moment in my life. Later when I finally fled out of the East, I came to this area, having no other place to go. I did not have to live in the streets as Doktor Wilhelm had, but was given a place to live in a refugee camp near Ingleheim. One day I went to Mainz to see if I could find a position teaching through the English department of the University of Mainz. Who should I find as the chair of the department—Professor Doktor Wilhelm! To my delight he recognized me instantly and came running around his desk and hugged me with tears in his eyes, a most atypical reaction for a German professor. Naturally, he found me a position in Mainz and thus I was repaid many fold for my small sacrifice of food.

During my stay in Mainz, I did not have a lot of contact with Otto. He was immediately put into a large bakery in Mainz Gonsenheim that was baking bread for distribution to the local citizenry and the many refugees. We did manage to get together now and then. I found him becoming more and more despondent. He had been offered a job by our old nemesis Sergeant Major Wauwau before leaving England. The sergeant major's family had a bakery in England where Otto could have gone if he had not chosen to come back to Germany. Seeing the destruction that the war had wrought on Germany and the poverty of the citizenry he definitely had second thoughts about having turned the sergeant major down. Our being held in the West was starting to bother all of us, but for Otto it was becoming too repressive of his desire to get home and see if he could salvage his life. Increasing numbers of soldiers were escaping and presumably returning to their home areas. Luckily, I talked Otto out of fleeing early because the soldiers who did leave were for the most part men the Russians were recapturing and sending to Siberia.

At last the day came and we were put on the Eisenbahn to be transported to a Lager at Bischofswerda, east of Dresden, where it was assumed we would be processed out of the military and allowed to go home. Upon arriving at Bischofswerda we found that freedom was not yet ours. We arrived in the middle of the night and were met by a strong contingent of Russian soldiers with many guard dogs. This was not totally a surprise because we had gotten our first taste of Russian occupation when we reached the demarcation line between the British zone and the Russian zone. The train was halted on an isolated spur track where we were detrained and formed into ranks. The Brits marched us down the tracks to a waiting contingent of Russians.

We witnessed a very terse ceremony of the changing of the guards to Russians. The English soldiers formed up and smartly marched back down the tracks to their own zone. Before the English had even started their brief parade, the Russians marched us to the east, and an awaiting line of freight cars, where we were hustled aboard amidst a hail of cursing and yelling.

Once in the camp at Bischofswerda we were not allowed to leave on work details. Our days were spent laying around in total boredom or in reeducation classes. It seemed we nasty Nazi dogs needed to see the error of our ways and learn about the glories of the new world and its adherence to the wonderful principles of the people's Socialism. Those of us who had been officers in elite types of units, Hitler's death troops as thry called us, were singled out and held up to the regular troops as criminals. Some of the higher ranking officers, Hauptmann and Major (there were no men of higher rank left in the camp) disappeared and were to my knowledge not seen again. I had long lost my last vestiges of uniform that showed my rank so they were never sure if I had been a Hauptmann or not. They knew I was an officer in the Luftwaffe Fallschirmspringer Korps and I let them believe that I was but an Oberleutnant, so I was not sent away.

Otto, not being an officer, was released much earlier than I. One day while I was sitting in the sun just waiting out the time, Otto came up to me and sat down. He did not say anything. I could see that something was bothering him.

"Otto, my old friend, you seem particularly depressed today. Don't worry, I am sure that we will be released soon and we will be on our way home."

"Yes, Erich, you are right today is a strange day for me, and you are also right about it being linked to our going home."

"Ha! See, your old commander still knows how to read your excuse for a brain."

"It will be a sad day in hell when an old Oberfeldwebel cannot outthink his officer, but this time I will not try, because this may be our last time to spar with words, my good friend."

"Last time? Have you word that they are going to shoot me?"

"No such luck; I doubt if even these ignorant swine would waste a bullet on you. No, I am here to say good-bye. I have just come from the bulletin board and have found my name. Tomorrow morning I am to be released."

"That is wonderful news, my friend but why are you so down about it?"

"Strange, isn't it? I have awaited this day for so long. Now it is here, and I am not jumping with joy, but shaking with fear. I am afraid to go home, Erich. What if there is no home when I get there, or perhaps it is so changed that all of the dreams I had for the future are no longer possible?"

"Yes, indeed, I know what you are talking about. I too am sitting here in the sun, wondering why I am so anxious to get home. Hell, I am not even sure if I really remember home. Perhaps I have built up some strange myth in my mind after all of these years."

"True. However, there is also another weight on my mind."

"And just what could that be, Otto."

"Tomorrow is a new day for me. Not just because the sun will come up anew, it is more. I have been a soldier for more than eight years, eight long years; some good, many bad, but all very, very real. As a soldier I have been someone, someone important to the welfare of others, a man of some power. Tomorrow I am nothing. I am a faceless man in a mass of defeated faceless people. For eight years I have shared jokes about the damn civilians and tomorrow I will be one. As a soldier I have had bonds of friendship far beyond what those who have not been to war could possibly know. Without being too sentimental, Erich, what I am trying to say is I think of you as more than a friend I happen to have shared some experiences with. Tomorrow we part ways, maybe forever, who knows." Otto quickly stood and offered his hand. I stood also and firmly grasped it. In the other hand he had a scrap of paper. "Here is where you may be able to find me if you ever get a chance."

"I will surely try and we will get together, you buy."
Otto spun quickly and walked away. Just as well because I did not want him to see the tears that had welled up into my eyes.

I didn't sit idle much longer. Shortly after Otto left, my classes got more intense. It started with a very intense interrogation. My first debriefing class was a rather calm experience. I was called into the class building and was met by a Russian officer. I did not know what his rank was because, having never served on the Russian front, I had never learned their rank insignia. He met me at the door, shook my hand, and waved me into the room.

"Well, Herr Oberleutnant, I hope you have gotten properly settled. I am afraid our accommodations are not very fine, but you must understand that we Russians had most of our national wealth destroyed by your army. Do you have any special problems I could take care of?"

"No thank you, sir; I understand that the war has been hard on everyone."

"Please have a cigarette." He offered me one from a silver case.

"Thank you, sir," I said as I took one and accepted a light from his lit cigarette. I almost gagged as I took the first draw. They were definitely not American cigarettes.

"I see you are not used to our Russian weeds," he stated as he noticed my reaction. "I see from your chart that you have been in America. They may be capitalist pigs but they do make good cigarettes; don't you agree."

"Yes, sir."

"How long were you there?"

"A bit over two years, sir."

"How unfortunate, did they treat you well?"

"Yes, sir."

"Please, Herr Oberleutnant, there is no need to be so formal. Please relax; I am not here to punish you. I am only trying to meet some of the men who are to become new citizens of the new Germany. What are your plans when you are processed out of the military?"

"I first plan to find my family, sir." I was still anything but relaxed. One does not relax when scared.

"Where do you think they may be?"

"Our home was in Potsdam, sir, but I have not heard from them since I became a prisoner."

"I am sure they will still be there. That is too bad that the Americans

280

were so cruel as to prevent you POWs from getting mail."

I knew this to be untrue because most of the prisoners had received mail. I thought it best not to argue the point, so I just shrugged and said, "No matter; now I should see them soon, shouldn't I?"

"Why, of course, we have no reason to hold you here long. However, you must understand that the proper processing must be done. And there is the case of security."

"Security, sir?"

"Yes. Unfortunately, we understand that the West" (I suddenly realized that Europe, if not the world, was now aligned in a new West/East configuration) "is trying to infiltrate our zone of occupation with capitalist sympathizers who are bent on creating havoc toward our peaceful process of rebuilding Germany. This we naturally must prevent. You do understand that, Oberleutnant, don't you?"

I failed to answer.

"I hope from your silence you are not one of those men. If it is found later that you are, I can assure you that it will be very bad for you. However, if you care to tell me such now, I will see that you are not harshly punished." He paused and looked directly at me and I at him. "Do you have anything to say to me?"

"No, sir, I do not understand the politics of the new world order, nor do I care to. I just want to get back to my family."

"I am sure you do," he said after another threatening silence. "I can guarantee that you will be out of here soon. First, though, I need a little assistance from you." He produced a pad of paper and a pen. "Just write me, in your own words, about the cruel way you were treated under the Americans and the English."

I stared down at the pad a moment, then said, "But, sir, I told you I was treated well."

"You are saying that you enjoyed your time as a prisoner?"

"No, sir, I am only saying that considering that I was a POW I was treated well."

"Perhaps you don't understand me, Oberleutnant. I stated that you should be released early if you choose to cooperate with us. If not, well . . ." He left off the sentence with a shrug. "Now perhaps you will try again. I will

281

leave you alone to write your statement of mistreatment."

He walked out of the room and closed the door. I could hear him talking to the guard. They both laughed.

I sat and stared at the writing pad. What did they want of me? Was I to make up stories, and if so, for what purpose? I knew that I should write something or I might be one of the men who were suddenly missing from the camp. At last I wrote:

> While being held in captivity in America I missed eating good
> German food, especially real bread. The American beer is also of
> poor quality.

I could think of nothing else to write.

Soon the Russian interrogator entered again. I realized that I still did not know his name. He picked up my pad, read it, and then asked, "I take it you meant to say that in America you were given very little to eat and drink, and what you did get was of despicable quality."

"Well, no sir; I just meant that I was not that fond of American-style food. We actually had plenty of food to eat and I am sure that it was quite nutritious."

The interrogator violently threw the pad on the ground, and began screaming, first in Russian and then in German. "You ignorant swine, you think you can make a fool of me! I am not so dumb as to not know what the conditions in America were. You obviously are a capitalist sympathizer. Why else would you try to hide the war crimes of the bourgeois Americans? I shall not waste any more time trying to be nice to such a swine as you. Guard, come and take this piece of shit back to his area."

Two big burly guards came in and grabbed me roughly out of the chair and half dragged and half threw me out of the room. They continued to poke and prod me all the way back to my hut.

I did not have any more contact with an interviewer for several days. At last I was called to the classroom area again. I was surprised to find that I had a different interrogator. He introduced himself as Herr Krupt. I was a bit taken aback that I would have a German interrogator. He asked me if I wanted to smoke, to which I nodded in the affirmative. We both just sat there a moment until I realized that I was to smoke my own cigarette. When

282

I brought out my pack (I still had Lucky Strikes) he reached for my pack and said "Do you mind?" He took one, handed the pack back and lit up. After he enjoyed his inhaled smoke and slowly blew it out, he began his interrogation.

"I must say I am a bit tired of the crap the Russians call cigarettes, but it is all that is available right now. Soon, of course, our own German manufacturers will be back in production." He paused to look at the contents of a folder (which I assumed to be a file on me). He occasionally grunted and shook his head. He slowly closed the folder and looked me in the eye.

"Kamerad, I see you had a bit of a misunderstanding with Major Stovanovich." At least I knew the name now. "You must understand a few things. I realize that you have been away for a long time. We appreciate the service you gave to das Vaterland, and understand the hardships you have endured as a POW. However, things have changed here; for the better, may I add. All of us, as probably you had, felt that the Third Reich was at last the instrument to move all of the German people into a new order that would allow us as a people to achieve the greatness that we all know is our rightful place in the world community. It is now clear that the path taken by the corrupt, evil group of self-serving murderers led by a madman has only left us Germans in total disarray and economic ruin. We have two choices left. We could follow the lead of America into a world where the rich control and the poor serve, or we could take the path leading to a world where the proletariat is in control of their own destiny and all work together for the equal good of all people. Yes, we all learned that communism was the worst evil in the world. However, one only needs to ask, 'Who was it that taught us that? Was in not the man whose immoral ways have left the German people shattered and shamed before the world?' I, Kamerad, have looked at this very closely and I assure you that what we learned about communism was wrong. We here in eastern Germany have realized our mistaken, evil past, and are working to form a new nation that will live by decent concepts and laws that make sure all people share in the prosperity and goodwill that will naturally evolve from such an enlightened movement."

"Furthermore, you must understand the role of the Soviet Union in

283

this new Germany. Yes, they are at the moment here in the capacity of an occupation force, but until we know that the last vestige of Nazi filth and hatred is exterminated for all time, it is good that they are willing to keep their occupational government and army in place. It should, therefore, be our duty as world citizens and proud Germans to help them in this endeavor. It is only by assisting them can we once again become a free, self-standing, prosperous nation. You do understand this, don't you?"

I nodded and tried to keep my expression from portraying any emotion one way or the other. He smiled and continued.

"I knew that if we talked, German patriot to German patriot, that you would understand. Now to the matter of the statement Kamerad Major Stovanovich has asked you to make. I understand your reluctance to sign anything, or write anything, that the government holding you as a prisoner may ask you to. Naturally, as a patriotic soldier you are hesitant to do anything that will bring dishonor to your people or yourself. However, that is not what our Kamerad has asked. He just wants you to help expose the capitalist swines to be the true heartless enemies of the German people that they are." He placed a writing pad and pen before me, asked for another Lucky Strike before turning to the window and saying: "It doesn't have to be long, just let our people know what terrible treatment you really had at the hands of the Americans and English."

I again found myself pen in hand wondering what I should do. I now knew what they wanted: for me to lie about my treatment in order to prove that the Americans and English still had hate and vindictiveness toward the Germans, their enemy. It would be an easy thing to do. Who would know, or even care, what I wrote? Then again, I would know. I would know that I would do anything, including lie, to prevent my own discomfort. I would also know that I, who had fought and killed men in battle because I truly believed that communism was evil was now being asked to be willing to address the world that I was a murderer. I would know that I may be in some part, no matter how small, responsible for keeping my own people from enjoying the prosperity that I witnessed in America. I carefully wrote:

I, as a member of the German military being held as a

284

prisoner, was occasionally mistreated by individuals put in charge of me. These incidences, however, did not seem to be the general policy of the governments that held me in the status as a prisoner of war.

In writing this I felt that I had successfully trod a neutral path.

Herr Krupt, upon noticing that I had finished strode over and picked up the pad. He read it, shook his head, then read it again. "Du Bloedmann!" he hissed. "I see that you are not the intelligent person I took you for. Well, so be it, Oberleutnant." He stormed out the door.

I heard him speak with the guard, but only briefly. I sat there tying to smoke a cigarette, but my hand was shaking so hard it was difficult. I knew what was coming. At last the door opened and I heard several men enter. Suddenly I felt a blow to my head and I fell, nearly unconscious, to the floor. I lay there in a state of dé jà vu. It was North Africa all over again. I half expected to hear a British voice cursing me; instead, it was a Russian. I received the anticipated kick in the ribs. Do all torturers go to the same school? On cue, I raised to my knees to receive the obligatory slap to my face; it came with stinging promptness. Again on cue my "bad guy" interrogator let me know that I should have cooperated with the "good guy". The screamer was not Major Stovanovich. I was hit from behind one more time and passed out. I found myself back in my hut. I remained there two days without any food or water. At last a German guard or prisoner, I know not which, came by and brought me some bread and sausage, and told me to go to the latrine and wash up because I had a class with Kamerad Stovanovich.

The major was short and to the point. "I have not much time to waste on enemies of the state," he said. "Tomorrow a load of such people is going for reeducation in the eastern USSR. If you would like to be on that train, fine. If not, I don't want to be nasty or demanding, but you must prove to me that you are not one of those enemies of the state." He shoved a pad and pen in front of me and then sat, lit a cigarette, and glared at me.

I knew that he was serious. The truth of the existence of the trains to Siberia was common knowledge in the camp. I thought about my family and started to write:

I, as a proud German, was treated very badly by the Western

285

Allies of the recent war. I understand that I had been wrong
in my support of the misguided Third Reich and its criminal
Nazi leadership. However, the powers and individuals who
held me in incarceration still should have been bound by the
rules of war to treat me in a respectful and civilized nature.

I pushed the pad over to Stovonovich.

He read it, then pushed the pad back to me. "Don't you think it proper, Kamerad, to mention something about your treatment under the Soviet army."

I added to my statement:
I appreciate the Soviet Occupational Government for
allowing me to see the error of my past thinking and
actions, and look forward to participating as a member
of the new Germany in building a nation dedicated to
living in peace and harmony with its generous neighbors
and benefactors.

I signed it, and again gave the pad to the stern-faced Russian.

He reread my statement, stood, and said, "I find this satisfactory, Kamerad, but I must tell you that, because of your early reluctance in cooperating, I am recommending that you receive some more classes instead of being released right away as was originally intended."

Over the next couple of weeks I spent a portion of each day attending classes about the glorious promise of socialism and the generosity and greatness of the Soviet people. Nearly every day I was given the opportunity to read my statement to the class, to which they always politely applauded. I watched as the classes grew smaller. At last it was my turn, and I was released.

CHAPTER THREE

THE LONG WALK HOME

You may remember that I told you that the officers were to be paid extra for our service once we were released from the military. Such was not the case. In fact we were released without any pay for services rendered. Those who questioned that oversight were laughed at and told to go find Hitler and ask him for missing pay. We were not even given a chit or money for transportation to our homes. We were just released onto the street with our few possessions. I had brought back some nice clothes and souvenirs from America, but I was released with only a small bag of clothing and a nice watch I had bought while in America. I was luckily wearing very nice clothing and even had an extra pair of boots in my seabag. I had also managed to horde away two cartons of American cigarettes. With one of those cartons I was able to eat and find lodging on my walk back to Potsdam. I had hoped to get rides on lorries from Bischofswerda to Potsdam, a distance of about 250 kilometers, but the only traffic I saw on the road were Soviet military vehicles. Naturally, I did not keep a journal of my journey home, but I will try to describe the trip in some detail because it will give you an idea of what things were like then.

On my first day out of camp (I was released in the morning right after breakfast) I decided to head west to Dresden. I was released with about twenty other men, none whom I really knew. Of the twenty, about ten of us were headed toward Dresden. It was a bright sunny morning and I felt so good about getting out of the Lager that I walked along at nearly a run. After only a kilometer there were only three of us together. The others either did not want to walk in a group, or were unable to keep up due to old wounds. For my part I just wanted to get as far away from Lager Bischofswerda as possible; before anyone changed their mind. I don't think the three of us even slowed down until we hit the village of Grosharthau, a distance of some five or six kilometers. Upon reaching the village I was quite heartened. After viewing Mainz I was afraid all of Germany was lying in a state of destruction. I had naturally seen towns intact on the rail trip to

287

Bischofswerda, but views seen through the slats of a freight car are somehow not real. Grosharthau seemed not to have been affected by the war. We all had pilfered some Broechen from the mess hall that morning, but had nothing to drink. Therefore, we decided to stop at a farmhouse at the edge of the village to ask for a glass of water. I knocked on the door. An old lady opened the door a crack, looked at me, and abruptly slammed the door in my face. I knocked again, with no response. The three of us looked at each other, shrugged, and headed on into town. We saw a lady hoeing in a garden, so we approached her. Upon seeing us she raised her hoe in a threatening manner, and began shouting.

"Go away, go away, we don't even have enough for ourselves."

"But lady," one of my companions said, "we don't want anything from your garden."

"I don't care what you want. We don't have it. Go away!"

Just then an old man came running around the corner of the house with a big pitchfork. He ran at us yelling, "You heard my Frau. Be gone with you. We have nothing to sell or trade." We three backed off quickly holding up our hands in defense.

The youngest of my two companions muttered, "Friendly place, isn't it? Perhaps we turned the wrong way and are in the Czech Republic."

We gave up approaching private homes. In the center of town we spotted a Gasthaus. "How about a Bier, my friends?" I proposed. They voiced their agreement, so we entered the dark confines of the small Gasthaus. No one was about, so I shouted, "Herr Ober bitte." Soon, the proprietor appeared. He looked at us very carefully. He obviously could tell we were strangers.

At last he said, "What do you want?"

"Is it too early to get a Bier?" I said.

"I don't know where you are from, but in Grossharthau it is never too early or too late for a Bier. Have you any money?"

"Well, no, that is our problem. Perhaps a trade?"

"That is everyone's problem nowadays; have you some silver or perhaps china?"

In a rather confused tone I echoed, "Silver? china?"

288

He laughed. "Oh, I understand. You three are mighty warriors just being released from Lager Bischhofswerda." We nodded. "Well, just what is it you do have to trade?"

"How about cigarettes."

"Ha ha, just what a man needs—a few of those foul weeds the Russians call cigarettes. Now, if you were to have some German cigarettes perhaps we could talk."

"How about American?"

His eyes opened wide. "Ami cigarettes you say? Why, I have not tried one, but I am told they are good."

"Then set up three Bier and I will give you three of the finest cigarettes you have smoked."

He thought a moment about this and turned around to his tap. He reached for a normal .5l glass, hesitated, then took a .25l glass and filled it, as well as two others. When he turned to set the glasses before us I already had four Lucky Strikes sitting on the bar. "One extra for being such a friendly man," I said as I raised my glass to my companions and to him. We all drank slowly and savored the fine brew. At last we were truly free.

When we brought out our meager portions of bread from our pockets the proprietor said, as he obviously enjoyed his smoke, "Perhaps I have some Wurst in the house."

"Enough to warrant the rest of my pack?" I said, as I laid the nearly full pack of cigarettes on the table.

He walked into the back and returned with a nice portion of Fleischwurst. I nodded and he set the meat on our table and took the cigarettes. I took a small bite of the Fleischwurst, chewed it slowly, and washed it down with a sip of Bier.

"Is this town always so unfriendly to strangers," the older of my companions asked, "or are they just against former soldiers?"

"No, my friend," the proprietor answered. "That is a result of war. You see, when Dresden was bombed what little food that was reaching the city no longer was available. Though thousands of people were killed and many fled, many had no place to go. Soon, to survive they began to swarm into the countryside in search of farm goods to bargain for."

"You say bargain for, wouldn't the farmers take their money?"

"You must have been away for a long time."

"About four years."

"No wonder. Let me tell you why. It is because we no longer have any currency that is worth anything. We have not had money that would buy much for nearly two years. First, there was the inflation. It got so bad that I remember racing to my friend's Baeckerei with a pocket full of Reichsmark that I had collected the night before from some passing soldiers, only to find that I only had enough to buy two loaves of bread. He only had ten loaves to sell that day. Naturally, I bought two loaves, knowing that that was all I would be able to get for the week. Normally, he would not sell me two loaves in one day, but as I say we are very good friends. As I left the Laden I found myself in the midst of my neighbors, who began to curse at me as I left with my valuable purchase under my arm. They cursed me for being so selfish not to share with them and for being so gluttonous as to buy two loaves. Well anyway, back to the trading. After the capitulation, Reichsmark were totally worthless. City people began to come out here to the country and trade their possessions for food. As the food has become even more scarce the value of the trading power of it has grown."

"That is very sad, but I have a question. If that is all true why did you trade such good Bier for three cigarettes and this Wurst for a few more? Are you a former soldier?"

"While it is true, my friends, that I am a former soldier (I was in the '14—'18 debacle), and I do have sympathies toward you, I must admit I trade only for other reasons. Cigarettes I can use; and these are good cigarettes, but china, silver, and nice clocks—I have a barn full of those now and none of them will feed my family or give me pleasure."

"Why didn't people we approached before coming to your fine establishment ask us what we had to trade?"

"Simple, they too have barns and attics full of traded goods, and besides that, they were sure you didn't come to trade. You see, the city people have pretty much run out of things to trade, even if we would deal with them, so they have begun to steal. A stranger in town now is most likely to be a thief. You are not thieves, are you?"

"No we are not thieves, at least, not yet. But maybe that is our fate for going away from our families to serve das Vaterland." I started to take another bite of my Wurst as I contemplated this frightening possibility. I caught myself, looked at it with a sigh, and put it with the small remaining piece of Broechen in my pocket. I drained the last drop of Bier and reached out my hand. "I thank you for your honesty and your hospitality."

"May your journey end in your family's arms," he said as he took each of our hands. "Where do you go from here?"

"We were heading for Dresden."

"I would avoid it if possible. It is not a sight you want to see, and it will be a hungry journey. Aufwiedersehen."

After we left the Gasthof, the older of my companions decided to take the advice of the proprietor and head directly north. The other two of us decided to press on to Dresden, which was only about twenty kilometers further. About halfway we came to a crossroads at a small Ort (villages). My friend was getting blisters, so he decided to stop. I continued on alone. Now, without companions to talk to, I found the walk more tedious. I was just thinking to myself that perhaps I could get a ride now that there was just myself. I heard a lorrie coming and stepped off the road, just as it was beside me I thought to myself, "How dumb, I should have tried to get a ride." I felt even dumber when I looked up as it sped by and I saw my friend waving at me from the back of a Russian army vehicle. I swore at myself and decided to wave the next one down. Naturally, none came by. About five kilometers further, in a grove of trees I found my friend alongside the road. He was sitting there nursing a broken nose and a host of other bruises. His generous Russians had stopped as if to relieve themselves in the woods and then jumped him, beat him up, and took his few belongings. I tried to help the poor man, but he claimed he was all right and that I should just go on without him. After that, I definitely tried to avoid any Russians.

Right before nightfall I reached Dresden. I decided to stay on the outskirts of the city for the night. I could see plenty of damage from street fighting, but nothing like the destruction of Mainz. Perhaps the Gasthaus proprietor in Grossharthau did not know what real destruction was. The next morning I found that he was very right. As I walked into the city, I

291

should say the remains of the city, I found a landscape of incomprehensible condition. It was as if a gang of super giant young boys had built a city of blocks and then tore it apart just to see things tumble. It did look the same as the very middle section of the bombed out Mainz, but on a much larger scale. I crawled over, and through, block after block of rubble in a daze. The city was strangely not without life. On almost every street I saw groups of ragged women and old men sifting through the rubble or trying to improve the condition of their former homes to the point where they could again inhabit them. I only stopped to talk to a few people. They were all very suspicious of strangers. I asked them where the young people were. "In the countryside," they answered, "looking for things to eat. We are to weak to cover the many kilometers it takes to find food." I did not stay in Dresden but worked my way along the Elbe on toward Meissen. I spent the night on the banks of the River Elbe, cold and hungry, having only had the bit of bread and Wurst the morning before. At Coswig, I turned north away from the river and headed for Grosenhain.

The road between Coswig and Grosenhain was full of refugees. There seemed to be lost people everywhere. They were not fleeing any place or anything. They were all looking for a place to live, or a scrap of food to eat. Those who did have food, having been successful in trading some of their possessions, avoided everyone they could. As you passed people, no one greeted each other or said a thing. This was very strange behavior for Germans. That afternoon it began to rain. It was a misty, cold spring rain. I was cold, wet, hungry, and miserable. In a grove of trees I saw a small group of refugees in a makeshift camp. They had several bonfires burning. I approached them to warm myself. Several young men in the camp stood and placed themselves between me and the fires.

"What do you want, stranger?"

"Just to warm myself and perhaps find a shelter to sleep in."

"Do you have any food?"

"No, I have not had anything to eat since yesterday morning."

"You will find nothing here. You should best move on."

I started to turn, then realizing just how cold I was, I turned back to them and said, "What has happened to my homeland when a cold man is turned away from a fire?"

The oldest of the men turned to the others and laughed, "Did I hear this fool right, brothers? Did he actually say, 'What has happened to Germany?'" He turned back to me and said, "Perhaps no one told you we had a war. Now, be gone with you before I get cold and irritable."

Just then an old lady stepped forward from the fire. "Johann, be still," she said to the young man. She looked at me and said, "Have you been away at the war, young man?"

"Yes, Gnaedige Frau, I have just been released from a prisoner of war camp. I have not seen my home since 1941."

"Is that where you are heading?"

"Yes, Gnaedige Frau, to Potsdam; I hope to find my family still there."

"Then come and warm yourself. Excuse my boys. They perhaps sometimes forget that Germans were once civil to others in need. You would not happen to have a small bit of food, would you?"

"Unfortunately not; I could find nothing in Dresden. I do, however, have a few cigarettes if your boys would like one."

That brought an instant response as the young men crowded to me to get a cigarette from my pack. They exclaimed that they had never smoked an American cigarette and so were quite excited about it. They started to ask me many questions about America. I was surprised to hear that they were not referring to Americans as enemies, but almost like they were old allies who would soon save them from the ruthless Russians. When I told them of the excess of food in America they all just made exclamations of ahs and oohs. To my delight, I was given a bowl of soup made from beets. It did cost me the rest of my pack of cigarettes, however. Before dark it quit raining so I moved on knowing that it may not be wise to sleep with men who may suspect that I had more cigarettes. By nightfall, I had reached Elsterwerda.

Early morning found me on the road to Liebenwerda and then on to Hersberg. By late afternoon I was very tired and very hungry. There was a chilly wind blowing with nothing to stop it in the low Heide (Heather) landscape I was walking through. Near Hersberg I found the remains of a small village that had been totally destroyed, evidently in a fierce firefight

293

between ground troops. I had just settled into the remains of a hay barn when a small convoy of Russian soldiers pulled up. They pitched tents, lit fires, and commenced to make dinner. The smell of ham and potatoes frying was nearly enough to make me come out of hiding and beg for food. However, I was not that desperate or foolish. After they all ate, out came the accordion and bottles of Schnapps. Soon they were all dancing and singing. About two hours after dark all became quiet. I could not detect any guards or men still awake. I could not hold out any longer. My old training came back and I low crawled into their camp. All of them seemed to be snoring in rhythm. I found my way to the lorrie I had seen them take food from. There, in the dim light of the dying fires, I was able to find a small ham, a loaf of black bread, and a couple bottles of beer. I was soon on my way down the road in the dark, making great haste to get away from the Russians before they awoke. I stopped several kilometers north of Herzberg and enjoyed a fine meal.

The next day was, as far as I can remember, uneventful. I did get a ride for a few kilometers on a farmer's wagon being pulled by an old ox. I did not ride long however, because it was just too slow. I was getting more and more anxious to get home. The next morning in a village north of Juterborg I was able to find a few wrinkled potatoes and a rutabaga in an old root cellar. I found a patch of brush near a small pond south of Trebbin and there, in an old pot I had picked up along the road, I made a wonderful stew with my remaining ham, the potatoes, and the rutabaga. Just as this fabulous meal was about ready to eat I looked up to see a man standing about three meters away looking at my fire and precious meal. I started to yell at him to go away, but then noticed how ragged he was and that he was using a crutch. I finally motioned him to come and sit by the fire. He did so without speaking, not taking his eyes off of the boiling pot.

"Have you come far, Kamerad?"

He nodded, then shook his head. "Excuse my rudeness, it has just been a while since I even smelled boiling meat."

I took note of his fine language. From his use of Hoch Deutsch I could tell that he had been raised in an educated family.

"Then when it is done would you join me for a small bite?"

"You are very kind. Are you sure you have enough to share with a wretch like me?"

"What is enough, I don't remember such a thing," I laughed. "We shall share the pot and pretend that we are totally satisfied. Would you like a cigarette now or after the meal?"

"Perhaps after would be more proper, with our fresh peaches and cream dessert, and perhaps a sip of fine cognac." We both laughed and shook hands.

"Have you been in the Wehrmacht?"

"Yes, I am just coming home from a prison camp in Poland. I was there since late '44, and you?"

I told him of my POW years and he shared some of his stories of war on the Eastern Front. We enjoyed our fine meal after it cooled enough to eat it with our fingers and drink the broth directly from the pot, having not even a spoon. In the morning we went our separate ways.

I had awakened very early and was on my way before dawn. I was in familiar territory and knew that by afternoon I would be home. I began to get more and more excited. Soon I was but a couple of kilometers from Potsdam. My heart was racing to the point that I forced myself to sit and smoke a cigarette. I had not had anything to eat since the shared meal of the night before, but I was far too excited to be hungry. Having gotten my racing emotions back in order I walked on into Potsdam.

I found a city that had obviously seen some heavy fighting, but it did not seem as if there had been a large-scale bombardment. My hopes grew that my family home may very well be unharmed. My parents actually lived in Bornstedt on the northern edge of Potsdam. I had to walk directly by the old Kaiserschloss, Sanssouci, so I diverted my path to look upon it. I came only close enough to see that it was a burned-out derelict. I did not investigate it more. I would just try to remember it in its glory. At last I came to my beloved village. I almost ran to my old neighborhood. However, before I could even see the house, I was stopped at a barbed-wire enclosure. There were Russian soldiers on the gate. As I approached, their rifles were brought to the ready and one of them yelled "HALT!" I froze in place until

295

one of the guards, obviously the sergeant in charge, he carried only a pistol, motioned me forward. He halted me several paces from himself and inquired, in very poor German, "What do you want?"

"I am trying to reach my father's house."

"I do not understand," he held out his hand as if to get something from me. "Papers?"

"I have no papers."

He pulled his pistol and yelled something to his guards. One guard locked and loaded his gun. (I was not so long out of war that the sound of that bolt slamming home didn't send chills up my spine.)

"Papers?" he again demanded.

I pulled out my identification booklet that I was given on leaving Bischofswerda, and the paper showing that I had been released from the military. He took them and carefully studied them. It took him a long time. It was as if he were memorizing them. He handed them back and demanded, "What do you want?"

"To see my parents. They only live right down the street in the house with brown shutters," I said, as I pointed down the street. He looked around to where I was pointing and shook his head.

"Nicht verstehen!" He waved back at the area behind him and said simply, "Raus!" He waved his pistol at me.

I knew that I would get nowhere but in trouble if I stayed there, so I left. I walked back through the village until I saw a butcher shop where I knew my mother used to buy her meat. The door was open. I went in to the Fleischerei and found the meat case bare; there were a few tins on the shelf.

"Hello, is anyone here?" I yelled.

A voice came from the back room, "Go away! We have no meat today."

I recognized the voice as that of Herr Gruber, the proprietor, and also a former classmate and very good friend of my mother. "Herr Gurber, bitte, it is I, Erich, son of Hildegard."

A head appeared around the corner. His hair was grayer and he was a bit thinner, but I recognized him. He looked at me closer and finally stepped out into the shop and with a big smile said, "Ach, Lieber Gott, it is

296

you." I was surprised when he came forward and hugged me. When he stepped back with his hands still on my upper arms I could see tears in his eyes. "How is your mother?" he asked.

"I have tried to get to the house but the Russians would not let me go there."

"Then she does not yet know?"

"Know what?"

"That you are alive, dear boy. We all thought you had perished in Africa. In fact, your mother received a letter from the Luftwaffe to that effect."

"That explains why I never heard from her. Do you know where she, Vati, and my brothers are now?"

"No, I am afraid not, Erich. I have not seen your mother and father since the Russians came and displaced all of the people in that neighborhood. It is now a large Russian army Kaserne. To my knowledge they did not deport them as I have heard they did in villages further east, but I don't know where they fled to. I am sorry."

I left Herr Gruber's in a bit of a daze. He had offered to let me stay the night, but I just wanted to start my search for my family. I decided to wander into town and perhaps go to the Standesamt, the city hall, to see if some records were kept as to where people may be located. When I got to the old building I saw a Russian flag flying and Russian guards at the door. I did not stop. I then decided to go to the police office. When I got there I was pleased to find it open, and that a German policeman was manning the desk. I noticed that he was not carrying a pistol. I went up too him and asked, "Are there still records of people living in the city?"

"Why do you ask?" he answered briskly.

"I have just returned from the war and am looking for my family."

"Have you papers?" he demanded.

"Excuse me, but I am here only to inquire about my parents."

"Have you papers, or not?"

"Yes, I have papers, but as I said I only want to inquire about my family."

A man in civilian clothes stepped up beside me, and with a strong

297

Russian accent, asked the policeman at the desk, "Is there anything wrong here?"

The policeman answered, "No, I think not, Herr Kommissar." Then he looked back to me and said, "Papers please?"

I shrugged and handed him my passbook and my release papers. The Russian looked over his shoulder, read the papers, and then stepped back. The policeman asked, "Are you planning to stay here in the Potsdam area?"

"I am not sure," I said. "It depends whether I find my family or not."

"Then you must register here. If you decide to go elsewhere you must come here and get a pass. Do you understand?"

Such procedure was the norm in Germany, even before the war, so I was not surprised. What was different was the presence of a foreigner, such as the Russian, overseeing the process. I filled out the form provided by the desk officer, handed it back, and started for the door. The Russian stopped me.

"One moment please, where do you plan to work?"

"I have not thought of work yet; first, I want to find my family."

"You can look for your family, but you must understand that in the new society there will be no one not working. What is it you plan to do?"

"I suppose I will look for a teaching job in my old school where I taught before the war."

"What is it you teach?"

"I am an instructor of English."

"English! Ha, that is good. Just where do you think you will teach English? Our children have no use for it in the new society. They must learn the language of your protectors, we Russians."

I wanted to question who the Russians were protecting us from, but decided not to, so I answered, "I can also teach German; will they have use for that in the new society?"

"You learn fast. You must be a brilliant university scholar. Just don't let your great mind get you in trouble, do you understand me? Now it will behoove you to know that your former school doesn't do the choosing as to

298

who works there. Such a concept led the old Germany to a closed system. We are in a new open society of the people; therefore, you shall report to the people's labor committee. They will place you in the best position for the people. You will find the hall on the square. Oh, and so that you don't feel that the new society will not take care of you, tonight go to the refugee shelter next to the Labor Hall and they will take care of you."

"But what of my family?"

"Yes, yes, of course, we will help," the German policeman answered. "Come back tomorrow and fill out an inquiry form, but don't expect much. There are thousands of displaced persons and we can only do so much."

I felt it best not to say anything other than, "Thank you," and left to go find the refugee shelter. There I was given a blanket and a straw sleeping mat. That evening I also was given some bean soup with chunks of good fat pork in it, and some dark bread.

The next morning I joined the other people at the shelter as they formed back in the food line, and shuffled up to get my handout. I was about as depressed as I could be. I had been years away from home; I was penniless; I could not locate my family; and it was now clear that I would be assigned to some menial job. Welcome home to defeated Germany. As I got my bread and hot coffee, not real coffee, it was made of roasted barley, I heard a familiar voice. "Well! I can't believe it. I think that is my brother. Erich, is that really you?" I looked up to see my younger brother, Friedrich. He seemed not even to have aged. He was the same ruggedly handsome youth. Soon we were at a table by ourselves.

"Erich, I just can't believe you are really here. You must know that Mutti and Vati got a notice that you had perished in Africa. I was at school when the notice came. I wanted to quit and join the military, but since you and Helmuth were already in, Mutti wanted me to wait until I was drafted."

"Please, Friedrich, tell me, are Mutti and Vati all right?"

His smiling face suddenly turned dark and somber. "Erich, Vati did not take the move from our house very well. I was in the Sudetenland when they were moved, but Mutti wrote to me nearly every day. Vati just was never the same. I am afraid he died last spring. Right after I got home."

We sat in silence for awhile, each staring at his own cup. At last I

299

asked, "And Mutti?"

"Yes! Yes! She is all right. She and Manfred live out on Uncle Rolf's farm." His face lightened back up. "You won't believe Manfred. He is as big as you and quite the hard worker. Uncle Rolf treats him just as a son and he loves the life of a farmer."

"Is Helmuth there also? He did make it through the war, did he not?"

"Yes, nothing could have killed old Helmuth. He came home several months ago. He is however, not in good health."

"Was he wounded?"

"Yes, I am afraid so, perhaps several times. He has an arm that is in poor condition, and he has a bad limp, but that does not slow him down. He seems to have had it rather rough in a prisoner camp in Russia, but he is the same tough old Helmuth. Except . . ."

"Except what, brother, is there something else wrong?"

"Well, I don't know how to explain this, Erich, but he is very unhappy. I think it has do with something he saw or did in the war, and then there is the matter of the new society."

"Ah, yes, the new society. Is that what you call this Russian occupation?"

Friedrich looked around and in almost a whisper said to me, "Erich, please do not be hasty in your judgement. Yes, we are under martial rule by the occupying forces, but there is more to it. I can tell you that they are working to help us build a new Germany, one that will function for the betterment of all people. Under Hitler, we were told that communism was evil, but now we know that Hitler was evil. I hope you will join me to develop our new Germany."

"Join you, Friedrich?"

"Yes, I have done well, I am now a well-respected member of the local committee."

I choose to believe my brother that perhaps a new start was exactly what Germany needed. There could be little doubt that Hitler and his Nazi party had led us in to near ruin. It was only later that I found out what a system based on communism really meant.

300

That very day Friedrich took me out into the country to see Mutti and Manfred. My mother must have held me tight for an hour as she tried to quit crying long enough to talk to me. Manfred was just as Friedrich had said, a man fully grown, and strong enough to whip us both. Friedrich also used his influence, which seemed to be considerable, to get me a position teaching Deutsch at one of the Potsdam schools. I moved into a small apartment in Potsdam with Friedrich.

It was several months until I was to see Helmuth. He was living in Brandenburg. There he worked for the Kreis (county) on road construction. Though Brandenburg is only 40 kilometers or so from Potsdam, travel passes were relatively hard to get. Helmuth was a small man; he took after my mother's side of the family. He was always a tough wiry man, a bit quick to temper, but a happy-go-lucky sort. He had been Friedrich's and my idol growing up. I had gotten bigger than Helmuth at a rather young age, but I never tried to challenge him physically. I knew damn well that he could whip me at any time he felt like doing so. The Helmuth I now saw was a small man in action, as well as in stature. His shoulders were stooped and his face was drawn and wrinkled. He was also prematurely gray. When we met I was expecting a fist to the shoulder and a hearty display of big brother dominance. Instead, I found myself being hugged and held tight while this near wreck of a man cried on my shoulder. At last he stepped back and said, "I am sorry, dear brother, but it is just that the word of your death, which I didn't get until I came home, was the final blow of this war for me. Now I find you home and more than that, looking so fit and strong, as if you have been away for a long vacation."

On our first few visits as a family, no one spoke much about the war. Friedrich was full of excitement and stories about the new German society. Helmuth and I were rather matter of fact about our work, neither of us very satisfied with it. Manfred spoke little. He would become a bit more lively and nod his head in agreement when Uncle Rolf talked of the farm, but otherwise would sit and listen to his older brothers talk. Mutti just scurried around and tried to make sure that her boys got what food was available and mended any rent or wear she saw in our clothes. It was several months before we three older brothers compared our experiences as soldiers.

301

I was the first to break the silence on the war. Manfred wanted to know about America. All of the family was spellbound as I told stories of the wealth and vastness of America. To my older brothers alone I spoke some of my time in France and in Africa. I did not get into some of the details I have told you. One would rather forget such horror and shame; however, I told of the good times and funny things that happened. For instance, my story about the flower girl was met with great laughter and returns of stories of their encounters with the opposite sex that were meant to top the one told before it.

Friedrich had been a paper shuffler in a headquarters unit. He did not have a lot of combat experience. His only combat time was actually the act of throwing down his weapon in a mass surrender as his unit was quickly overrun by the Russians near the end of the war. In the prison camp his administrative skills were put to work in the political commissar's office. There he had been enthralled with the concept of the new German society. When I had related my treatment in the camp at Bischofswerda he assured me that the only problem I had had was my stubborn adherence to the evil education and society which we had been subjected to in our childhood years.

Helmuth was very reluctant to talk about his time in Russia, and his treatment as a POW. He only told us, as a family, of some of the fun exploits he experienced. When he told of the Polakken girls, or his wild times in The old Czech Republic, he would become his old self and laugh at the "harumphs" and protests of Mutti. When Uncle Rolf or Friedrich would ask him about the times when he saw combat, he would just wink at me and say something like, "Oh yes, the Russians at Saint Petersburg, well, I jumped up from my foxhole and yelled, 'I have come from Uncle Adolf to shoot you bastards.' Most ran in terror back to the city, and others just laid down their arms and begged me not to harm them."

One evening, he and I were sitting in a local Kniepe having a Bier (the only product that seemed to be readily available), when he became very serious and told me about the Eastern Front.

"Erich, I cannot in this lifetime explain to you how horrible it was in the East. I was asked to do things and to endure things that I thought no

302

man could. I know that you in the Afrika Korps were brave soldiers, and stood strong against the English until the end. I was in such an army at first, especially in France, but when we went to Russia things changed. I must tell you this because someone needs to know. The truth is that at times we changed from being soldiers to being killers. The Russians were great fighters and they were a vicious enemy. That naturally led to a strong hate that grew in our guts as we saw so many of our companions die, but it can not excuse the wanton death and destruction we were ordered to rain down on the common citizenry. My company was once ordered to go into a village and kill every single person and try to blow up every building and dwelling—all because a sniper had killed an officer."

I interrupted Helmuth and told him of the torture of my Hauptmann and the resulting order for me to kill prisoners with a flamethrower. He but shook his head and said, "May God forgive us, brother, for I am sure the world will not."

He went on to tell me of his time in prison. How different it was from my internment in America. Just the fact that over half of his Kameraden, his entire company, or what was left of them after they had surrendered together, died in the prison camp was a great contrast to the treatment I received. Many died from the torture they were constantly subjected to, but perhaps more died of hunger and dysentery. Helmuth himself only weighed about 54 kilo (119 lbs.) when he was released. When my brother finished his story all I could think of doing was to order another Bier. When the Ober brought it, before I could raise it in a Prost to better times, my brother put his hand on my arm.

"There is more, Erich. There is more that I must tell you."

I lowered my Bier and asked, "What could be worse than what you have told me? It was war brother, and in war horrible things happen."

"What I am about to tell you is not the result of war. It is the result of our country's policy. Before I got to Russia on the second tour, I had been sent back to Goerlitz to heal from my wounds, I was coming back to Russia by hitching onto one convoy or transport train after another. The transportation links were a mess. On several occasions I passed trainloads of people crammed into animal-transport and third-class freight cars. These trains were very heavily guarded. I thought it strange to transport common prisoners by train when rail transport was in such a premium to get troops and supplies to the front. The rumor was that they were Jews being taken to work camps. On two occasions, I came by camps where large numbers of prisoners were held. Most seemed to be Jews, but I think many were Poles and other Eastern peoples. I saw with my own eyes stacks of bodies awaiting burial in mass graves. From the large area of disturbed ground and new mounds of earth I think the practice had been going on for some time. In one camp there stood large smokestacks and one could smell the odor of burning bodies. Believe me, brother, I smelled enough charred human flesh in battle not to mistake the odor. Yes, they were burning their prisoners. I don't have any proof of what I say, Erich, but I am sure that our government was not taking the Jews to work camps, nor the many Poles we sent to be relocated to new areas; they were deliberately exterminating them. Is this what we fought for and our friends died for, Erich?"

"Helmuth, I don't know from what you speak, but I do know that you and I, and our many living and fallen Kameraden, fought for a better Germany; perhaps we were wrong, but how were we to know?"

We three older brothers tended to treat Manfred with care; after all, he had been too young for military duty and really knew nothing of war. When we did talk of the war we kept it light so as not to disturb him. One day when I was in a terrible mood, my teaching position was a disappointing experience at best, Manfred interrupted my complaining.

"Brother Erich, can't you just take things as they are? The war is over and we lost, we must now adjust."

I blew up. "Adjust, you say? After all we lost? Perhaps you didn't lose much, little brother. You didn't see your friends die. You didn't even know there was a war other than perhaps you didn't have your belly full at times. Who the hell are you to tell me to adjust?"

Manfred, looking shocked at my tirade, started to say something, bit his lip, then got up quickly and left the table. My mother quietly got up, cleared his place, and started for the kitchen. She stopped in the doorway and turned back to me. "I know that war was not a good experience for you, son, but it gives you no reason to be so insensitive. Manfred may never have

304

worn a uniform, but I guarantee you that he experienced the horror of war far too close." She turned her back on me and walked into the kitchen. I looked to my uncle, but he just lit his pipe, popped open his newspaper, and commenced to read. I sat at the table for a few minutes and tried to make sense of what my mother had said. I got up, took my dirty plate to the kitchen, set it on the sink board, kissed my mother on the cheek, and went out to find Manfred.

I found my young brother cleaning out the milking stall. Uncle Rolf no longer had a milk cow, but did have an old ox they used for plowing. I picked up a fork and began to help Manfred. As we finished, I asked him, "Manfred I guess there are things I do not know. Would you please tell me about what things have been like here."

Manfred took the handles of the wheelbarrow and headed for the Mist pile. I followed along as he dumped the load of manure on the pile. He started to tell me his story. "As you said, war here was mostly one of waiting. We lived only to get letters from you three at the front. Vati, hardly talked, and Mutti tried to stay busy knitting and making things for the boys at the front. As you indicated I was hungry most of the time. I remember once I traded my pocketknife to a passing soldier for a whole loaf of bread. I brought it home as if I had found a treasure of gold. Mutti scolded me for giving away the pocketknife you had given me. I hope you are not mad, but I just want you to know that you were right. My main worry was keeping my belly full. I am sorry."

"It sounds like a fair trade to me. I have heard of people who got far less for far more."

"You are also right that I didn't really understand the horror of war until the end."

"What happened then, brother?"

"Right at the end most of my classmates were called up as members of the Volkssturm. I was sick with influenza and could not go. We were still in our old house and I remember them marching by singing a patriotic song as they left town to go to the north to help set up the defense of Berlin. I was ashamed to show myself in the village. I should have been with them. In less than a week the Russians were here. That is when they first kicked us out of

305

our house. We did get it back, but not for long. That is when we came here to Uncle Rolf's. Anyway, not long after the first Russians were here we heard that there was a terrible battle just about 10 kilometers from town. It was not long after we heard about that battle when it was rumored that Berlin had fallen. One day a convoy of Russian soldiers came around and picked up all the men and we older boys who were left and took us north. We came to the area of the big battle. There we were ordered to clean up the area. Everywhere there was burned out equipment and dead soldiers. The Russians had removed their dead soldiers, at least we did not find many. I was put on the burial detail. We would walk through the area until we found a body, or more often several. They were not hard to find since they had been lying there for over a couple of weeks and were very bloated and stinking. We would dig a big hole and drag all of the bodies close to it and dump them in. We would then fill dirt over them. At first I could not touch them. I would just back off and gag, but the Russians shot another boy who refused, so I soon learned to control myself enough to do it. Sometimes the bodies would be so badly damaged, or so decomposed, that a part like an arm would come off when you tried to drag the body. My friend and I made some long hooks and used them to drag the bodies. By the third day I was starting to get so numb to the horror that I dragged the men to their crude burial with no more feeling than if they were old pig carcasses. Then we came to an area were I recognized the bodies. That day I buried four of my classmates. I swear to you that I did not use the hook. Those we could, we picked up and carried to the holes. I have since taken their families to the graves and they moved them here to the cemetery. I understand that many of the bodies did not get moved and there is a monument there for them. I also found one Russian soldier. He was in a foxhole. He was just sitting there as if asleep. I knew him to be dead, of course, by the stench. I did not report his body because I would have been made to crawl in that hole and fetch him out. I just shoveled dirt over him. I have thought about telling the Russians where he is, but have been afraid they would punish me for not reporting him when I found him.

"I have no real idea what you three brothers as soldiers saw in war, but I hope it was not worse than I. Please forgive me for my comments to

306

you. You have every right to complain, but please remember we at home also know something of the horror of war."

I put my arm around Mandfred's shoulder and said, "Enough of this talk of war, let us go get a Bier."

After that I tried not to complain around my family so much, but I was becoming more and more upset with the new Germany. My brother Friedrich may have been right to work with the Russians to try to pick up the pieces, but from my perspective it was not toward a good end. As a teacher I was very regulated. In the classroom I was to teach a German free of the old classics. I also was not to have my students read anything written in the last ten or fifteen years. We were to teach nothing that would give our young students a false pride in being a German. I also got so little compensation that I don't know how I could have lived without the fact that my family had a farm, and my brother was a member of the local committee. It was because of this that I began to think of trying to get to the West.

During this time I was able to get in contact with two of my old Kameraden, Otto Schmidt and, to my delight, Juergen Beckmann. Otto had found work as a baker in his old hometown. From his letter I could tell that he was also in love. It seems that one of his childhood sweethearts was still unmarried and had made it her cause to see that the old wounded veteran was comforted and given proper hero status. Otto's wounds were still bothering him but he was unable to get further treatment. Otto, like I, seemed to be very skeptical about the new Germany. His letters were not specific on it; however, I could read between the lines of his disappointment and fears for the future. No doubt, he was hesitant to write his true feelings, as I also was to him. Past experience had made us aware that letters are not necessarily private, and serious consequences could result from foolishly expressed feelings. I had plans to visit Otto, but expenses and the difficulty of obtaining the necessary travel passes made it impossible.

Juergen responded back to me with only one letter. His situation helped to push me into acting on my desire to leave the teaching position I was in. Juergen had gotten home before I had. His status as an American citizen had caused his separation papers to go much smoother than it had for Otto or me. He returned to a family in distress. His father had owned a

307

rather large farm before the war. He had returned from his five-year stay in America with enough cash to purchase a nice farm. Though he was originally from the Ulm area he had migrated to the east were land was cheaper. During the war his farm had been used as an army headquarters on several occasions since the farmhouse itself was a large structure that had once been the hunting lodge of Kaiser Wilhelm. When the army would settle into his house he was also required to feed them. This had seriously taxed his resources and left him ill prepared for the economic collapse accompanying the war's end. Juergen found himself struggling as a field hand to try and help his father to farm enough without proper draft animals and tools to scratch out a living. The Russians were also demanding a stiff tax.

One day, Juergen's father had returned from town with sobering news. He had found out that it was possible for American citizens to leave Germany if they left within the week. Juergen's father took Juergen aside and told him of the development.

"Juergen," he said, "you must take this opportunity to leave this stifling situation."

"No, Vater," Juergen protested. "I cannot leave you and Mutti alone to try to rebuild the farm. I am sure with my help things will get better."

"Yes, son, together we could get this old place back into shape, but there is more at stake here. You must not just think of yourself; think of your sister. Several times already she has barely escaped the fate of so many of our young German girls." (Though the early days of rape and pillage by the advancing Russian troops had waned, the girls were still targets for the occupying Russian soldiers.) "She is a beautiful girl and getting more so each day. She is now fifteen and will perhaps be required to work in the village. There I cannot protect her. You are both Americans and I have gotten your visas to go to America. You must take your sister away from this horrible climate. You know how much I love both of you, and how much Mutti and I will miss you, but there is no choice."

Juergen's letter to me, in answer to a letter I wrote to him, was written the day before he left. It was not a letter written by a man whose dreams were to come true by migrating to a new rich land. It was a letter from a scared young man who was carrying out a duty to his father with the same sense of loyalty he had shown me as his officer in combat.

I have never heard from him again, but my bet is that when you go back to America you could find him in the area of Wisconsin where he was born.

My opportunity to leave my home came one day when I was at a teachers' meeting in Brandenburg. I had been sent there as a part of a district committee to discuss the writing of all new textbooks. Actually, the content of the books had already been dictated by the state, but we were to approve them. I took the opportunity of being in Brandenburg to visit each evening with my older brother. One night as we met in a local Gasthaus he guided me to a back corner and told me of a way to get to the West. He told me that road crews from the next county were able to get very close to the demarcation line between the English zone and the Russian occupational zone. He told me that the crews, though accompanied by a guard of Russian soldiers, were not watched very close and he knew that one could slip away. From there one could get across the line fairly easily since there was not as well a regulated patrol as there would be if it were a recognized border. He could get me on such a crew if I could come up with a proper bribe.

I was in luck. I had brought along with me the new pair of boots I had carried home from America. I had little use for them as a teacher and they were too small for Manfred, so I had brought them with the idea of seeing if Helmuth could use them. I showed the boots to Helmuth and he was very excited. He was able to trade the boots in for a good bribe and some extra traveling money. In fact, he was able to pick up some contraband Western zone script. We were to leave in the next few days.

I did not even hesitate, such was my anxiety to get out of the East. At dawn two days later I found myself, with five other men, including my brother, in the back of a lorrie on the way toward the West. We were being followed by a Russian armored car holding three armed "overseers". I had loaded onto the truck in the work yards and no one asked for any ID. I am sure the others knew that I was a brother of Helmuth's, but they said nothing. I carried nothing with me other than a small bag of food. All the workers carried such a bag. Mine was a bit fuller, but no one commented on it. Not far to the west of Brandenburg we came to a section of road that was in

309

bad repair. It was obvious that it was still torn up due to war damage. We unloaded and commenced to work on it. We were joined by a crew from Genthin which is in the Kreis to the west of Kreis Brandenburg. During the break for the midday meal, Helmuth motioned me to come with him and we sat under a tree away from the other workers. We were soon joined by a couple of workers from the other crew. Helmuth whispered to me, "When we begin to load up to go home tonight, you join these two men and board their lorrie."

"Won't they see the two of us?" I protested.

"I am not coming with you, and no, no one will say anything. It has been arranged."

"But, brother you must come. We are in this together."

"No, Erich, I am too weak to go. Besides, it would cause a problem, so do as I ask. Just don't forget me."

I started to protest, but just then a Russian walked over to us and waved his gun to indicate that it was time to get back to work. All afternoon I had trouble concentrating on my shoveling. I would look over to Helmuth, but he would not let his eyes meet mine. Before I realized that the time had gone by, the crews began to load their tools. I hesitated and looked to my brother. He only nodded and with tears in his eyes walked over to his lorrie. I turned and headed for the other lorrie. No one said anything or acknowledged me as I boarded.

That evening I was taken to the home of one of the men. The next morning I found myself with a new crew heading north. That day another exchange took place and I found myself spending the night in a new home near the city of Stendal. From there I was transported on a freight lorrie taking supplies to Gardlegen. The next morning I was on a crew that went to work on a bridge over a canal in the small village of Niendorf. That evening I slipped away when the crew stopped in the village to buy a Bier for the road. That night I walked to Boesdorf as instructed, and then west. Sometime during the night I crossed into the British zone. The next day I hiked into Wolfsburg. I must say that there was not a lot of difference between the East and West. People were still wary of refugees and I had a hard time finding some one willing to sell me some bread and Wurst. Using

310

the script Helmuth had gotten for me (I have no idea how), I was able to get a ride to Hanover.

In Hanover I was pleased to see the main rail line operating and was able to hide away on a freight heading south. I was far from alone. The train was full of refugees of all ages. Some were seeking a place to settle, but it seemed most were in search of other members of their families. It took me only three days to get to Mainz. The train was occasionally searched and all refugees kicked off, but we would all just hustle down the track and hitch onto the next passing freight, sometimes the same one we had been on.

I had chosen Mainz as my destination, only because I knew it from my stay as a prisoner there, and because it was the city of Gutenberg and his first printing press. Somehow, I felt that qualified it as a fitting place for a teacher to settle.

I was surprised at the level of progress I found in the rebuilding of the city. Back in the East there was little movement toward repairing anything but the most basic infrastructure. The Mainz area was by then under the occupational jurisdiction of the Americans and was beginning to come back to life. I heard that the university was trying to get reestablished so I went there to ask about employment. I was sent over to the English department. Lo and behold, who should I find as the chair—none other than Professor Doctor Wilhelm. Needless to say, I was met with open arms. Professor Doctor Wilhelm soon found me a position at the school I still teach in.

CHAPTER FOUR

THE CIRCLE IS CLOSED

Before I leave this story of my friend's experiences meeting his enemy, I think it proper that you should know what happened to his English friend, Vera. I will let her tell the story.

I stood in the dark in the street and watched the figure of Eric walk away until the dark swallowed him. I stood for some time rooted to the spot knowing that he would come running back to tell me he would stay in England. He did not return. I don't think I even cried on the way home. The tears were to come later and in full force. At last I realized that he was right; he could not have stayed in England. How foolish I had been. In my head I knew that our romance was over, but in my heart I still held a strong desire to hold him again. This desire overruled any good sense that I may have had and caused me to walk toward the camp every evening for the longest time. Sometimes I would go to the shepherd's hut, and sometimes to the wooded hill near the camp. After a couple of weeks it was pretty clear to me that Eric was either not in the camp or would not be coming out. I did still continue my nightly vigilance because it allowed me to sit in the quiet and dream of our foolish but exciting clandestine meetings. The last day I went to the camp it was a Saturday and I realized how quiet the camp was. I walked down to the main gate and found it open. Inside there were some soldiers kicking a ball around, so I went on in. I finally got their attention. A couple of blokes ran over to me.

"Miss, can we help you?" the older and more handsome of the two asked me.

"I was just curious, what happened to the prisoners?"

"We've sent the buggers home. Why, was your boyfriend one of them?" They both laughed.

"Unfortunately not," I said with a grin to cover my real thoughts. "I hear those Germans were some tough and handsome blighters."

"Tough? Tough you say to the boys that whipped them? If it's tough

312

you want, you have come to the right fellows, luv. As for handsome, I think you need look no further. What do you think, pretty miss?"

"I think maybe the war has made you daft, laddie. Will the camp be a closing now?"

"Aye, but not for a few weeks, while we lock her down. Enough time for us to become good friends. Say, starting tonight, luv?"

"Though as tempted I might be, my hubby the major might not agree."

The cheeky fellow stepped back so quickly he ran into his mate, who started to chuckle. "Just kidding Mrs. . . . uh . . . Major. Can I help you locate your husband, ma'am?"

"No, I know where to find him." I turned and started to leave, then turned back to them and said, "Oh, by the way, I was kidding. I know you boys are the toughest blokes on the globe, and as for handsome, your friend there is a real knockout."

That caused a big grin on the young soldier's face, and the older to wince a bit.

That very evening I went home and packed. The next evening found me back at my unit to take my punishment. The morning after I got back I had to report to the colonel. He tried to act mad, me having been AWOL for several months, but I could tell he was actually glad to have me back. As I said, women in the British army were not treated very roughly after the war. I was put to work processing damage reports and other such boring tasks. I again discovered that the sight of a woman in uniform was no longer a come-on to the men. In fact, I was treated a bit oddly, as if the men felt I was not really a woman if I didn't want to go back to the kitchen stove. After only a few months I knew that the party was over and asked for a discharge, which was not long in being granted.

I returned home and hired on as a secretary in a small woolen mill. Life settled into a slow boring routine. I did find a group of girls my age to run around with, which was good because men were really in short supply. Those who had survived the war now found village life too boring and most headed for the cities. I did have a few fellows I dated, but they were not very exciting types. I would find myself comparing them to Eric and

313

then get mad at myself for being so foolish. I had come to realize that my fling with a German POW had to be the stupidest thing any girl had ever done.

Things changed one evening when I was out with the girls at a local carnival. I ran in to Ronald. I had known Ronald in school and had gone out dancing with him a few times. I found that he had been in Burma and had just returned home. Ronald was a tall, dark, handsome man, and his father had a nice feed mill near the town. He was considered quite the catch. We began seeing a lot of each other and soon I could tell he was falling in love with me. Unfortunately, I just did not feel the same way. I found myself again thinking of Eric and wished that I would at least get a letter. No letter came, of course. I finally confided in my mother about my feelings. She really got upset, and then told my father. I had never seen him so upset. Luckily, they didn't tell anyone else or I would have been thrown out of the village.

Ronald began to grow more and more insistent and impatient with me. My parents also began to put on the pressure. At last I realized that life must go on, and that Ronald was a very nice man. I agreed to marry him. I was still hesitant enough about the union to talk him into a long engagement. I used the excuse of the need for the two of us "to let the war air out of our brains a bit" before we made the final leap. He reluctantly agreed and we set a date several months out. As the day came closer, I warmed up to the idea and actually started to look forward to it. My mother was all aglow. One evening, about a month before the big day, she said, "See Vera love, all things work for the best. You and Ronald will soon be married and you can quit your job and settle down here in the village for a long happy life. Just think how horrible it would have been if that Hun fellow had ever stolen you away to a life behind a plow somewhere in a backward German village." Her mention of Eric made me think of him for the first time in weeks. Also, I started to think about living my life in that little quiet, dull, village. I could just see myself, like the other women in town, dragging my children out once a week to the only social event, church services, while my man sat in the bloody pub telling war stories. I started to get really cold feet. I went back to long evening walks in the countryside. After several arguments with myself I decided that once again I was being foolish and that marriage to

314

Ronald would be best; love would surely come later.

At last, the night before the big day came. I was all packed and had my luggage standing in the front room, ready to go. Mother and I sat down for a nice cup of tea. She even let me light a cigarette, right at the table. I sat looking into my cup hoping, I guess, to read a good fortune in the leaves. A knock came at the door. I felt it was probably my girlfriend coming to get last-minute instructions as my maid of honor. I opened the door and there stood Eric. My heart jumped into my throat and I could not say anything. Neither did he, nor did we move toward each other. I have no idea how long we stood there before he said, "Are you ready to go?" I don't think I paused very long. I looked back to the luggage and then to him and said, "Yes."

316

EPILOGUE

ERICH AND VERA

Vera and Erich were married shortly after returning to Germany. They settled in Mainz, where they were when I met them in 1968. They were able to return to East Germany several times to meet with Erich's family. After the Iron Curtain became a reality, Erich was not able to go back, even when his mother died. Vera was never really happy in Germany. She told me that, though they had many friends, she always felt that they treated her as an outsider. She never became a "German," other than in a legal sense, being that she did take out German citizenship. Erich remained a teacher in the Mainz area until his retirement. Shortly after I had the opportunity to meet them and hear their amazing story they moved to South Africa, where Erich took a positon in a German school. They did not return to Germany until after I left for the United States. I was never to see Vera again, as she died rather young. I did have the opportunity to meet again with Erich on several occasions. On these visits I urged him to write his story, but he never did. I hope I have done it in a manner he would approve of.

OTTO

The man I have called Otto in this story and his wife came to America in 1954 with little in their pockets. They were sponsored by a farmer to settle in central Wisconsin. There they were given a small shack, with no electricity or indoor plumbing, on the cranberry marsh he was given a job on. Later, he moved to Wisconsin Rapids, Wisconsin, where he worked in a paper mill until his retirement. His wife was to die before his retirement and he subsequently married a German widow from the area. He now lives in Stevens Point, Wisconsin, with his second wife. He has occasionally attended VFW functions and was given veteran status by them as their token German.

JUERGEN

The man from whom I drew much of the character of Juergen Beckmann and his sister were also sponsored to settle in Wisconsin. This Juergen married a local farmer's daughter and eventually purchased his father-in-law's farm. He remains on the farm, though he is retired and has sold the operation to one of his sons. He still owns the family farm in northern Germany, from which he and his sister emigrated to the United States.

ERICH'S BROTHERS

Oldest brother Helmuth committed suicide not long after Erich fled to West Germany. No one knows if it was from his reluctance to face life in pain as a near cripple or because of his war memories. I know little of the fate of the other two brothers other than the middle brother, Friedrich, served in the East German Army Reserve. To my knowledge, they never did come to the West for a visit with Erich and Vera.

I will end this story of the meeting of enemies with a couple of comments made on my last visit with Erich before he and Vera moved to South Africa. We were sitting in a Gasthaus on the Rhine River near his summer place. He had just told me about his return to Potsdam. He summed his story up by saying, "Art, if you will meet your enemy as a friend you will have no enemy." Later, we were joined for the evening by his friend, the owner of the Gasthaus. On the television a popular variety show was in progress. The show was hosted by a well-known German actor, a Jew.

The Gasthaus owner looked up and said, "Look, Erich, they are back."

To this slur, Erich responded, "Yes. You see, Art, it was all for naught."

Footnotes

1 [14] It was very common in the German army for the clergy to be in the army as medics. No chaplain corps was allowed. Several priests have told me that they wore their vestments under their uniforms. Everyone knew they were priests and they were called upon to do such things as last rites, but never officially. (pg. 17)

2 [15] Erich was a member of the elite airborne troops of Herman Goering's a force (Luftwaffe). The term fallschirmspringer means paratrooper. (pg. 21)

3 [16] I distinctly remember my reaction when Erich said this. I was suddenly mad. How could this man tell me in such a calm voice that his first reaction to killing what could have been my father or uncle was to find enjoyment in a new brand of cigarette? It was only my resolve to find out what the war was like from the view of a German soldier that made me sit quietly and drink my beer as Erich continued. (pg. 46)

4 [17] I have changed the name since I am not sure I remember it right and also don't want some possible relative to feel it is their Hans I am writing about. (pg. 46)

5 [18] Erich later told me that years after the war he had attempted to located the family. What he would say to them he was not sure. He never located them. (pg. 46)

6 I have spoken with other German veterans about this rumor of American prisoners being used as forced soldiers. This rumor was not uncommon. Several veterans of the German forces at Normandy had heard this rumor. (pg. 46)

7 [19] The fact of the matter is that homosexuals in the Third Reich were severely dealt with. They were sent to the death camps, especially Dachau. (pg. 88)

8 [20] It may be of interest to you to know that in later life one of Erich's true delights was to go on summer tours aboard merchant vessels, especially those that plied up and down the African coasts. (pg. 93)

9 [21] High German, that is without a distinct local dialect (pg. 94)

10 [22] The tale of the man I have chosen to call Otto Schmidt in this story perhaps deserves

to be written in its entirety on its own. I confirmed Otto's story with the man himself, and found it even more enthralling than as related by Erich. However, I have chosen here only to enhance Erich's tale to me slightly with more details as given to me by his friend, that I have chosen to call Oberfeldwebel Schmidt (Otto). (pg. 97)

11 [23] What the POW's did not know was that the contractors paid the government as much as forty-two cents per hour for the men's labor. This put millions of dollars in the government's coffers. (pg. 140)

12 [24] These graves are still to be found at the Fort Douglas Cemetery, Salt Lake City, Utah. (pg. 195)

13 [25] Vera always used the English pronunciation of Erich's name. (pg. 246)